JESUS,
A JEWISH
GALILEAN

JESUS, A JEWISH GALILEAN

A NEW READING OF THE JESUS-STORY

SEAN FREYNE

T&T CLARK INTERNATIONAL
A Continuum imprint
LONDON • NEW YORK

Published by T&T Clark International
An imprint of Continuum

The Tower Building,
11 York Road,
London, SE1 7NX

15 East 26th Street,
Suite 1703,
New York, NY 10010

www.tandtclark.com

British Library Cataloguing-in-Publication Data

A catalogue record for this book is available from the British Library

ISBN 0-567-08457-4   (hardback)

ISBN 0-567-08467-1   (paperback)

Typeset by Tradespools, Frome, Somerset
Printed on acid-free paper in Great Britain by CPI (Bath), Bath, Somerset

For Gail, Bridget and Sarah
and
in memory of my parents
John Vincent Freyne, died 1940
and
Lucy Ellen O'Flaherty, died 1984

CONTENTS

MAPS

PREFACE

Yet another attempt to discover the historical Jesus! This topic has been so overworked in recent decades that soon it must surely be due a sabbatical rest. Yet there is always the temptation to believe, naïvely no doubt, that a particular aspect of the topic not yet discovered, or at least not properly treated, could, perhaps, hold the key to an adequate understanding of the issue, which in its present form has been with us for over 250 years. My particular vista has a Galilean angle, prompted by the way in which the Galilee of Jesus has been constructed by different scholars in the more recent past. One occasionally gets the impression that the quest for the historical Jesus is in danger of becoming the quest for the historical Galilee, with all the attendant hermeneutical pitfalls that that particular enterprise has given rise to.

The more immediate context of this particular study has been the invitation to deliver two series of guest lectures on various aspects of contemporary Galilean studies – the Gunning lectures at the University of Edinburgh (1998) and the J. J. Thiessen lectures at the Canadian Mennonite University in Winnipeg, Canada, in 2002. I am grateful to the staff and students of both institutions for their friendly reception of my ideas. Their critical engagement has helped considerably in sharpening the focus, even if they will not immediately recognize the final form in which my ideas have emerged. This applies particularly to the 'long view' which I have adopted in approaching the various topics from the perspective of the Hebrew Scriptures. The subject of Jesus and the Ecology of Galilee (chapter 2) is, to the best of my knowledge, novel in contemporary study of the historical Jesus. I am grateful to the organizers of the Manson lecture at the University of Manchester for providing me with the opportunity to present my first reflections on this topic (2003), which have here been expanded and revised to provide the horizon within which to develop other aspects of Jesus' career.

I must acknowledge the patient and gentle prodding of Dr. Geoffrey Green of T&T Clark since this project was mooted several years ago; he must have thought that the manuscript would never see the light of day. The practical encouragement of Rebecca Mulhearn of T&T Clark International (Continuum) has helped considerably in concentrating my efforts over the last several months. I have had a ready forum for debating my ideas with colleagues and students of the School of Religions and Theology and the Joint Programme for Mediterranean and Near Eastern Studies at Trinity College, Dublin. However, an author must take responsibility for the ideas expressed and trust a sympathetic, if not uncritical readership for their final evaluation. My thanks to my friend, calligrapher Mr. Tim O'Neill, for assistance with the maps. I owe a special word of thanks, as always, to my family who have allowed me the time and space to devote myself to this project.

Sean Freyne
Trinity College, Dublin
May 2004

ABBREVIATIONS

Standard abbreviations are used for the Biblical books, apocrypha and pseudepigrapha, Dead Sea Scrolls and Rabbinical writings. Biblical citations are from the New Revised Standard Version with Apocrypha and the Loeb Classical Library translation of Josephus is used.

BASOR	*Bulletin of American School of Oriental Research*
BTB	*Biblical Theology Bulletin*
BZ	*Biblische Zeitschrift*
CBQ	*Catholic Biblical Quarterly*
ESI	*Excavations and Surveys in Israel*
HTR	*Harvard Theological Review*
IAA	*Israel Antiquities Authority*
IEJ	*Israel Exploration Journal*
INJ	*Israel Numismatic Journal*
JA	*Jewish Antiquities* of Flavius Josephus
JBL	*Journal of Biblical Literature*
JSJ	*Journal for the Study of Judaism*
JSNT	*Journal for the Study of the New Testament*
JSNTSS	*JSNT Supplement Series*
JSNTSS	*Journal for the Study of the New Testament Supplementary Series*
JSOT	*Journal for the Study of the Old Testament*
JSOTSS	*Journal for the Study of the Old Testament Supplement Series*
JSP	*Journal for the Study of the Pseudepigrapha*
JW	*Jewish War* of Flavius Josephus
Life	*Life* of Flavius Josephus
NTS	*New Testament Studies*
RHPR	*Revue d'Histoire et de Philosophie Religieuses*
SNTSMS	*Studiorum Novi Testamenti Societas Monograph Series*
TSAJ	*Texts and Studies in Ancient Judaism*
WUNT	*Wissenschaftliche Untersuchungen zum Neuen Testament*
ZDPV	*Zeitschrift des deutschen Palästina-Vereins*

1

JESUS, JEWS AND GALILEE:
INTRODUCING THE ISSUES

The ebbs and flows of the scholarly quest for the historical Jesus have been a constant preoccupation of western theology for over two centuries, yet no final consensus has been achieved about the identity of Jesus and his movement. It is usual, if somewhat schematic, to number three stages to the modern 'quest' provoked by the posthumous publication of H. S. Reimarus' *Fragments* on the topic by G. E. Lessing in 1786. These stages are: the nineteenth-century liberal lives of Jesus, so trenchantly exposed as modernizing accounts by Albert Schweitzer's *The Quest of the Historical Jesus* (1968), the post-Bultmanian 'new quest' with its somewhat minimalist approach to the question in the mid-twentieth century, and finally, 'the current third wave', mainly, but not exclusively associated with the Jesus Seminar in North America during the 1990s.[1]

The distinguishing feature of this most recent chapter of Jesus-scholarship in contrast to its predecessors is the interest in the social, as distinct from the religious aspects of Jesus' life. This shift of emphasis can undoubtedly be attributed to many factors operating within late twentieth-century western society, which have led to an increasing 'secularization' of New Testament studies. Whereas previously the debates were about the various titles that Jesus might have employed as self-designations (Messiah, Son of Man or Lord, for example), or discussions of his role as prophet or charismatic religious leader, today he is typically characterized as a social reformer, a peasant activist or Cynic dissident. It is somewhat ironic, though inevitable that in an age of globalization recent studies of Jesus have been concerned with the local setting of his public life, thus giving rise to a renewed interest in Galilee also.

The Gospels and the Historical Jesus

This shift of emphasis from the universal to the particular, far from simplifying the task of the historian of Jesus, demands an increased critical awareness across a number of disciplines. Not merely is it necessary to adopt a position on the hotly debated question of the historical nature of the gospels, it is also now important to combine insights from ancient history, archaeology and the social sciences, particularly, cultural anthropology. Ideally, such a project calls for a group of scholars engaged in an interdisciplinary study, yet such is the fascination with the topic that there has been no shortage of scholars essaying the task over the past 25 years. Inevitably, these studies have given rise to varying discussions about the correct procedures to be adopted and methodologies to be employed. Amid such a variety of opinions it becomes imperative to outline, however briefly, the perspective being adopted in this study, if only to give the reader some orientation with which to judge the adequacy of the enterprise.

    The most obvious dilemma facing any researcher in the field is surely how to avoid the criticism of some future Albert Schweitzer with regard to modernizing Jesus. Imaginings of the past always involve our awareness of the present, and to the extent that the figure of Jesus can be made to support our own best insights and dreams, it is difficult not to avoid the temptation of co-opting him for our cause. Despite this obvious pitfall, there are those who believe that while a thoroughly 'objective' account of the historical Jesus is an unattainable ideal, it is still possible to avoid the *cul de sacs* of previous scholarship on the subject. Thus, John Dominic Crossan, one of the most prolific members of the Jesus Seminar in the USA, has stated his views on the topic in his usual elegant and trenchant style in the introduction to his best-selling 1991 study. Describing the current situation of many different portraits of Jesus as 'an academic embarrassment', the aim is that his study should 'not add to the impression of acute scholarly subjectivity in historical Jesus research'. He is concerned, he informs us, 'not with an unattainable objectivity but with an attainable honesty', and to this end he exhorts other scholars to follow his 'triple triadic' process, which involves the interplay of an interdisciplinary approach, including the social sciences, a scientific stratification of the Jesus traditions and a critical use of this inventory for historical reconstruction.[2] Likewise, John Meier, who independently, but contemporaneously with

Crossan, undertook the task of 'rethinking the historical Jesus' is cautious about 'objective' as the proper classification for his study.[3] Yet he believes that striving for such an ideal allows one to avoid 'a rampant subjectivism'. Meier makes the helpful distinction between the 'real Jesus' (problematic though that term is with regard to any past figure) and 'the historical Jesus'. This latter is a modern construct which may, by the use of modern scientific methods, 'give us fragments of the real Jesus'. Even then, however, it becomes difficult to disentangle completely 'the historical Jesus' as a figure in the past from 'the historic Jesus', as the one whose memory continues to influence history, either in a general sense or in the more specifically Christian sense of Jesus as the Risen Christ, the object of Christian preaching and belief as he is represented already in the earliest documents.[4]

The hesitation of both these scholars on the issue of objectivity in regard to the historical Jesus underlines the specific nature of our primary sources, the gospels. Crossan is quite explicit in regard to the problem involved. 'The gospels are neither histories nor biographies, even within the ancient tolerance of such genres', he confidently asserts.[5] It is this understanding of the nature of the gospels that has led him to engage in the elaborate process of stratification of the traditions with a view to establishing potentially authentic material. From the limited database which he thereby establishes, he is prepared to accept only those items for which there is double attestation in two independent sources, thereby leaving himself open to the charge that he has rejected perfectly good historical information, either because it only appears in one source, or because he is not prepared to explore the possible historical information about Jesus that may be contained in the upper, 'redactional' layers of the gospels according to his and his Jesus seminar colleagues' adjudication of the evidence.

In my opinion this judgement, scientifically rigorous though it may appear to be, is too restrictive and does not take sufficient account of the nature of the gospels. The alternative to this position is not to return to a naïve historicism that seeks to bypass the critical study of the gospels or minimizes the differences between them. More modest, but realistic goals need to be set on the basis of the character of the evidence which we do possess. This involves the recognition that the gospel frameworks are not random inventions as the Form Critical school had suggested, but seek rather to provide a narrative frame for the *kerygma* about Jesus, once the impetus arose to provide such an account among the second-generation Christians. This implies that there is no 'pure' historical evidence available in the gospel traditions, no matter how much one seeks to refine the criteria. The gospels themselves are narrative expressions of the *kerygma* or early preaching, and it is impossible to separate out brute historical facts from their kerygmatic intent. Either we accept that the early followers of Jesus had some interest in and memory of the historical figure of Jesus as they began to proclaim the good news about him, or we must abandon the process entirely and adopt the position of Rudolph Bultmann that 'we can know nothing about the life and personality of Jesus, since the early Christian sources show no interest in either, are moreover, fragmentary and often legendary'.[6]

As a reaction to this historical scepticism of his teacher and mentor, Ernst Käsemann expressed the matter trenchantly in his programmatic 1953 paper. 'The exalted Lord,' he writes, 'has almost entirely swallowed up the image of the earthly Lord, and yet the community has maintained the identity of the exalted Lord with the earthly.... The question of the historical Jesus is, in its *legitimate* form, the continuity of the Gospel within the discontinuity of the times and the variations of the *kerygma*.'[7] It was important for Käsemann that continuity between the early Christian preaching *about* Jesus and the preaching *of* Jesus could be established on critical grounds, since in his view this was the nature of early Christian belief from the beginning. The early preaching insisted that it was *Jesus* who had died and was risen, and it was this conviction that prompted the development of a narrative about him which made no distinction between the earthly and the risen Lord. Corresponding to this kerygmatic interest in the question of the historical Jesus, there has been a strong tendency to see the gospels as unique documents that cannot be compared with other 'biographic' types of narrative, a position which, strangely, Crossan, as just cited, also seems to espouse. Neither Käsemann, nor Gunther Bornkamm, another influential representative of 'the new quest' for Jesus after Bultmann, were interested in the local aspects of Jesus' proclamation as represented in the gospel narratives. It was the fact of Jesus' existence, and not the details that was important from their perspective. The uniqueness of the message brought forth a unique literary response, it is claimed.

However, this judgement is based on theological rather than on literary-historical grounds, and more recent discussions have situated these early Christian writings within a larger context of the biographic encomium genre of Greco-Roman antiquity, which includes a historical as well as a propagandistic intention. Thus, the gospel narratives can and should be critically evaluated in terms of their portrayals of Jesus and his ministry while making full allowance for their other perspectives and the modifications that these might bring to the historical intention.[8] To put the matter concretely in terms of the present study, when the evangelists portray Galilean situations in the life of Jesus, it will be necessary to ask whether these merely serve the later interests or whether they might not also reflect judgements about the historical Jesus, since such an interest cannot a priori be excluded from the writers' intentions.

Recent comparative studies of the gospels in terms of genre suggest that they do in fact bear a 'family resemblance' to other ancient Lives, all of which originate from a tripartite 'basis-biographie', comprising of a beginning (*arche*) dealing briefly with the origins of the subject, a middle (*akme*) concentrating on the high-point of the subject's public life, and an end (*telos*) relating the subject's demise and possible vindication.[9] All the gospels fit easily into this basic structure which allowed for numerous additions, expansions and adaptations, but whose essential character is recognizable. Traces of such a 'biographic' interest in Jesus can be detected in Christian writings other than the Gospels also: Q (Lk. 3.3, 4.1, 7.1, 10.13–15, 13.24), Acts (10.37–41) and the Pauline letters (1 Cor. 11.23–26, 15.2–4; Gal. 4.4; Rm. 1.1–2). This is equally true of Josephus' brief account of Jesus when stripped of its later Christian interpolations (*JA* 18.63f.). The socio-rhetorical function of the encomiastic (praising) and propagandistic (apologetic) aspects of such works needs to be considered in evaluating their historical intent, but that is also true of other ancient sources, even Josephus' *Life*.[10] Furthermore, in the case of the gospels the role of the biographic impulse within a Jewish matrix needs to be considered. In this regard the books attributed to the great Israelite prophets, Isaiah, Jeremiah and Ezekiel, for example, combine the personal experiences and oracular utterances as a single message. For that very reason the historical circumstances of the prophet's life becomes particularly important within a Jewish context.

Thus, when all due allowance is made for the literary considerations, we do less than justice to the intentions of the evangelists if we do not take seriously this 'historicizing' tendency of their work. Their frameworks are discarded as 'later' and unreliable at the expense of a very different narrative account of our own making, one that often has little to do with real life situations in first-century Galilee. In recognizing the historical intention of the gospel writers, we should, at least initially, show a greater trust in the various leads which they suggest with regard to the course of Jesus' ministry. Even when their actual knowledge of Galilee may be sketchy or not based on personal experience, as first-century Mediterranean people they are much more in tune with situations such as urban/rural tensions and ethnic relations in antiquity than we could ever hope to be through our 'outsider' perspective.

Galilee and Jesus

The modern historian of Jesus must come to the discussion equipped with more than a critical understanding of the gospels, however. The shift of emphasis from the universal to the local in modern studies of Jesus has shone the torch on Galilee in a way that was not obvious 25 years ago when Professor Martin Hengel of Tübingen suggested to me that a study of Galilee could make an important contribution to our understanding of early Christianity.[11] Little had been written on the subject, and even standard histories of the period merely repeated certain stereotypes of Galilee and the Galileans from the ancient sources. I quickly became aware of the potential dangers of dealing only with the actual period of Jesus' ministry in the reign of Herod Antipas, Apart from having to deal with the vast amount of secondary literature concerning the historical reliability of the gospels, there was the obvious temptation to create a picture of Galilee that would provide the suitable backdrop for the particular role that different scholars wished to attribute to Jesus. These ranged at that time from violent revolutionary to pious *hasid*, and since then the list has been considerably increased, most notably by the introduction of the Cynic-like Jesus.[12] Perhaps the most shocking example of such a manipulation of the evidence was Walter Grundmann's suggestion in his 1941 study that Galilee was pagan (*heidnisch*) and that 'with greater probability, Jesus was not a Jew'.[13] What in my judgement was called for, therefore, was a study of Galilee that would not focus primarily on Jesus and his Galilean ministry, but which would seek to establish the distinctiveness of the region by adopting 'the long view', one which stretched from Alexander the Great to Hadrian, a period of 400 years, during which there were many changes. Only in this way would it be possible to avoid the danger of a distorted understanding of Jesus and his ministry, however unconsciously. The picture of Galilee that emerged in that first attempt has had to be revised more than once in the intervening years, as new evidence began to emerge from the intensive archaeological work in the region. Key sites such as Sepphoris have been uncovered and regional surveys have helped to identify the changing patterns of settlement and ethnic identities over time.

What was the nature of the Galilee that Jesus inhabited and how did he relate to that environment? My second book was intended to answer that question, but with hindsight I did not sufficiently integrate the literary approach to the gospels and the historical investigations in the second part of the book, as its subtitle suggested.[14] The present study is intended as a renewed effort to explore the issue of Galilee and Jesus from a different perspective. At the outset it is important to realize that Galilee was not the only theatre for Jesus life and ministry. Some recent studies have tended to minimize or even ignore his Judean roots and subsequent ministry, basing themselves on a perceived opposition between Galilee and Judea/Jerusalem, and in the process ignoring the leads suggested by the Fourth Gospel, which depicts Jesus as a companion of John the Baptist in the Judean desert and concentrating his ministry on Jerusalem, with Galilee functioning as a virtual place of retreat (Jn. 4.1–2, 45).[15] The historical plausibility of these connections and the role that Jesus played within the variations of first-century regional Jewish identities will emerge more than once as this study proceeds.

Another issue which will emerge as highly significant in this study has been raised recently in a stimulating manner by the Norwegian scholar Halvor Moxnes.[16] He rightly points out that in discussing Jesus' identity many studies have concentrated on his distinctive conception of time, ignoring the importance of place in establishing and maintaining identity. Moxnes' reflections are based on recent social-scientific discussion of the meaning of place, and more particularly the loss of the sense of place in modernity, other than as a stage on which to engage in the tasks of a globalized world, driven by market capitalism. Time and progress become synonymous, and the successful person is therefore not tied to any one place, but is a global citizen. A Jesus-figure, related to a particular location is of little significance in such a culture. It is not surprising, therefore, that an interest in Jesus in his own place has arisen, as Moxnes astutely notes, in third-world situations, where people who are often the victims of western economic exploitation find in the stories of Jesus and his engagement with the marginalized of his own place a powerful motive for resistance to their oppression.[17]

Once the idea of place is retrieved in regard to Jesus and his ministry it is important to note that it is not an unproblematic concept. For many people today, having a sense of place is a bulwark against what they perceive as the instability and uncertainty of modern life. Place becomes a static, immovable concept with rigid boundaries and unchanging identity. This attitude can function at the personal, but also at the national level, in support of aggressively nationalistic policies. In contrast to this understanding, Moxnes suggests a fluid sense of place as a human construct that is constantly being negotiated and redrawn as different interest groups struggle for control of the social structures which define a particular place. Thus, places and their identities should be seen as unfixed, contested and multiple. 'Instead of seeing places as bounded enclosures,' writes Moxnes, 'we should see their identities as formed in interactions with the outside and with others.'[18] Moxnes' study proceeds to view Jesus' ministry in Galilee from a spatial perspective at both the micro level of redefining domestic space and the macro level of establishing an alternative regional identity which had been defined and controlled by the Herodian ruling elite. We shall have occasion to engage with his insights throughout this study at various points.

When one looks at the modern history of Galilean studies in the light of Moxnes' reflections it becomes clear that Galilee has been constructed in various ways by different interest groups over the past 200 years. Such interests do not necessarily disqualify the results, since from the perspective of place considered as a human and social construct, and not a given and static entity, it is possible, even probable, that multiple Galilees co-existed in antiquity. However, the plurality does remind us of what Historian of Religions, Jonathan Z. Smith says: 'Human beings are not placed; they bring place into being.'[19] How has Jesus' Galilee been constructed in the modern period and whose interests have these portrayals served?

Galilee as such does not feature in the nineteenth-century Lives of Jesus, because Galilee did not matter except as a stick with which to beat Judea and Judaism. The French scholar Ernest Renan is one fascinating, if disturbing example of this trend. He wrote his celebrated *Vie de Jesus* in 1863 as he was engaged in a project for the

French government of mapping Phoenicia (modern Lebanon). He had formerly been a Catholic seminarian, who had rejected his Christian faith, but with his fascination for Jesus as a historical figure undiminished. The romantic tone of his *Vie* is touching, written in a hut in southern Lebanon, with the whole of Galilee stretched out below him. 'The landscape,' he writes, 'is like a fifth gospel, torn but still legible.' The lush verdant terrain can be favourably contrasted with the barren Judean hills farther south, a contrast that mirrored the attitudes of the inhabitants of both regions, especially their religious attitudes. 'The north alone made Christianity,' he wrote, whereas 'Jerusalem was the home of that obstinate Judaism, which, founded by the Pharisees and fixed by the Talmud, has traversed the middle ages and come down to us.'[20] This thinking reflected a common nineteenth-century ethnographic assumption that there was a causal connection between the natural environment and the character of the inhabitants of a region. The German scholar, David Friedrich Strauss, whose study of Jesus had greatly influenced Renan, wrote: 'The Galileans had simple and energetic minds, whereas the Judeans had a higher culture and much more foreign intercourse. However, they were fettered by priestcraft and Pharisaism.'[21]

Not merely did Renan and Strauss share the false assumptions about the relationship between ethnicity and place of their own day, they also shared western colonial attitudes towards the Middle East. Idealization of the great centres of civilization such as Egypt, Mesopotamia and Palestine, the land of the Bible, co-existed with denigration of the present inhabitants of the region. This reflected the deeply anti-Semitic mindset of much European scholarship of the period, especially directed towards Jews and Judaism, as exemplified in Renan's caricature, which was equally standard description of those Jews of his own day who refused to assimilate to the Enlightenment values. Inevitably, therefore, Jesus had to be distanced from Judaism, and the portrayal of Galilee as different from the south, even to the point of being racially mixed, served this purpose well. Thus, a trend was established, traces of which, as in the case of Grundmann noted above, could re-surface at any time, and to which modern scholarship is still not totally immune, even from our post-holocaust perspective.

At the very time that Renan, Strauss and others were denigrating ancient Judaism and using their particular portrayal of Galilee and Galileans for this purpose, many European Jews were still coming to terms with the emancipation from the ghetto in the wake of the French Revolution, by seeking to participate fully in the academic and social life of the period. While some Jews freely assimilated to the dominant culture of the day, others sought to preserve their specific Jewish identity by embracing the critical methods of the Enlightenment in the study of their own past. Thus was born the Science for the Study of Judaism (*Wissenschaft des Judentums*), with its critical but apologetic aims. One aspect of this movement, associated with such scholars as Abraham Geiger and Heinrich Graetz, was a reappraisal of the figure of Jesus, resulting in a much more positive understanding of his role in contrast to the negative portrayals of the Rabbinic texts and the medieval *Toledoth Yeshua*.[22] Instead of the impostor/magician figure of these works, Jesus now emerges as a thoroughly Jewish figure, and thus was born the process of 'the bringing Jesus home to Judaism' – a trend that continued on in the twentieth century, but with quite different results in the work of Joseph Klausner, Leo Baeck, Martin Buber, David Flusser and others.[23] This movement arose originally as a response to the de-judaizing of Jesus in Christian theological writing that was heavily influenced by the theologian, Friedrich Schleiermacher. It was also aimed at presenting an account of Jewish history which would explain the origins of the Christian movement without denigrating Judaism itself as a monotheistic faith, something which Christian, mainly German, scholarship of the period was all too prone to do.[24]

A Jewish Jesus required a Jewish milieu in which to operate and Jewish historians inspired with the spirit of *Wissenschaft des Judentums* were busily engaged in such an enterprise for reasons to do with the origins of Rabbinic Judaism in Galilee. Despite the dubious reputation of the inhabitants in the Rabbinic texts, such as the frequently quoted statement of Johannan ben Zakkai – the sage to whom is attributed the renewal of Judaism after the catastrophe of 70 CE – 'Galilee, Galilee, you hate the torah; your end will be destruction' (PT *Shabb* 16.8), or the Babylonian Rabbis' denigration of the Galilean 'people of the land' because of their alleged ignorance and non-observance of torah, Galilee took on an importance for Jewish scholars because of its role as the centre of Palestinian Judaism in the period after 135 CE. Several studies by Adolf Büchler and Samuel Klein from the early part of the twentieth century fall into that category, the former dealing with social aspects of Judaism in the region, and the latter being concerned with topographical and historical issues of the Jewish settlement there.[25] Inevitably, a very different picture of Galilee emerged from these studies to that of Renan and Strauss earlier. Galilee was now seen as being both culturally and religiously Jewish, and such centres of Jewish learning as Sepphoris and Tiberias began to emerge from the shadows of Nazareth and Caphernaum, those villages which were associated with Jesus' ministry in the gospels and which had come to prominence in the itinerary of Christian pilgrims visiting the Holy Land from the Byzantine period.

In her study of the work of Abraham Geiger, one of the pioneers of this nineteenth-century movement in Germany, Susannah Heschel points to the fact that certain strands of current North American scholarship about Jesus (which has largely taken over from Germany as the home of the industry) continue the trend of its nineteenth-century German antecedent.[26] There are some notable exceptions, however, such as E. P. Sanders, whose 1985 book on Jesus together with his earlier study of Paul (1978) represented a potential paradigm shift in New Testament scholarship with regard to the Jewish world of both Jesus and early Christianity.[27] Another North American scholar, Bruce Chilton, has also consistently sought to locate Jesus firmly within a Jewish religious milieu by working with the Targumim, or Aramaic paraphrases of the Bible, which were used in synagogue worship.[28] Yet these voices were drowned out by the noises emanating from the Jesus Seminar with its deliberate use of the mass media to popularize their work on the historical Jesus.

We may well ask why, given the climate of good will between Jews and Christians in the post-holocaust era, the notion of a Jewish Jesus did not have greater appeal. One possible reason is a trend, associated with 'the new quest' of the 1950s, to formulate objective criteria for unearthing unimpeachable, 'bed-rock' tradition about Jesus, foremost of which was the principle of dissimilarity. As described by Norman Perrin in his influential *Rediscovering the Teaching of Jesus* (1967), 'the uniqueness of Jesus is found not in the things that he shares with his contemporaries, but in the things wherein he differs from them'.[29] However, in speaking of Jesus' uniqueness Perrin was not primarily interested in identifying certain aspects of Jesus which differentiated him from his contemporaries in the way that all religious reformers adopt a distinct identity, while remaining within their own tradition. Uniqueness here is a theologically loaded term, and the danger is that the resultant picture of Jesus will set him over against his Jewish inheritance, thereby also paving the way for an understanding of Christianity that superseded an outmoded and discredited Judaism.

Recently, the notion of adequate criteria has been thoroughly revised by a number of scholars, most notably the Heidleberg New Testament Professor, Gerd Theissen. Instead of dissimilarity, with its tendency to provide a minimalist amount of authentic tradition, he now proposes a criterion of historical plausibility as the most suitable formulation to address the issue of the historical Jesus as currently debated. Plausibility is explained with reference to both influence and context, thereby broadening considerably what can in principle be judged as authentic within the Jesus tradition by giving priority to coherence over dissimilarity. His formulation of the criterion seeks on the one hand to build bridges between Jesus' own understanding and formulation of his mission and that of the movement that arose in his name (his influence), and on the other, to locate Jesus firmly within the cultural milieu of his Jewish co-religionists (his context) – aspects of his history that the criterion of dissimilarity had by definition excluded. Theissen formulates his ideas about this latter aspect as follows:

> Whereas the criterion of difference requires that it should not be possible to derive Jesus traditions from Judaism. . . . the criterion of plausible historical context requires only a demonstration of positive connections between the Jesus tradition and the Jewish context, i.e. between Jesus and the land, the groups, the traditions and the mentalities of the Judaism of that time.[30]

Theissen has thus opened the door for historical Jesus studies to enter the field of Second Temple Jewish studies as the proper context in which to debate the distinctive voice of Jesus, even when that voice is at times in conflict with other trends within that broader setting. Ironically, in the very period in which the most intense recent debates about the historical Jesus were taking place (1980–2000) the task of documenting that polyphonic world of Judaism was being pursued with vigour and expertise, yet the two projects rarely seemed to engage with each other. Jewish and Christian scholars working closely together engaged in the production of the two-volume edition and translation of the The Old Testament Pseudepigrapha (1983 and 1985) and in the publication and elucidation of the Dead Sea Scrolls. Both corpora of writings provide a unique documentation of the variety and diversity of what previous scholarship had simply labelled Judaism, as it struggled with placing Jesus in his proper milieu.

The Contribution of Archaeology

While historians of both Judaism and early Christianity have mainly relied on the literary sources in constructing their different pictures of Galilee, archaeology as a discipline has gradually begun to establish itself independently of the literary sources.[31] The social sciences have provided the archaeologists with models for interpreting their data and have helped to broaden the horizons of the discipline to engage in more sophisticated analysis of various aspects of ancient societies that are not treated at all, or only lightly touched on in the literary sources. Thus, archaeologists, no less than historians have been engaged in the construction of Galilee as place, both regionally and locally, providing a different, and sometimes, conflicting view of the regional particularities to that which can be gleaned from the literary sources.

It is significant that the impetus for intensive archaeological exploration of Galilee in the twentieth century has not been due to historical Jesus studies in the first instance. The initial focus was on the origins of Israel in late bronze age Canaan on the one hand, and the development of synagogue art and architecture in the Byzantine period on the other.[32] True, sites associated with Jesus' life and ministry, especially Caphernaum and Nazareth were explored under the direction of the Italian Franciscans as Keepers of the Holy Places, but the results of their work had little or no impact on the scholarly community and were deemed – often unfairly – to be more devotional than scientific. In the light of the discussions about human construction of place it is important also to recognize that archaeologists, despite the popular impression of objectivity that their work of 'digging up the past' gives, are also engaged in the interpretative activity of re-imagining places. The Department of Antiquities in the modern state of Israel has been highly active in exploring and displaying the traces of the national heritage as these have been recovered throughout the land. Similarly, religious interests, Jewish and Christian, can also be at work in the identification and explication of various sites, and revisionism is as important in this discipline as in any other area of human investigation. These cautionary remarks are not intended to suggest that an ideological bias is actively present in the modern archaeology of Galilee; quite the contrary, in my experience. What they do point to is the fact that different questions are of interest to different schools of archaeologists. In this regard it is significant to note that whereas the so-called Israeli school of archaeology is understandably interested in cultural/ethnic indices, the American approach focuses rather on the economic and social markers that help in producing a fuller picture of life in a particular location. Insofar as this generalization holds true, Galilee has been well served by a mixture of both approaches and the results can assist considerably in contemporary discussions of Galilee as place in relation to Jesus' ministry.

There are three crucial issues to do with Jesus' Galilee that in my opinion continue to be considerably illumined by the archaeological study of the region. These are: 1) the extent and nature of the impact of the spread of Greek culture in the region; 2) the identification of Jewish ethnic markers at various sites; and 3) the changing nature of the social and economic conditions under Herodian rule. All three issues can be construed in terms of Moxnes' notion of contested place. The epithet 'Galilee of the Gentiles' has applied to the region, not only in ancient sources, but also in modern scholarly construals, with, as we have seen, possible application to a non-Jewish Jesus. Some recent discussions of a Cynic, or Cynic-like Jesus require a Galilee that was thoroughly Hellenized in cultural terms to be plausible. Even if one were to allow for this in the urban centres it is not at all clear that the same ethos would have obtained in the village culture where Jesus' ministry seems to have been conducted. What needs to be explored is the nature of the Jewish encounter with Greek culture, which, as Martin Hengel has shown, was one of acceptance of many aspects of Greek life – education, commerce, political structures and technical skills – by all branches of Palestinian Judaism by the mid-second century BCE, without any compromise on ethnic identity or religious belief and practice.[33] As used since the Enlightenment 'Hellenism' and 'Judaism' are idealizations of what in reality was a highly complex cultural exchange, one that in fact pre-dates by several centuries Alexander's dream of a one-world culture. The awareness that it is more appropriate to speak of confluence rather than conflict calls for more nuance in dealing with the evidence, therefore. Did enculturation/assimilation apply differently in different regions? What strands of Jewish culture could be accommodated to the new world-view in the light of continued contact with the Greeks, even before the advent of Alexander the Great? These and other similar questions need to be explored in detail in assessing the ethnic mix of Galilee, and the archaeological evidence has much to contribute to that discussion, as we shall see.

Closely related to this issue is the nature and history of the Jews in Galilee. The literary sources are sparse in the amount of information that they have to impart, and consequently the role of archaeology is crucial in filling in the blanks. Many scholars today prefer to speak of Judeans rather than Jews, since historically the name applies to the inhabitants of the territory of Judah. However, gradually it came to be applied to all those who adhered to the customs and practices of the Judeans, irrespective of their place of origin or residence. The discussion as to the proper nomenclature does raise the question of the population of the north in the centuries following the fall of the northern kingdom to the Assyrians in 732 and 721 BCE. Archaeological surveys suggest that there was a noticeable break in the settlement pattern in Galilee from the seventh to the fifth century BCE, thereby indicating a large-scale devastation and deportation, as the Assyrian records suggest. Unlike the fate of Samaria to the south some twelve years later, Galilee was not, it seems, resettled to the same extent with non-Israelite peoples. Further surveys in upper Galilee and the Golan point to a gradual upsurge in settlements from the fourth century onwards, many of them showing signs of a Judean presence in the material remains. This evidence is seen as confirmation of the accounts of the Maccabean expansion to include the north as part of the inherited land in the second and first centuries BCE.[34] Among modern students of Galilee, Richard Horsley does not agree with the scenario of an Assyrian devastation and claims that an Israelite, as distinct from a Judean presence continued in Galilee over the centuries, developing its own customs and practices in the interim. The Hasmonean expansion is then viewed as a colonization by Judeans of their Galilean Israelite cousins, thereby giving rise to a highly conflictual situation in the Galilee of Jesus' day.[35] Jesus' presence in and ministry to Galileans takes on a very different character depending on which of these scenarios one adopts. While archaeology cannot decide definitively on the matter it can, as we shall see in a later chapter, offer plausible evidence for deciding on the more likely of the two alternatives.

Whereas the two previous issues deal with cultural aspects of Galilee, the third topic on which archaeology has much to offer deals with Herodian influence on the social and economic fabric of the region. Here the excavation of Sepphoris is potentially of crucial importance, since Josephus tells us that Herod Antiaps, the son of Herod the Great and ruler of Galilee in Jesus' day, 'made it the ornament of all Galilee', giving it the name *autokrator*, or 'sole ruler' to honour Augustus. Furthermore, he founded Tiberias as a new city beside the lake, 'compelling people from everywhere to live there' and offering them plots of land for so doing. Both foundations must be seen as expressions of a policy of intensive Romanization in order to win favour from the imperial patrons. Because of present-day conditions the archaeological investigation of the former site has been much more thorough than that of the latter. Sepphoris has yielded up some of its splendour as a result of intensive exploration by various teams of archaeologists, Israeli and American. In visiting the site, however, one must be careful to distinguish between the Sepphoris of Jesus' day and that of later times, to which belong the most impressive of the finds, especially the Nile house, the Dionysus villa with its exquisite mosaic and the Synagogue floor, as well the underground water storage system.[36]

It is, therefore, difficult to assess the impact of 'imperial architecture' in the Sepphoris of Jesus' day, but there are other pertinent questions that can and are being put to the evidence. These have to do with the understanding of a pre-industrial city as an economic and social system, and the likely impact that such changes might have had on the inhabitants of the nearby villages, including Nazareth. Ongoing excavations at sites of differing size and importance in the region such as Jotapata, Khirbet Qana and Kefr Hanania, and lately Nazareth also, can provide comparative evidence in terms of lifestyles in urban and village centres, as well as the changing character of the villages themselves in the early Roman period. Furthermore the presence of coins, ceramic ware, both domestic and commercial, as well as other artefacts such as lead weights, inscriptions, figurines, etc. can all function as important clues to the networks of supply and demand that operated in the region, and the likely impact that these might have had on the peasants' lives, living under the shadow of Herodian opulence.

Outlining the Approach of the Present Study

One sometimes gets the impression from popular articles and TV programmes that archaeology can unlock the secrets of Galilee, and that 'the torn, but still legible landscape' can act as a fifth gospel, to borrow Ernest Renan's colourful expression. This, however, is far from the full truth, even though one should not underplay its significance, when the results are judiciously evaluated and brought into dialogue with the literary accounts. Since the evidence is always partial and capable of multiple interpretations, due modesty is called for with regard to any claims about our re-figuring of Galilee in the first century and Jesus' role there, however much we would like to see the full picture. Some scholars have shown a heavy reliance on sociological models to provide the framework within which both the archaeological evidence and the literary data about Jesus can be arranged to tell his story in a modern key that sounds suitably scientific. However, as Marianne Sawicki, herself a long time student of Galilee and the author of a perceptive study on the topic, reminds us: 'the generalised model provides no new evidence'. And she goes on to suggest that 'Jesus-historians have been reading sociology too reverently and texts too suspiciously'.[37]

It should be clear from the above discussion of the salient aspects of recent studies of the historical Jesus and Galilee that I prefer to be a critical, but not an overly suspicious reader of texts, employing sociology as a tool to provoke interesting questions rather than to provide a framework for a re-telling of the Jesus-story in its Galilean setting. Luke records the basis-biography that underlines all the gospels, including, in my opinion, the Fourth Gospel, in his second volume, *Acts of the Apostles*, when he attributes the following speech to Peter in a Roman setting:

> You know the message God sent to Israel, preaching peace through Jesus Christ. (He is Lord of all). That message spread through all Judea, beginning in Galilee, after the baptism that John announced: how God anointed Jesus of Nazareth with the Holy Spirit and with power; how he went about doing good and healing all who were oppressed by the devil, for God was with him. We are witnesses of all that he did in Judea and in Jerusalem. They put him to death by hanging him on a tree; but God raised him on the third day and allowed him to appear, not to all the people, but to us who were chosen by God as witnesses, and who ate and drank with him after he was raised from the dead. (Acts 10.36–41)

As the most self-consciously historical of the evangelists, Luke throughout his work shows a Thucydidean awareness of the role of speeches in history-writing. One did not need to be present to record the sentiments expressed. All that was required was to imagine what was suitable to the occasion, according to the great Attic writer, and here, as elsewhere in Acts, Luke shows himself as master of the art. In essence Jesus' life consisted of a beginning with John the Baptist, a middle 'doing good in Galilee' and an end in Jerusalem that, though it appeared to be failure, was in fact a vindication by God. The narrator is Peter who can with historical realism be made to claim the role of privileged witness to these events. By taking our cue from this brief outline we will at least be in a position to explore what the historical Jesus meant to his first-century followers, thus satisfying, it is to be hoped, Theissen's criterion of plausibility of effect. This three-point outline provides the perfect platform for exploring aspects of Jesus' life as this can be re-imagined within the Galilean and Judean worlds of the day. In fact the outline hints at three, not two places that Jesus engaged with in his career: the desert, Galilee and Jerusalem, and these three locations provide points of departure for the three opening chapters of this study.

However, in the light both of Moxnes' discussion of place as a contested space and the insights which the archaeological evidence (in conjunction with the literary accounts, as appropriate) can provide about the changing face of Galilee, it will be important to recognize that Jesus enters the region from the desert not 'to go home' to the old Galilee, but on a mission to remake it in accordance with his vision. Galilee is not a stage on which he acts out the drama of his life and which determines its direction. It is rather a challenge to compete for his version of Galilee in relation both to the external and the internal relations that existed in the region. Following the lead of various theoretical discussions Moxnes distinguishes three dimensions of place: the *experience* of place, namely, how it is managed and controlled; the *legitimation* of place, i.e. the ideological underpinning of the dominant controlling view; and the *imagination* of place or the way in which an alternative vision of place can be developed as well as the strategies that are required to implement the new vision. Helpfully, he makes suggestions as to how each of these categories applies to first-century Galilee. The experience of place relates to the existing spatial practices, for example the ownership and use of land, the flow of goods and the demands for any surplus that might accrue. The native elites, especially Herodians, legitimated their control through the claim that this pattern corresponded to the natural order of things: the annual tribute to the emperor and the agricultural and other offerings for the temple ensured that the highest authority's claims were clearly established, and as the immediate representatives of this twin authority, client rulers and Jerusalem priests, were entitled to their share by association.

To categorize from the perspective of place the exploitation and legitimation that obtained in Galilee as elsewhere in regard to land-ownership, taxation and other forms of control, is both novel and helpful, and we shall return to these aspects of the situation in the later chapters. However, the third dimension of 'imagined place' has particular resonance for the present study, since it raises directly the issue of the imaginative resources available to Jesus in order to develop his alternative view of Galilee. If we are to claim that 'doing good in Galilee' and 'hanging on a tree in Jerusalem' were more than mere accidental occurrences in terms of Jesus' sense of his own mission, then it should be possible to identify the stories, oracles and events that helped to shape his vision. In order to achieve that, however, the Jesus tradition, both in its general outline and in its details needs to be examined within the context of the larger Jewish story as this had been expressed and was accessible in the first century, keeping a particular eye on those aspects that might resonate particularly in Galilee. Only in that way is it possible to identify which currents of his diverse and multi-faceted Jewish inheritance shaped his vision and purpose. In a word, what were the most likely wellsprings that Jesus could draw on in order to challenge the prevailing sense of place that was Herodian Galilee, and how might he have sought to legitimate for his followers his particular strategy to realize his vision?

In most studies of Jesus' Jewish background there would appear to be a reluctance to envisage the idea that he himself, as distinct from his followers, might have been influenced by the Jewish Scriptures of his day. Scholars have turned to the more esoteric collections such as the Dead Sea Scrolls or to apocryphal works such as 1 Enoch in their search for suitable 'background'. I do not wish to minimize the importance of this material since much of it represents the ongoing living tradition of Judaism as this had been developed in various circles during the Second Temple period. On the evidence available to us it is not possible to draw a definite line between canonical and non-canonical writings in the Judaism of the first century CE. Clearly, some books were deemed to be authoritative but there does not seem to have been a fixed order or number of books that was universally acceptable, in the way that became standard in later Christianity. Writing about the year 130 BCE, the grandson of Jesus ben Sirach informs us in a prologue to his Greek translation of his grandfather's work that he was familiar with 'the law, the prophets and the writings of the fathers', a summary that sounds very like the tripartite division of the Hebrew Bible as we know it today. Elsewhere we hear of the law, the prophets and the book of psalms (Lk. 24.44) or 'the book of Moses, the prophets and David' (4Q MMT 7.10). Yet books like 1 Enoch and Jubilees, for example, would also appear to have been authoritative in the Qumran community on the basis of the number of manuscripts that have been found in the caves, thereby suggesting to one expert in the field that 'these texts had some form of authoritative status at some point in the history of the Qumran community and its antecedents'.[38] These works belong to a category of Jewish writings which, somewhat anachronistically have been described as rewritten Bible insofar as they take episodes (the flood, for example) or characters (Enoch, Noah, Abraham, Elijah, for example) from what later became identified as Biblical books and develop these quite independently of their original context. Thus, on this evidence the tradition was alive, imaginative and free, and the great variety of this interpretative literature shows the potential and impetus that existed to find new meanings from earlier texts to meet present needs.

Allowing for this fluidity and diversity within various streams of Judaism, which in some respects would appear to have been quite similar to the early Jesus-movement, it is still somewhat strange that scholars have for the most part not explored other possibilities also in their search for Jesus' Jewish background. It seems highly improbable that Jesus would have been unfamiliar with the foundational story of Israel as this was recorded in the *Torah*. Likewise, the oracles of salvation of great prophetic figures of Israel continued to be highly relevant for later generations also, again on the evidence of the Qumran community, but also in the composition of the *Lives of the Prophets*, a first-century CE introduction to the various prophets of Israel's history, and the erection of monuments over their tombs (Mt. 23.29).

One can suggest several reasons for this apparent blind spot, which calls for some comment. An obvious reason might be the belief that as a Galilean craftsman, Jesus would not have had the necessary levels of education in order to read or the means to study such texts. A recent study by Catherine Hezser suggests that literacy among Jews was no higher than among other Mediterranean people and that only the elite or the upper level retainer class could read and write.[39] It was one thing, therefore, for the Jerusalem scribe Jesus ben Sirach to have knowledge of the *Torah* and *Nebiim* and the other writings, but a Galilean peasant was a different matter. However, we have no way of knowing the social status of Jesus' family, and even if we did, it would prove very little. He had, after all, joined the Baptist circle, among whom presumably, as among its near cousins, the Essenes, study of torah was a daily exercise. The myth of 'the ignorant Galilean fishermen' (cf. Acts 4.13) was used to their advantage by the followers of Jesus as part of their claims about the truth of their message, and this characterization may have been applied to Jesus also in modern consciousness as well as in ancient attempts to vilify him (Mk. 6.2f.; Jn. 7.15). Even if Jesus belonged to the predominantly oral culture of his day, this did not mean that he was uneducated in terms of his own tradition, knowing what we do today about oral cultures and the role of memory in such societies.[40] Familiarity with Israel's story was to be communicated orally in the home, according to the Passover Seder (Exod. 13, 14). In addition, the Aramaic Targumim were intended for those who could not read or did not understand the Hebrew text, and the studies of Bruce Chilton, previously mentioned, have shown that there is a considerable degree of correspondence between the language and speech patterns of the Isaiah Targum and the recorded sayings of Jesus.[41]

There is, one suspects, another more telling reason for this rather glaring omission in contemporary study of Jesus, namely the criterion of dissimilarity, which ultimately separated Jesus from both his own Jewish roots and his followers' understanding of him, as previously discussed. Another possible reason for ignoring the importance of the Hebrew Scriptures in the life of Jesus by modern scholars is the fact that until recently, critical study of those writings, especially the Pentateuch, has been mainly concerned with exploring their historical nature in relation to Israel's origins. This has been the main focus of attention in Galilean studies also insofar as the Patriarchal and conquest narratives have entered into discussions about the Israelite character of Galilee in the late bronze and early iron age.

However, we are currently experiencing a paradigm shift in regard to the dating and the purpose of the Pentateuch. We cannot here enter into the hotly debated issue as to whether these texts contain historical traditions about early Israel or whether Israel itself is merely a construct of post-exilic Judah that has been retrojected back to earlier times. However, there seems to be a growing consensus that the Pentateuch not only reached closure in post-exilic times, but that more importantly, it addressed issues that were of particular importance then as the community sought to deal with questions of identity and diversity in the Persian period. This new awareness of the dating and concerns of the Pentateuch in its present form makes it possible to see it as part of the extraordinary literary output of this period, and it would explain also the fact that books such as 1 Enoch, Jubilees and The Testaments of the Twelve Patriarchs emerged as adaptations, elaborations and expansions of the foundational stories of Israel in such a free manner. Furthermore, given the fact that it was produced at a moment when Judah was a mere truncated portion of 'all Israel' as represented in the Pentateuchal narratives, these stories of origin function not so much as history but as prophecy, concentrating more on how Israel might and could be rather than how Israel once was.

Once the immediacy of the Biblical stories for the concerns and difficulties facing Jews in the Greek and Roman periods is recognized, there seems to be little good reason to deny to Jesus, as a reforming prophet endowed with the Spirit, a familiarity and engagement with those stories in whatever form they reached him. If at a very early stage indeed the early Christians turned to the Scriptures in order to understand the things that happened to Jesus (cf. 1 Cor. 15.2–4), it would seem somewhat perverse to deny such a facility to him also in the various circumstances he encountered, even when we cannot always cite the chapter and verse which might have inspired him. Such a concession would seem in all the circumstances to conform rather well with the criterion of contextual plausibility in regard to Jesus' relationship with his Jewish inheritance, assuring the coherence between Jewish matrix, Jesus himself and the Jesus-movement which is required, if we are to do justice to the historical relationships involved in the rise of early Christianity. It is with this working hypothesis that we will now attempt to put the criterion to work by reading in chapters 2–4 aspects of the Jesus-story in its broad outlines within a Galilean setting. In chapters 5 and 6 we will continue to operate within the same horizons, focusing now, however, on those aspects of Jesus' story which led to the ending in Jerusalem.

2

JESUS AND THE ECOLOGY OF
GALILEE

Three regions are recognised as regards the law of removal ... The Galilee
is divided into upper Galilee, lower Galilee and the Valley. From Kfar
Hananiah and northward, all places where the sycamore does not grow are
regarded as upper Galilee. And from Kfar Hananiah and southwards, all
places where the sycamores do grow are regarded as lower Galilee. And the
region of Tiberias is regarded as the Valley. (M.Sheb. 9.2)

This brief description of Galilean sub-regions is taken from the
tractate *Shebiith* (seventh year offerings) of the Mishnah, the Jewish
law-book compiled in the second century CE. The tractate deals
with the various obligations associated with the seventh year, when
according to Biblical law the land was to be left fallow. The
statement cited here occurs in a discussion of when precisely
harvesting must cease so that the farmers would not be seen to be in
violation of the seventh year regulations. Since harvest-time differed
from one region to another on the basis of local climatic conditions,
it was important to define those regions precisely. This vignette
illustrates well how closely Jewish religious attitudes were related to
the variations of the seasons and the natural conditions of the land.
None of the gospel writers mention these regional variations with
regard to Jesus' public ministry, yet it would appear that they are
familiar with the changing landscape of Galilee also, as we shall see.
On the other hand, Josephus, our other main literary source for
Galilee in the Roman period, signals the regional differences, even
though his main interest is on the region as a whole, the
governership of which he had taken over in 66 CE on behalf of
the Jewish revolutionary council.

In the light of the discussion in the previous chapter regarding
current trends in historical Jesus research, it is somewhat surprising
that very little has been written about his attitudes to the natural
environment. As was noted previously, a concern with the social

aspect of Jesus' ministry has replaced the dominant religious interest of a previous generation. Such a climate, one might have expected, would have meant that ecological issues in the ministry of Jesus would have been a focus of scholarly attention. Ironically, however, the change of perspective, though fuelled by concerns about justice for the marginalized, did not include eco-justice within its purview, despite the fact that clear evidence from third-world situations points to a direct link between despoliation of the natural environment by western commercial interests and the erosion of the traditional way of life of exploited peoples. The obvious explanation for these omissions in the past is that Biblical scholarship was mainly concerned with the divine-human message of the Biblical books. Salvation history was the dominant focus for various theologies of both the Old and New Testaments, produced by Christian scholars, and the natural world was of no particular interest or importance within the dominant European theological paradigms of the twentieth century.[1] Creation was subordinated to redemption and what distinguished Israel from her neighbours, it was claimed, was the rejection of the nature divinities of the surrounding peoples in favour of a God who was Lord of history.[2] The archaeology of Israel had not yet achieved the independent status it has today when its chief dialogue partners are not only social scientists, but also botanists, geologists, chemists and other material scientists. Biblical Archaeology in Palestine was formerly conducted as a service to Biblical studies, often of a conservative theological nature, whereas Near Eastern Archaeology, the preferred description of this branch of the discipline today, employs all manner of scientific analysis of the material remains of sites in order to understand aspects of humans' engagement with the natural world as well as with one other.[3]

More recently, the various social scientific models employed by Biblical scholars for understanding the world of Jesus have largely concentrated on economic and social factors, failing to take account of human connectivity with the eco- and bio-spheres. The interest in Jesus as a social revolutionary has led to an incomplete picture insofar as it ignores aspects of his respect for the natural environment also. While the recovery of his programme of inclusion of the marginalized has increasingly also included discussion of the role of women,[4] it is still based on models that do not take sufficient account of the challenge that gender analysis poses to the stereotyping of women and nature, and therefore does not explore the possible ecological implications of Jesus' challenge to his contemporaries in this regard also.[5] This calls for an exploration of the extent to which Jesus is indebted to those aspects of his inherited tradition that include an understanding of the earth as God's creation, and the implications of such a perspective for human interaction in his view. In responding to a question by a rich young man, Jesus is reported to have combined Israel's distinctive understanding of God, based on the *Shema'* (Deut. 6.4), with the Genesis idea of a good God: 'Why call me good? One is good, God' (Mk. 10.17). Did this awareness of the goodness of God as expressed in creation (Gen. 1) make him more sensitive to the natural world also, and if so, how did this awareness affect his understanding of the way that humans should behave towards one another and towards the gifts of the earth? The rich young man is advised to be rid of his possessions and follow Jesus' itinerant lifestyle. Are there ecological as well as social implications in this advice?

In discussing Jesus' attitude to the earth in the context of the Galilean environment, it is important to bear in mind the idea of place, not as a closed container in which human life is determined by the physical environment, but as negotiated space, as touched upon in the previous chapter. This is particularly important in the case of ecological discussions where the temptation of a romantic under-standing of nature and its influence can lead to very distorted and determinist views of human nature. A classic example of this attitude in regard to Jesus and Galilee is that of Renan, who, we have seen, equated landscape and human characteristics in an alarming manner. Describing the influence of lower Galilee on Jesus' views, he writes in the same vein:

> Such was the horizon of Jesus. This enchanted circle, the cradle of the kingdom of God, was for years his world. Even in later life he departed but little beyond the familiar limits of his childhood. For yonder, northwards, a glimpse is caught, almost on the flank of Hermon ... And here southwards the more sombre aspect of those Samaritan hills foreshadows the dreariness of Judea beyond, parched as by a scorching wind of desolation and death.[6]

No less fanciful is the description of geographer George Adam Smith. Commenting on the plentiful water supply of the Galilean region, he writes:

The difference in this respect (supply of water) between Galilee and Judea is just the difference between their names – the one liquid and musical like running waters, the other dry and dull like the fall of your horse's hoof on her blistered and muffled rock.[7]

Neither view has any place in a discussion of Jesus and the Galilean environment, especially when they are couched in such anti-Semitic terms. The focus here is on the two-way interaction between the natural environment and human cultivation in first-century Galilee, and the impact which this might have had on Jesus' own reactions to what he experienced in that environment and his consequent understanding of God's call to him. In order, to evaluate properly his response, however, it is necessary first to come to an appreciation of the manner in which the inherited traditions of Israel viewed the gifts of the earth.

Ecological Factors and Human Culture

The Genesis accounts of creation set the tone for Israelite views about the earth and human relations with it, even though one finds elsewhere, especially in poetic contexts, traces of different mythological ideas of Yahweh restraining the waters of the deep and overcoming the monsters that continue to threaten earth life.[8] The opening chapters of Genesis, however, provide a more ideal, if static view of creation: Gen. 1.1–2, 4 deals with God's ordering of the heavens and the earth in the six days of creation, and Gen. 2.5–24 describes the state of the first couple before and after the expulsion from the garden of Eden. The account of the creation of humankind (*adam*) in the first Genesis version would appear to give humans a dominant role over the animal and plant life, irrespective of what the precise meaning of the Hebrew verbs translated as 'have dominion' and 'subdue' (Gen. 1.26, 28) may be, since only humankind, both male and female, are said to be made in the image of God (Gen. 1.26, 27). This is usually described as the Priestly account, suggesting that the rest of the created world is oriented to human use, since humans are God's representatives on the earth, while also emphasizing that all of nature is the result of God's creative word, and therefore expressive of God's goodness.

By contrast, the second, or Yahwistic account touches only briefly on the details of the creation of the universe, focusing its attention instead on the two different conditions of humans – the blessings of

Eden before they disobey God's command and the curse of hard labour and toil with which they are afflicted after having been put out of the garden. Here the idea of the human struggle with the environment finds expression in the difficulties encountered both in generating life and in sustaining it. As the narrative of the primordial history unfolds, this struggle leads to violence and bloodshed, so that 'the wickedness of man was great upon the earth' (Gen. 6.5). The flood narrative which follows might appear to signal the return of the primordial chaos as the waters of the deep engulf the earth, leading to the destruction 'of every living thing from the face of the earth' – all, that is, except Noah and those with him in the ark (Gen. 7.23). However, Yahweh repents, promising never again to threaten the order he originally established: 'As long as the earth remains, sowing and reaping, cold and heat, summer and winter, day and night shall cease no more.' Yahweh makes 'an eternal covenant' not merely with Noah's descendants but 'with every living creature to be found with you ... There shall be no flood to destroy the earth again' (Gen. 8.22–9.11). Thus, when the next great act of human hubris occurs with the erection of the tower of Babel, Yahweh is true to his word. Humankind are scattered over the face of the earth, so that they no longer could understand each other, but 'the eternal covenant' with the earth is maintained. The call of Abraham to mediate the divine blessings to all 'the nations of the earth' now defines the future of both humankind and the earth, also. The 'eternal covenant' is still intact and God's blessings will endure (Gen. 15.18, 17.1–8).[9]

When the two accounts of creation in the opening chapters of Genesis are read within this broader context of the primeval history as a whole, the human dominance over the material world that is apparently suggested is considerably curtailed. The larger context shows that the redactors of the Pentateuch were deeply conscious of the fractured and ambiguous situation in which humans find themselves in their relationship with the natural world. As 'earth-creatures' they are an integral part of the material world, sharing with animals, birds and fishes the breath of life that permeates God's whole creation, and yet that world in all its animal and plant diversity appeared to have been ordered for human good. The invitation to Adam to name the animals in the second account seems to go even further, a sign of the divine condescension in 'the hierarchy of creation' that allows humans to complete God's creative word. Disobedience has turned what was intended as a blessing into a curse, resulting in alienation between them and the earth and between humans themselves, when harmony and bliss was their intended lot. These stories anticipate Israel's story, as this will unfold in the subsequent narrative of her precarious occupation of the land. Thus in the accounts of the tribal blessings (Gen. 49; Deut. 33), animal traits can be freely employed to describe the tribes' varied characteristics and their struggles to establish themselves within their allotted territories, without any pejorative intent. The different blessings that sea, mountain and plain have to offer various tribes are fully acknowledged, while also proving to be highly ambiguous, as it turns out.

Whereas previously, scholars have understood the descriptions of the tribal characteristics as reflecting the conditions that obtained in early Israel with the shift from the nomadic to the settled way of life, more recent scholarship points to a later date of composition. Israel's occupation of the allotted land continued to be precarious over the centuries, as various imperial powers – Assyrians, Babylonians, Persians, Greeks – had all controlled Israel at various junctures of her history. It was as a response to the continued threat posed by this history that the mythical stories of creation were intended to function, offering consolation and reassurance to those whose position seemed to be highly precarious, caught between the poles of stability and ruin, creation and devastation. In detecting various aspects of the conquering nations' mythical world-views in the Israelite creation and flood accounts, scholars have by implication pointed to the way in which Israel had co-opted the stories of her conquerors to respond to the human and national crises that she was experiencing through their domination. An essential component of the reassurance that these stories offered was the acceptance that it was Yahweh, not Tiamat, Marduk or Assur, that had created the world, and that his original intention, manifested to Israel through liberation from slavery in Egypt, was to maintain the good earth that he had created, despite human wickedness. The earth and its blessings were the guarantee of Yahweh's continued favour, his eternal covenant. It behoved Israel to respect that earth, and this was enshrined in her law codes.

The Ecology of the Promised Land

As the home of the northern tribes, Galilee was the first region to suffer at the hands of the Assyrian ruler Tiglathpilesar III in 731 BCE, and it was only natural that the blessings of the land and the awareness of its variegated and distinctive natural features were more keenly felt. This situation may well be reflected in the book of Deuteronomy, where the author portrays Yahweh as the warrior Lord who is the rightful owner of the whole land, having driven out the previous owners (the Canaanites and others) in order to bequeath it to Israel in a divinely sanctioned treaty. The richness and fertility of the land is stressed in order to entice Israel to observe the conditions of the treaty, foremost of which is the rejection of any other gods except Yahweh alone.[10] Two aspects of the treatment are highly significant for our inquiry into possible ecological dimensions of Jesus' career. These are the contrasts drawn between Israel and Egypt on the one hand, and that between the conditions of life in the promised land and those that obtained in the desert on the other. It seems possible to detect behind both contrasts echoes of the creation stories, and their underlying theological concerns.

> The land which you are about to enter to occupy is not like the land of Egypt, from which you have come, where you sow your seed and irrigate with the foot, like a garden of vegetables; but the land which you are crossing over to possess is a land of hills and valleys, watered by rain from heaven, a land which the Lord your God cares for; for the eyes of the Lord your God are always upon it, from the beginning of the year to the end of the year. (Deut. 11.10–12)

Once Israel has entered into the land (the book is an address of Moses, set in a desert context), her life will be blessed because she will have inherited a blessed land in terms of its natural resources. In particular the importance of water for human life is underlined, and the contrast with Egypt in that regard is sharply drawn. There, human labour is required for irrigation in order to cultivate a garden of vegetables, but in Israel the rain comes as a gift from heaven and the earth drinks it up, since God cares for the land and that care is the source of its fruitfulness for Israel, 'a land flowing with milk and honey' (Exod. 3.8; Deut. 6.3, 11.8).[11] In this perspective the land is not cursed and there is no sense of the labour and toil that is to be the lot of humans according to the Genesis account of the expulsion of Adam and Eve from the garden of Eden (Gen. 3.1–17). This fertile land is pure gift. However, the presence of the desert always looms close at hand, should Israel disobey the covenant demands.

The contrast between life and death, blessing and curse, which is laid before the people at the end of the book (Deut. 30.15–20) can equally be expressed in the contrast between the land of Israel and the desert. In a remarkably lyrical description of the land, north and south, both its natural fertility and its geological texture, the Deuteronomist draws this contrast as follows:

> For the Lord, your God, is bringing you into a good land, a land with flowing streams, with springs and underground waters welling up in valleys and hills, a land of wheat and barley, of vines and fig trees and pomegranates, a land of olive trees and honey, a land where you may eat bread without scarcity, where you will lack nothing, a land whose stones are iron, and from whose hills you may mine copper. You shall eat your fill and bless the Lord your God for the good land he has given you. Take care that you do not forget the Lord your God by failing to observe his laws, his ordinances and his statues ... When all that you have has multiplied, do not exalt yourself forgetting the Lord your God who brought you out of Egypt ... who led you through the great and terrible wilderness, an arid wasteland full of snakes and scorpions. He made water flow for you from flint rock and fed you in the wilderness with manna, that your ancestors did not know in order to humble you and to test you and in the end to do you good. (Deut. 8.11–16)

The richness of the land can be a temptation to Israel to forget that Yahweh was the donor, however. Such forgetfulness will bring down a curse, not only on the Israelites, but on the land itself. Wasteland conditions will be established and the land will cease to produce its fruits no matter how much they toil; they shall neither drink the wine nor anoint themselves with the oil, both highly pertinent crops in a Galilean situation (Deut. 28.38–40). Later, another set of stark images is employed to underline the permanent devastation of the land: succeeding generations will suffer from the ecological conditions which Israel's sinfulness will have brought about: 'all its soil burned out by sulphur and salt, nothing planted, nothing sprouting, unable to support any vegetation, like the destruction of Sodom and Gomorrah' (Deut. 29.21–23).

While the Deuteronomist's description of the ecological conditions suggest a northern colouring, prompted possibly by the Assyrian devastation, the Priestly Code in Leviticus chapters 17–26 dates from the time of the exile, when Judah had suffered a similar fate to the north at the hands of the Babylonians. Again, however, it is possible to detect a similar process at work, namely, an idealized picture of conditions in the land and the Israelites' relationship with it compensating for the sense of loss that had been experienced in exile, and the changing social conditions that this had brought about. Central to the legislation is the idea that Yahweh is the owner of the land and Israelites are tenants with the somewhat restricted rights of aliens (*gerim*, Lev. 25.23). The basis for Yahweh's ownership is not, as in Deuteronomy, one of conquest, but rather the claim that the land is temple-land that belongs to the deity, and therefore shares in the holiness of Yahweh who is present in his temple and throughout his land. The emphasis, therefore, is not on the natural fertility of the land but on its holiness, and Yahweh's ownership has to be asserted every fiftieth year, when, in addition to the regular cycle of a seventh year Sabbatical, a special Jubilee year has to be observed at the end of seven sabbatical cycles.[12]

It is against this background that the regulations for the Sabbath and Jubilee years (Lev. 25.1–55) must be understood which reflect a major development from previous legislation to do with the land and its produce. While the Deuteronomic Code also dealt with the Sabbath (but not the Jubilee) year, the emphasis was on the obligation to care for the poor by the remission of debt (Deut. 15.1–11), not on the relationship with the land. In Leviticus, however, this aspect of restoration of right relationships within the community is associated with the Jubilee, or fiftieth year, where it is extended to the return of property acquired since the previous Jubilee to its original owners and the freeing of Israelite slaves (Lev. 25.8–55).

Concern for the earth is developed in quite a radical way in the legislation for the sabbatical year in this Code (Lev. 25.1–7). The more ancient law of leaving a fallow field every seventh year, which was designed to assist the poor and the wild animals (Exod. 23.10–11), is radically transformed so that the Israelite peasants should not perform any agricultural activity at all in the seventh year. The reason for this is that the land itself must rest by being returned to its owner, Yahweh. The motivation is religious rather than humanitarian or ecological, as in the Exodus law, therefore. Commenting on this legislation, Norman Habel insightfully remarks:

> The link between Israel's obedience and a future in the land is a common theme elsewhere, but here the focus is on the land itself playing a role, yielding or not yielding its produce, depending on the relationships of the Israelites to their land-owner ... The land is a living reality with rights to be respected.'[13]

While the land will enjoy its Sabbath from human cultivation of any kind, human and animal needs will be taken care of. To the question: 'What shall we eat in this seventh year if we do not sow or harvest the produce?', Yahweh replies that his blessing will ensure a plentiful supply in the sixth year to cover that year, the seventh or sabbatical year and the eight year, until the new harvest arrived, 'since the land will yield its fruit, and you will eat your fill and live securely' (Lev. 25.19). Such a utopian plan was totally dependent on Israel's obedience to Yahweh as the land-owner, but also on the belief that the land itself would do his bidding because it shared his holiness. As a practical programme it would, if enacted, have wrought havoc to a peasant economy, given the diversified ecological situation within the land, and in the light of the obligation to pay tribute in kind to foreign overlords.

Prophets and the Natural Environment of Israel

While the Deuteronomic and Levitical law codes give two different, though highly pertinent views of the role of the natural world in Israel's life and destiny, the prophets are also deeply conscious of the rich symbolism of the natural world as expressive of Yahweh's relations with Israel, when describing both present infidelity and future restoration. Surprisingly, Hosea can view the desert as a place of refreshment (Hos. 1–3), but more typically both he and Amos view the future restoration in terms of a renewal of the natural beauty of the earth and the rich abundance of the harvest (Hos. 14.6–7; Amos 9.13–15). Jeremiah also employs these same images for the restoration to come (Jer. 24.6, 31.27–28, 32.41). This prophet has deeply personal feelings for the land's pollution and its suffering because of the sins of the people: 'I am in anguish, I writhe in pain, my heart is throbbing', he declares, as he relates his vision of apocalyptic destruction of the creation: the earth is a formless void, the lights of the heavens have gone out, the mountains are quaking and the birds of the air have vanished, as Yahweh prepares to execute his judgement (Jer. 4.19–31).

Isaiah also relies on images from the world of nature and the animal kingdom to describe both the desolation of judgement and the renewal to come. Judah's land is desolate as after the fall of Sodom; Zion is left like an abandoned lean-to in a vineyard (Isa. 1.7–9), and the vineyard itself (Judah) will be devastated, so that thorns and weeds will grow where once the hoe was used to till the vine (Isa. 5.1–5, 7.23–25). He reserves his most vivid use of the imagery of natural devastation for the punishment of enemy nations:

Babylon will be ravaged so that even a nomad will not pitch his tent there and jackals will roam through its once splendid palaces (Isa. 13.19–22); Edom is turned into a wasteland (Isa. 34). Yet future restoration has an Eden-like quality, a restoration of the original harmony both in natural world and in humans' relations with it (Isa. 11.1–9).

For both parts of the Hebrew Bible – the Law and the Prophets – human life and the life of animals and plants are inextricably bound together for good and ill. God's eternal covenant (*berit olam*) embraces both animal and plant life (Gen. 8.22–23) as well as human (Gen. 17). It is a gratuitous gift from God, whereas his covenant with Israel is conditional on observance of the pattern which Yahweh had established in the creation and which was expressed in God's resting on the Sabbath (Exod. 31.13–17). In all pre-industrial societies human life is heavily dependent on the fruitfulness of the earth, giving people a deep sense of bonding with the natural environment. However, the Israelite experience went deeper still because of the belief that the earth was Yahweh's alone, since he had created it and seen that it was good. Israel stood between a blessed and a blighted land, between Eden and Sodom, depending on its willingness to acknowledge its total indebtedness to Yahweh as expressed in the covenant stipulations. While Yahweh's use of the natural world to punish and reward Israel might appear capricious and even devaluing of the earth, the assurance of the new creation of which Isaiah in particular speaks (Isa. 65.17, 66.22) and which finds its way into the New Testament through Paul (Rm. 8.18–25), indicates that in the Biblical perspective human redemption can only be considered in conjunction with the redemption of the earth itself. This was the case because human life could not be considered apart from earth life. Both shared the same fate, because both were inextricably bound together as expressions of God's creative goodness.

Wisdom and Creation

The Israelite tradition as received by Jesus had, in addition to the Law and the Prophets, another highly significant strand, that of Wisdom, which, like the Mesopotamian creation myths, was also derived from the larger international environment. Here the notion of creation as expressive of divine wisdom provides a more stable view of the natural world than that presented by the mythic pattern of the conflict between good and evil affecting the material universe also. While the Israelite wisdom tradition bears all the hallmarks of its international provenance, at its higher level it has been thoroughly integrated into Israel's theological framework, especially in terms of the personification of Wisdom as Yahweh's helpmate in creation (Prov. 8.22–31), and through its identification with the Torah of Moses (Sir. 24.27). The links between Wisdom and Apocalyptic are also well established in Daniel and 1 Enoch, pointing to wisdom as heavenly and esoteric, calling for divine revelation in order to unlock its secrets.

We shall have occasion to discuss these aspects of the Wisdom tradition in later chapters, but here it is popular wisdom, exemplified particularly by the proverb or gnomic saying, which is of special interest. The fact that this type of wisdom could be incorporated into the scheme of higher wisdom with its creation-centred perspective, suggests that the rhythms of the created world were a primary source of its inspiration. As in all peasant societies, Israelites also had to rely on their powers of observation in coping with the everyday problems of home and field, sky and earth. Wisdom, honed down to short, pithy statements that encapsulated a lot of human experiences and experiments in dealing with everyday problems, offered practical advice for living. As Gerhard von Rad puts it, even seemingly 'naïve observations have an involved intellectual pre-history'.[14] This was based on the observation and contemplation of a large number of similar occurrences, giving rise to an awareness of certain patterns both in nature and in human life. Knowledge of these was important if one was to negotiate successfully the difficulties that are encountered in the course of the everyday. However, these patterns were never understood as laws by which the hidden meaning of the world could be discovered. Human life and natural life often replicated each other, so that likenesses are easily observable: 'Clouds and winds and yet no rain. So is a man who boasts of gifts and never gives' (Prov. 25.14). Because life is mysterious and there are no laws governing it in the way that the Greeks could speak of a law of nature, there is a certain playfulness about the popular wisdom tradition, an ability to observe the ironies of life and learn from them. Thus the riddle, presenting some enigmatic problem was a favoured form, as the story of the Queen of Sheba's visit to Solomon, mentioned by Jesus (Mt. 12.42; Lk. 11.31), famously illustrates (1 Kgs. 10). There was a serious side to this style, however, since it was intended to engage the hearer in an active discovery of the underlying truth. Unlike the higher wisdom of the scribes or the revealed wisdom of the seer, popular wisdom did not presuppose a school setting but could be pursued at any level and in any context, because the raw material of life's struggles was all that was required.

Because the Israelite doctrine of creation did not understand the world as a free-standing entity, but as an extension of Yahweh's self-disclosure, popular wisdom could be easily fitted into more theological modes of thought and discourse. For such a mentality the insights into the working of the world attained through popular wisdom are nothing short of the disclosure of the God-self that lies behind and beyond those patterns, and makes their operation both possible and intelligible. Faith in the creator God identifies the presence of God in the seemingly most insignificant and mundane aspects of the creation. Longer poems can bring this characteristic Hebraic insight to a more profound expression in a striking manner. In these instances the centrality of the human person within the creation is emphasized as in Sirach (Sir. 16.24–18.14, 42.13–43.33), whereas at other times the variety of the natural world itself becomes the object of the poets' contemplation (Pss. 19, 104; Job 38.1–39.30). Yet behind these extended compositions lies a poetic imagination that operates with the single insight that Israel's proverbial tradition had captured in a profoundly simple manner.

Paul of Tarsus, with his two-culture background, expressed this understanding in his adaptation of the traditional *Shema'* prayer (Deut. 6.4): everything that exists has come *from* the one God and exists *for* the one God. To this basic Jewish formulation, Christ as the one *through* whom are all things and *through* whom they exist, is added, without any sense of disloyalty to his ancestral piety (1 Cor. 8.6). The Greek philosophical colouring is apparent in the use of prepositions to express causality, but the possibility of including Jesus Christ in the formula as the instrumental cause of creation arose from the creation theology of the Wisdom tradition, that could speak of Lady Wisdom being present with the creator in the foundation of the world (Prov. 8.22–31). What Paul's cosmopolitanism could express in this way for his Corinthian congregation who claimed wisdom for themselves (cf. 1 Cor. 1.24), Jesus' parabolic discourse could articulate more concretely in and through the popular wisdom of his Galilean peasant audiences who lived close to nature and depended on it for their subsistence.

Jesus and the Micro-Ecologies of Galilee

The discussion of the ecological aspects of the Hebrew Scriptures provides a rich set of images reflecting the nature of the land, its diverse landscapes and its varied floral and faunal life. Despite their different perspectives all strands of the tradition share a common understanding that the natural world is an expression of Yahweh's creative power as 'Lord of Heaven and Earth'. Indeed when one reads the Hebrew Scriptures with a view to their appreciation of the natural world it is impossible to agree with the charge that Israel's monotheistic faith as expressed in these writings contributed to the de-sacralization of nature.[15] Despite the changes of political regimes over the centuries and the attendant social and cultural upheavals, it still remains true that the inherited religious attitudes with regard to the world of nature remained alive and operative and continued to shape Israel's sense of her own destiny. The Rabbinic movement of the second century CE produced the Mishnah, which has been described by Jewish scholar Jacob Neusner as the work of scribes based on the perspective of priests, but reflecting the social world of peasant householders living in the land and responsible for the maintenance of purity as this was defined in the Biblical laws, especially the Holiness Code of Leviticus.[16] This emphasis becomes evident in the amount of attention that is paid to agricultural matters in the first two divisions of the Mishnah, those of Appointed Times and Agriculture. Undoubtedly, Jewish farmers like others in the Near East were familiar with Greek and Roman technical knowledge in agricultural matters – as the archaeological record clearly indicates – yet the religious thinkers continued to develop the ideas that had been prompted by the Scriptural views on the obligations surrounding agricultural produce in maintaining the holiness of Yahweh's land.[17]

The Jesus-movement could equally be described as originating within a similar social matrix, but with rather different concerns. It too was heir to the Scriptural views of nature as God's creation and operated within the village, as distinct from the urban culture of Galilee. The fact that it was not concerned with the holiness of the land as defined later by the Rabbis, does not mean that either Jesus or his first followers had abandoned the sense of God's presence to them in their everyday world of plants, animals, natural environment and the processes of life and death that the agricultural cycle of the year proclaimed. Because the gospels are the narrative accounts of aspects of Jesus' life as he engaged with humans, and are, presumably, written for a largely urban clientele towards the end of the first century, one might easily get the impression that at best the natural world provided a background, a ready-made source of images for Jesus' theocentric and anthropocentric message, and that nature as such was of little consequence to his concerns.

However, that would be a superficial reading, given Jesus' rich heritage of seeing human life within the context of all life, and his deep sense of God as the creator of heaven and earth and all that is in them. The importance of Jesus' belief in the creator God is something that we shall encounter in more detail in later chapters. Here one only needs to recall those aspects of his piety that are expressed in the few recorded addresses of Jesus to his God: 'Abba/Father' (Lk. 11.2; Mt. 6.10) and 'I thank thee Father, Lord of heaven and earth' (Lk. 10.21; Mt. 11.25). The address to God as Father, while coming under criticism from a modern feminist perspective, needs to be understood in the context of Jesus' own situation where the notion of kinship is central to his understanding of his community. The role of father is that of provider of the necessities of life, thus making it a suitable image for God as creator and sustainer of all life. 'Lord of heaven and earth', likewise, has clear allusions to Yahweh's creator-role against the backdrop of the Genesis story of God creating the heavens and the earth (Isa. 40.12, 42.5, 48.13).

Ancient observers of Palestine such as Strabo and Pliny were more conscious of any unusual features of the flora and fauna or the landscape, the former mentioning that the precious balsam tree grew in the Plain of Genneserath (though he may have confused this with lake Huleh to the north), and the latter noting the hot springs of Tiberias.[18] However, it is the Jewish historian Josephus who gives the most detailed statement of the relationship between landscape and people in regard to Galilee of Jesus' day. After outlining the political boundaries of the first century, he writes as follows:

> With this limited area, and although surrounded by such powerful nations, the two Galilees have always resisted any hostile invasion, for the inhabitants are from infancy inured to war, and have at all times been numerous; never did the men lack courage nor the country men. For the land is everywhere so rich in soil and pasturage and produces such a variety of trees that even the most indolent are tempted by these facilities to engage in agriculture. In fact it has all been cultivated by the inhabitants and there is not a single portion left

waste. The cities too are plentiful and because of the richness of the soil the villages everywhere are so densely populated that even the smallest of them has a population of over fifteen thousand inhabitants. (*JW*. 3.41–43)

Even allowing for Josephus' well-known penchant for exaggeration, his account of the links between Galilee's fertility and its dense population is a good example of the interaction between place and people that modern social theory highlights. His basic description of Galilee when he was in charge of the first revolt in the region in 66/67 CE is borne out by modern geological studies of rock and soil formation as well as by archaeological surveys of the dense settlement pattern in the countryside.[19] In the more mountainous region of upper Galilee aerial photography has shown the outlines of extensive terracing of the slopes where the vine and the olive were cultivated, suggesting high-density population and intensive cultivation. This aspect of Galilean life is reflected in place names such as Gush ha-lab (Gischala), 'the valley of the olive', and Beth ha-kerem, 'the house of the vine'. Josephus describes Gischala as 'rich in olive oil' as he tells the story of John's shameful exploitation of his co-religionists in Cæsarea by selling them oil produced in the region at double the going rate (*JW* 2.590–592).

Unfortunately, the gospels are not as specific as Josephus with regard to Galilean geography in their telling of the story of Jesus. Nevertheless, expressions such as 'throughout all Galilee', 'the surrounding territory of Galilee' and 'through cities and towns' which are employed to describe the movements of Jesus in the region, all reflect a generally accepted view that his was an itinerant ministry, which was replicated in the sending of the disciples to the towns and villages also. When some actual places are mentioned as, for example, Mk. 7.31, the evangelists have sometimes been accused of ignorance of, or misinformation about Galilean topography.[20] In making such judgements scholars are operating with our present maps of Galilee in mind. However, recent attention to peasant ways of viewing the world from a local perspective that has only a limited knowledge of or interest in regions lying beyond the periphery of their immediate locale, casts a different light on gospel geography.[21]

The Sea/Lake of Gennesareth is undoubtedly the centre of the Galilean action, even though all the gospels seem to have much more detailed information of Judean and Jerusalemite topography. Nazareth is firmly established in the traditions as Jesus' home-town

(*patris*) even though Caphernaum can be described as his own city
(*ten idian polin,* Mt. 9.1; cf. Mk. 2.1). While the Fourth Gospel
highlights Jesus' visits to Cana (2.1, 12, 4.43f.) it also recognizes the
tradition about Caphernaum (Jn. 2.12). The earliest topographical
references to Jesus' public ministry are probably the Q sayings
condemning the towns of Bethsaida, Corazin and Caphernaum
because of their refusal to repent (Mt. 11.20–24; Lk. 10.13–15).
Other stories such as the healing of the Gadarene demoniac (Mk.
5.1–19); the encounter with the Syro-Phoenician woman (Mk.
7.24–29) and the discussion with the disciples in the region of
Cæsarea Philippi about his identity (Mk. 8.27–30), all suggest that
Jesus' travels took him through different sub-regions of Galilee –
towards the coastal plain, upper Galilee and across the Lake to the
Golan region, each ecologically as well as politically and culturally
diverse.

One plausible view of this outline presentation in terms of the
historical Jesus, which will be explored further in the following
chapter, is to recognize here the contours of a scheme that seeks to
represent Jesus as having covered all regions of the northern part of
the inherited land of Israel, inspired by his ideas and hopes of Jewish
restoration eschatology. With this working hypothesis it is
interesting to pose the question as to how Jesus might have reacted
to the different natural, as distinct from cultural environments that
he would have encountered on his travels. These different sub-
regions had given rise to different modes of human interaction with,
and opinions about the natural world. How might his experience of
and reflections on these regional variations have coloured his actual
sense of his ministry and mission in the light of the received
tradition? We shall follow him on some of these movements seeking
to discern in the recorded sayings and deeds some of his responses to
the changing natural environment he would have encountered on
such journeys.

From the Desert to Lower Galilee

The earliest phase of Jesus' public ministry that historians can reliably
trace is that of a close connection with John the Baptist and his call
for repentance together with a ministry of baptism beyond the
Jordan. The Fourth Gospel is the most explicit in that it speaks of
Jesus also engaging in a ministry like John's (Jn. 3.21). The Q
document is an important earlier witness to Jesus' avowed

admiration for John and his lifestyle: 'Of those born of women there is no one greater than John' (Mt. 11.11; Lk. 7.28). In both Mark and Q John is represented as a 'desert figure' living on 'locusts and wild honey' and far removed from the urban lifestyle of Herodian elites. John's gospel locates him along the Jordan, at Aenon, near Salim, whose location is unknown, or more generally in Perea (Jn. 3.22–24, 10.40–42). Josephus would seem to support this latter location by declaring that John was imprisoned in Machaerus, a fortress east of the Dead Sea. The two traditions (Q/Mark and John/Josephus) can be easily harmonized, once 'the desert' is understood in terms of the Judean desert, where indeed, human life, either nomadic or sedentary, was sustainable, as the residents of Qumran and other figures such as Josephus' teacher Bannus, testify. Two different Hebrew terms – *arabah* and *midbar* – are translated as *eremos*/desert and they can refer either to a desert in the strict sense or to a wilderness where there is little or no human habitation. Either landscape contrasts sharply with the arable land of either the coastal plain or the central highlands, and Josephus' remark that the Jordan river wanders through much desert (*eremian*) on its way from the Lake of Gennesareth to the Dead Sea (*JW* 3.515) allows for plenty of latitude in determining the theatre of John's and Jesus' activity.[22]

In Jewish religious memory the desert had particular associations to do with Israel's origins when Yahweh was close to them in their wanderings, but also as a place where Israel had put Yahweh to the test, because of the dangers, real and mythological, that were associated with such a barren location. Then, as now, the desert, though threatening in terms of human survival, was a place that facilitated a deeper encounter with the self and the discovery of a new purpose, freed as one was from the encumbrance of life as lived in 'the real world'. It was natural, therefore, that various Jewish dissidents are to be found in the desert as part of their protest against the existing religious establishment, the Qumran Essenes being the foremost example from the first century CE. Significantly, the evangelists seem to be conscious of this dimension of Jesus' own personal story when they present him at prayer, typically in a desert or lonely place. In their view, like Elijah before him (1 Kgs. 19.8), he had never totally abandoned that primal location and could return there as his own needs demanded.[23]

If Jesus had been a disciple of John's and had shared his desert experience, his return to Galilee marked a very definite shift of environment, therefore. The distinction between upper and lower

Galilee suggested by the Mishnah is based on natural features to do
with the (fig) sycamore that is most frequently associated with the
Shephelah region in the south, according to the literary sources
(1 Kgs. 10.27; 2 Chron. 1.15; Amos 7.14), but is mentioned for the
Carmel region also.[24] In fact the Shephelah and the Nazareth range
both share the same type of rock – semi-pervious chalk and marl
which produces soil-cover to the top as well as springs. In this
respect the Nazareth hills differ from the other three ranges (Tiran,
Yotvath and Shagor ranges) which divide lower Galilee into a series
of valleys running in an east/west direction. These three more
northerly ridges consist of hard and craggy limestone from the
Cenomanian age and are uninviting for human habitation. Springs
are to be found on or near the floors of the valleys. This means that
the basins between the ridges are fertile with deep soil suitable for
cereals and other crops, most famously, the Bet Netofah plain.
Consequently, the settlements are all located close to natural springs,
the result of minor faulting, or man-made cisterns. The Nazareth
ridge, by contrast, has villages, including Nazareth itself situated near
the summit, because of the possibility of cultivation that it offers
right to the top of the range (see Map 1).[25]

   The question has been raised, but to my mind not adequately
answered, as to why Jesus' ministry took on a very different style and
strategy to that of his erstwhile mentor, John, once he arrived in
Galilee.[26] One element of an adequate answer must surely be this
shift of environment, once this is not understood romantically as in
the nineteenth century, but in terms of the ways in which human life
was lived and had adapted in the different habitats. The contrast for
human living between what the Deuteronomist describes as 'the arid
wasteland with fiery snakes and scorpions' and 'the land with
flowing streams and with springs and underground waters welling up
in valleys and hills' (Deut. 8.7–15, 11.13–17) must have been
blindingly obvious. The extent to which such an 'exodus'
experience might possibly have caused him to reflect again on his
understanding of God's call and his own role, especially in the light
of the inherited belief in the gift of the land, cannot be properly
assessed in isolation from other aspects of his ministry. Yet, it seems
altogether plausible to suggest that the contrasting experience of the
potential blessedness of life in the land, must have touched him to the
point of re-evaluating the present as a graced moment rather than
one of awaiting God's imminent judgement, cathartic though the

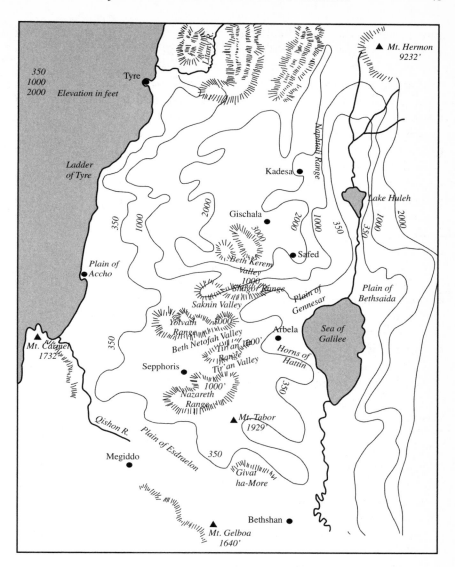

Map 1   Physical Features of Galilee

desert environment had been viewed by various Jewish reformers, before and after him.

The phrase *potential blessedness* in that suggestion is crucial, since the effects of Herodian rule in Galilee as elsewhere meant that the resources of the land were not equally shared by all its inhabitants as was intended in the Deuteronomic and Levitical ideals. A different and more immediate challenge was posed, namely, to raise an awareness of how the present as lived in the land was such a distortion of the original vision, and to offer an alternative that might be different, indeed may we say, messianic. Jesus may have left the desert conditions behind him when he returned to the environs of lower Galilee, but he brought with him values that were reflected in his erstwhile mentor, John's, diet, namely, locusts and wild honey. On his return to Galilee Jesus' lifestyle was inferior to that of the animal and bird world: 'Foxes have holes and the birds of the air have nests, but the Son of Man has nowhere to lay his head' (Mt. 8.20; Lk. 9.58). Neither sought the comfort of familial homes, not to speak of royal palaces, and in true prophetic manner both sought to challenge not just in words, but in lifestyle also, the prevailing values of the culture.

Recent excavations in the grounds of the Scottish Hospital suggest that Nazareth was a farming settlement in the Roman period. The excavated farm shows considerable human development in terms of watch-towers, terracing, grape presses and a field irrigation system. This was supplied by water flowing in a nearby wadi, which originated in a spring higher up the hill.[27] Presumably this would be typical of other villages in the neighbourhood, all of which were situated on the ridge because of the good soil-cover and the plentiful supply of springs on the summit. The village culture that such an environment created was that of small-scale farming with peasant land-owners and their families the most common type of resident. These settlements represent Jewish colonization of the Galilee from the mid-second century BCE, in the wake of the Hasmonean expansion.[28] In order to ease the population pressures in the south, allotted land was granted to army veterans and others willing to migrate north in the newly (re)captured territories deemed to have been part of the ancestral land. Such settlers remained staunchly Jewish and pro-Hasmonean and never willingly accepted the Herodians or their lifestyle. The Nazareth farm project supports the idea that they were not just mere subsistence farmers, but like all colonizers in the Mediterranean as elsewhere, worked the land intensively, participated in the redistributive system and were able to support a relatively comfortable lifestyle. The main crops would be the traditional Mediterranean ones of cereals (mainly wheat and maize), olives, figs and grapes. This should not obscure the fact that their way of life was still precarious, and heavily dependent on factors outside their control such as annual variations in the weather patterns and demands on their resources from passing armies or other impositions by absent rulers.

In Jesus' day the rebuilding of Sepphoris 'as the ornament of all Galilee' inevitably put extra pressure on the traditional way of life of the peasant land-owners in the villages in its immediate vicinity, such as Nazareth. Human as well as natural resources, including, or especially the water, were required to maintain the luxurious and decorative lifestyle of the urban elites, with their fine garments and royal palaces, adorned with fountains and bath houses. It was from such people that John the Baptist had maintained his distance, according to Jesus' characterization (Mt. 11.8; Lk. 7.25).[29] Payment of the tribute that was due to Rome in addition to Antipas' personal allowance of 200 talents, required that the land should be intensively cultivated and harvested each year. Several of Jesus' sayings echo this constant struggle of the peasant with the elements, expressed in typical proverbial form:

> Are grapes gathered from thorns or figs from thistles? (Mt. 7.16; Lk. 6.48)
> The rains came and the wind blew and they beat upon that house. (Mt. 7.25/Lk. 6.48)
> God makes his sun to rise on the wicked and the good, and the rain to fall on the just and the unjust alike. (Mt. 5.45; Lk. 6.35)
> In the evening you say it will be fine weather for the sky is red and in the morning it will be stormy today because the sky is red. (Mt. 16.2–3; Lk. 12.54)
> The ravens do not have to sow or reap or gather into barns. (Mt. 6.20; Lk. 12.24)

As the demands coming from the centre grew, the margins for the smaller land-owners and their families were reduced, driving many of them to penury and brigandage. This pattern led in turn to the development of larger estates which were located in the better agricultural land of the plains of Jezreel to the south and the Bet Netofa valley to the north of the Nazareth ridge, as well as in upper Galilee.[30] Such a conclusion is corroborated by various literary references and clearly reflected in Jesus' parables. 'The land of a rich man produced a good harvest', demanding that he extend his storage capacity, according to Luke (12.16–20). Josephus speaks of the imperial granaries in upper Galilee, which were the envy of a local entrepreneur, John of Gischala, whose designs he was able to foil (*Life*, 71–73). On another occasion he describes how he himself was able to confiscate a large quantity of grain belonging to Queen Bernike, an Herodian princess, 'which had been collected in the neighbouring villages and stored for her at Besara', a village on the borders of lower Galilee and the territory of Ptolemais/Acco (*Life*, 119f.). Both incidents indicate how middle men or self-appointed leaders stood to gain from getting their hands on produce which had been collected from the peasants, either as part of the tribute due to Rome, or from private estates. The gospel parables are also highly informative about the diverse types associated with these estates – absentee landlords, farm stewards, slaves, hired servants and day labourers, often recruited or possibly press-ganged from the surrounding villages, such as those on the Nazareth ridge.

As noted above, this rapidly changing economic situation inevitably also brought about a change of values among this ever-increasing group of deprived and harassed small land-owners. The system of tithes and other agricultural offerings had been devised to underline Yahweh's ultimate ownership of the land, but they also helped to highlight the sacral character of the land and its produce and the need to care for it as part of God's creation. The loss of land lead to an erosion of such values. The supplanting of a mode of production based on trust in Yahweh's seasonal blessings to Israel, for one driven by greed, opulence and exploitation, inevitably fractured the tenuous connection between land, people and religious concerns. Elites, on the other hand, had no particular attachment to the land other than to exploit its resources to the maximum, literally and metaphorically draining it.

The elaborate water system at Sepphoris, which still today beggars belief in terms of its range and technical sophistication, is a classic example of elite attitudes to natural resources. Human manipulation of the environment for their own needs could occur without any consideration either of its impact on the local water supply of the land-owners of the Nazareth ridge, or their value system. This would have prompted Jewish peasants to view the plentiful supply as a gift from a caring God, not the result of human resourcefulness – the land soaking up the seasonal rains 'which welled up again in valleys and hills' (Deut. 8.7). In all, 13.5 kilometres of aqueducts have been uncovered, dating from the first and second centuries CE, which together carried some 4300 cubic metres of water into a large underground reservoir that has been hewn out of the soft local rock to bedrock. The earlier part of this system certainly dates from Antipas' reign and carried water from two springs at the foot of

Mt. Yedaya, near to the sites of two local villages.[31] We can only speculate how this development affected the lives of the local villagers, but presumably it made extra demands in the need to draw water or be dependent on what could be gathered in cisterns in the rainy season.

It was to hard-pressed people such as these villagers that Jesus' declarations of beatitude were addressed and intended as good news: 'Blessed are the poor'; 'Blessed are those who are hungry now'; 'Blessed are those who weep now' (Mt. 5.2–8; Lk. 6.20–21). These sayings seek to reassure people who have to face the prospect of being reduced to conditions of impoverishment, hunger and mourning, and who felt the right to rail against such conditions in the light of the promise of 'a land flowing with milk and honey'. The promise that had been made to their ancestors was now being enjoyed by outsiders – veterans of Herod the Great's armies and other pro-Herodian favourites who had been given shares in the best land of the country as a reward for their loyalty. To name this situation a blessing, and not a curse, as the Deuteronomic theology would have suggested, called for a bold religious imagination. Jesus' call for unconditional trust in the heavenly Father in the face of deep anxieties about food, drink and clothing – the very basics of human life – was indeed a strange demand (Mt. 6.25–34; Lk. 12.22–31). The rhetoric of the passage, expressing the anxiety in the form of a question: 'What shall we eat, what shall we drink, wherewith shall be clothed?' as well as the circumstances, have clear echoes of the Sabbatical year question of the Israelites (Lev. 25.20). In that context, as now also with Jesus, the answer is to examine the way in which Yahweh shows his care by ensuring the fruitfulness of nature for all his creatures.

Jesus invites his audience to consider the lilies of the field whose lives are so brief, and the birds of the air who are deemed of little value because their number is so great. Yet in both cases God cares for their needs. Within this 'chain of being' humans may have a special place, but that should not lead them to ignore God's care for the apparently least and most insignificant elements of his created world, of which they also are a part.[32] It is surely significant that the occupations mentioned here – agricultural activities of sowing, reaping and gathering into barns, on the one hand, and domestic chores of toiling and spinning, on the other – reflect the village economy of Nazareth and other such places. Jesus may not have actually declared the Jubilee in his hometown in the manner that

Luke suggests (cf. Lk. 4.16–30), but sayings such as these together with his itinerant lifestyle clearly pointed to the Jubilee and Sabbatical values. These expressed a total confidence in God's care when faced with the demands of the urban economy, which was eroding the lifestyle of the Galilean villagers and generating deep anxiety. The people of Nazareth were unimpressed with his wisdom, we are told, describing him as a 'craftsman' (*tekton*), and thereby disqualifying him as a source of wisdom according to the system of Jerusalem and its scribes (Mk. 6.2–4; Sir. 38.24–39). Yet, the source of his wisdom would appear to have been a deep appreciation of the natural world and its processes reflected on in the light of the Hebrew Scriptures and the creator God of which they spoke.

From Nazareth to Caphernaum

Jesus' option for the lake-front rather than the home-town of Nazareth and its environs, as the principal site of his ministry represented a major shift of micro-regions and by implication of human cultural activity in relation to the eco- and bio-spheres of Galilee. The reasons for the choice are unclear and it would be entering the realm of the speculative to be definitive on the matter, though several possible suggestions can be put forward: acquaintance with some of the Baptist's disciples from Bethsaida; rejection by his own people; searching for suitable labour; option for a more open, cosmopolitan environment; avoidance of Herodian presence at Sepphoris, close to Nazareth; a healer in search of suitable air and water .... For purposes of this chapter it is more important to reflect on the implications of the change of environment for Jesus' own response in the light of the particular ecological conditions in each sub-region and the ways in which humans had adapted to these.

The Valley region, which in the Mishnah is linked with the district of Tiberias, should be extended to include the whole surround of the Lake, which was deemed to be an important natural resource, according to the tribal blessings (Deut. 33.23). Unlike the Dead Sea farther south, which was also below sea level, the Lake of Gennesareth and its immediate surrounds were blessed by a plentiful supply of water by the various streams that flowed from both upper Galilee on the western side, and from the Golan on the east, as well as by numerous springs. The Jordan river, whose headstreams originated in the foothills of Mt. Hermon, provided a direct ecological link with the storied mountain to the north. Flowing south, the river passes through the Huleh basin which is described as a marshy area of Lake Semechonitis, and afterwards it descends rapidly through a deep gorge before entering the Lake of Gennesareth below the town of Bethsaida/Julias (*JW* 3.515).[33]

The Valley differed from both upper and lower Galilee in that its rock formation consisted of basalt, due to the more recent volcanic activity, which had caused the rift valley from Lebanon to the gulf of Akaba. This type of rock produces rich and fertile soil, thereby creating another highly distinctive micro-ecology within Galilee, something that Josephus was well aware of when he describes the fertility of the Plain of Gennesareth in such glowing terms (*JW* 3. 516–521). In this small area the natural fertility of the soil, combined with the plentiful supply of water and the very warm temperature to produce every kind of fruit and plant. Indeed Josephus could be accused of sharing the Romantics' view of the region when he writes: 'One might say that nature had taken pride in thus assembling the most discordant species in a single spot, and that by a happy rivalry, each of the seasons wished to claim this region for her own.'

A move to the lake-front entailed very definite ecological and climatic changes from that of the Nazareth area, therefore, even though the political presence of the Herodians was never far away, with the founding of Tiberias close to the hot springs beside the Lake in 19 CE. It is noteworthy that while allotments of land were granted to those who were compelled to dwell in the new city, presumably as the service personnel for the elite, the upper, Herodian class owned estates across the Jordan in the fertile Golan region (*JA* 18.36–38; *Life*, 33). This is significant information, since it suggests that despite Josephus' glowing description of the fertility of the Gennesareth plain, cereal-producing land was at a premium on the south-western side where the nearby hills come close to the shore. This points to a mixed and diversified economy, one based on the traditional agricultural patterns, making due allowances for the distinctive ecological features already discussed, on the one hand, and the fish industry associated with the Lake, on the other. As an outsider to this region, Jesus had no stake in either, but as a *tekton* or craftsman there would undoubtedly have been plenty of demand for his skills, especially in the boat-building industry that must have been flourishing in the region. However, it is as a prophetic figure, who challenges the values of both farmers and fishermen, that he appears in the gospel narratives. James and John, the sons of Zebedee, and the brothers Peter and Andrew, were summoned to abandon their family fishing enterprises and join his permanent retinue as a new form of family (Mk. 1.16–20, 3.31–35). The inhabitants of Capernaum, Corazin and Bethsaida, all three settlements located on the fringes of the fertile plain at the north-west corner of the Lake, were upbraided for their refusal to respond to his call to adopt a different set of values to govern their lifestyle (Lk. 10.13–15; Mt. 11.20–24).

The names of two of the places associated with Jesus' followers, Bethsaida and Magdala, indicate their association with fishing, and in addition Tarichaeae, the Greek name for Magdala, refers to the industry of salting fish. Furthermore, surveys around the Lake reveal abundant remains of harbours, break-waters and fish pools datable to the Roman period.[34] In addition to the gospels, other literary evidence also stresses the fish industry. Thus Strabo (*Geographica* XVI. 2, 45) mentions the salting of fish at Tarichaeae as well as the fruit-bearing trees in the region, and Josephus reports that 'the lake contains species of fish, different in taste and appearance from those found elsewhere' (*JW* 3.509). He later mentions the fact that a fish found in the lakes near Alexandria, the *Coracin* (apparently a type of eel) is found in a spring nearby, and that because of the similarity some people think that this is a tributary of the Nile (*JW* 3.520).

Reference to the Nile is interesting in this context, since papyrological evidence from Ptolemaic Egypt indicates that the fish trade was highly developed and tightly controlled by the royal authorities there, suggesting that it was an important source of revenue. Since we also know from the Zenon papyri, dating to the middle of the third century BCE, that the Ptolemaic regime introduced new techniques of viticulture at the estate of Bethanath in the Bet Netofa valley in lower Galilee, it is highly likely that it was in that same period that Magdala (Migdal Nun) the House of Fish became Tarichaeae, the Fish-Salting Centre.[35] A dedicatory inscription from an association of fishermen from the harbour of Ephesus indicates the social standing and the economic significance of such centres and those who manned them. A fishing customs-house is dedicated to the emperor Claudius, his mother and wife, as well as the peoples of Rome and Ephesus, by the fishermen and the fish-sellers of the city from their own resources. A long list of names is attached indicating the amount given by each and the items for which the donations were given.[36] From this list it can be inferred that this was an impressive building, and while Tarichaeae was unlikely to be in a position to compete with Ephesus in this regard it does indicate the social standing and the affluence of those engaged in the industry.

The view of Ferdinand Braudel that fish did not play an important part in the economic life of the Mediterranean generally because 'the waters were geologically too old ... biologically exhausted' has been vigorously challenged by a recent provocative study of the Mediterranean region by Horden and Purcell.[37] They suggest that the marginal nature of much of life in the Mediterranean, especially in the east, where the Fertile Crescent is a narrow strip between sea and desert, challenged human resourcefulness in many different ways. This factor can be easily underestimated in our modern perspective. Once this wider canvass is employed, however, the significance of the salted fish industry takes on entirely new dimensions. The possibility created by the technique of salting fish for export to various markets such as Rome was highly important for local economies. A surplus could be treated as the equivalent of a cash crop and consequently the technique was practised widely from the Black Sea to Spain in the west, and in the Orontes basin in the east. Tarichaeae falls within this network and its impact on the Galilean environment must be assessed in that wider context. 'Salt is good' is a saying attributed to Jesus in relation to his own message (Mt. 5.13; Mk. 9.59), but its value was viewed very differently, one suspects, by those of his hearers who were directly or indirectly engaged in this thriving industry around the Lake. Tarichaeae was merely the depot and outlet for much of their labour, and ancillary industries such as ceramic-making, boat building and repairing, sail making, and salt collection were all dependent on its continued success.[38]

What would Jesus' likely reaction have been to this developed natural resource close to the heartland of Galilee? It might appear that he would have approved of the resourcefulness that could exploit the natural produce of the land for human living, an excellent example of progress as 'dominion' in accordance with the first Genesis account of creation. The blessings of the tribes as articulated in the Scriptures highlighted this natural fertility of the different regions, including the lake. Yet there were dangers attached, as in the case of those tribes who did put the enjoyment of the fruits of the earth and sea before their Israelite identity (Asher and Dan, Judg. 5.17). The imagery of fish and fishing does not figure as prominently as do those taken from agriculture in the Jesus tradition. In addition to the call to the first followers to 'become fishers of men' (Mk. 1.19), fish are mentioned together with bread as the staple diet of the average small householder who was likely to have made up the bulk of Jesus' audiences (Mt. 7.9–11; Lk. 11.11–13). Furthermore, the net cast into the sea occurs, at least in Matthew's gospel, side by side with images of the merchant in search of fine pearls and the hidden treasure in the field, to describe the mysterious and surprising nature of the kingdom of God (Mt. 13.44–49).

The call to the disciples to leave their boats and nets to follow him on a greater errand as 'fishers of men', even when couched in the language of their erstwhile activity, suggests that for Jesus there were more important tasks than those of the everyday, however laudable and necessary these may have been. There is no condemnation of fishing or the fish industry, only the call to view their association with him in terms that would be understandable to those familiar with such an enterprise. What prompted that call and how might we explain the ready response, as described in the Synoptic gospels? Was it perhaps that the lifestyle of fishermen was more in tune with his own itinerant mode (Mt. 8.20; Lk. 9.58) than that of peasant farmers, tied to the land and still seeking to maintain the essential link between ownership of land and blessedness, in accordance with Israel's founding story? Or was it the fact that fishing was a relatively lucrative occupation that caused Jesus to challenge these people and their commercial values, or did a possible shared background in the circles of John the Baptist, as suggested in John's gospel, play any role in their readiness to choose another way? Despite Josephus' linking of the sailors of Tiberias with the destitute class of the city (*Life*, 33), one suspects that Galilean fishermen in general were far from the bottom rung of the social ladder of Roman society. Indeed Mark suggests as much by mentioning that Zebedee had 'hired servants', suggesting a commercial rather than a subsistence occupation (Mk. 1.20). Furthermore, the fish industry presumably involved women as well as men in various aspects of the salting process. Their presence in Jesus' permanent retinue, notably the Magdalene, Mary, might well be related to the fact that she and the other 'Galilean women' were engaged in chores other than the purely domestic, making it easier for them to join a wandering charismatic prophet.[39]

There is, however, another aspect of Jesus' activity by the sea which is at least worth considering before following him further on his journeys. Gerd Theissen has noted the sense of 'local colouring' that is involved in describing this inland mass of water (12 kilometres wide by 20 kilometres long) as a sea rather than a lake.[40] Both Luke and Josephus with their greater sense of the importance of the Mediterranean, speak consistently of this as a lake/*limne* rather than following Mark (and Matthew) in speaking of the Sea of Galilee, or simply the Sea (nineteen times in all). While the expression 'Sea of Galilee' is undoubtedly a translation of the Hebrew *yam kinnereth* or *yam ha-galil*, there is, according to Theissen, a further dimension to this usage, namely, the sense that the Great Sea, the Mediterranean, had little significance for the peasant population of Galilee, land-locked as their region was by the powerful presence of the Phoenicians who had controlled the Mediterranean for generations.

Within such a perspective, which Jesus would have shared, the Sea of Galilee could take on definite symbolic significance also. Mark or his sources certainly think so with his two stories of the Gadarene demoniac (Mk. 5.1–19) and the stilling of the storm (Mk. 4.31–34), both reflecting the mythological sense of the Deep where evil monsters dwell, which Yahweh as creator God had conquered and could contain in check (Isa. 27.1; Ps. 74.13, 89.5–11). This reflects a very old and widespread Ancient Near Eastern mythological point of view, expressed most famously in the Enuma Elish epic, and undoubtedly passed on orally in popular tradition. Wherever people lived in an environment dominated by water and had to struggle with the possibilities and dangers that such a location offered, the threat of the Deep was present. The more the natural resources of the Sea of Galilee could be exploited for human need, the more such mythological ideas were likely to recede in people's consciousness. Yet for Jesus, behind such 'ancient' and 'outmoded' notions there was a more important truth, namely, his belief in the creator God, whom he dared to call *Abba*/Father, and whose care for all his creation, expressed in overcoming of the chaos that constantly threatened, was a central element of his Jewish faith and hope.

The Surrounding Region of Galilee

The third 'journey' on which it is proposed to follow Jesus in the ecological tour of Galilee is that which took him to the surrounding regions (*perichoron*) of Galilee, and which Mark has described rather awkwardly at 7.31. Such a journey would inevitably have taken Jesus to upper Galilee, a region whose physical contours and resultant climate is quite distinctive from that of lower Galilee and the Valley, as was acknowledged in the Mishnaic passage cited at the outset of this chapter. Whereas none of the ranges in lower Galilee exceeds 1000 feet, those of upper Galilee reach to more than 2000 feet. The highest peaks are those in the south, where the Meiron massif rises to almost 4000 feet above the Beth ha-Kerem valley that marks the northern extent of lower Galilee and through which the Acco/ Tiberias road ran in antiquity. The rock formation of upper Galilee is the same as that of the three most northerly ridges of lower Galilee, namely, Cenomanian limestone and dolmen. Because of the height of the mountains and the inclination of the hills there is a plentiful rainfall, however.[41] The fact that the southern escarpment with its rugged and barren features is the highest point in upper Galilee means that there is a striking and sudden change in the landscape as one ascends north of Kfar Hananya, 'above which the sycamores do not grow'. In upper Galilee further faulting in a north/south direction creates a number of hills and valleys, sloping west towards the coastal plain and south towards the rift valley. As a result of these features, communications between upper Galilean villages is some-what more restricted than in lower Galilee, and the area was never subjected to the same degree of urbanization in the Roman period.

A journey from lower to upper Galilee in antiquity would have either involved travelling through the narrow gorges of the Jordan rift, or via the steep climb through the Meiron pass above Kfar Hananya. The political boundary with Tyre varied at different periods and in Jesus' day it seems to have been as far south as Qadesh, so that effectively for him to reach the region of Tyre would have involved going through upper Galilee. Despite these political issues, the region formed a natural hinterland for Tyre, and had a ready outlet for its grain, wine and oil produce, as we shall discuss more fully in the next chapter. The plentiful rainfall ensures excellent crops in the well-sheltered valleys, but this would have had to be collected in cisterns during the rainy season, as the hard limestone made it difficult to locate the springs at the higher levels. Effectively, the tradition suggests that Jesus moved in non-Jewish territories, but it is more reserved in its declaration that he crossed the Jew/Gentile divide, as the story of his dialogue with the Syro-Phoenician woman indicates (Mk. 7.24–30).

These encounters took him not just to different micro-ecological regions, but also to areas where traditional human engagement with, and appreciation of the environment was different to that which obtained, at least in principle, in the Israelite/Jewish territory. This difference was expressed most obviously in the variety of different deities, some local, some universal, worshipped in these regions, many of them having a background as nature deities, even when they bore Greek names. Recent study of Israelite origins in relation to their Canaanite predecessors in the land, especially in the light of the discovery of the Ugaritic texts from Ras Shamra, suggest that the break with the older culture of 'nature religions' was not as sharp as the Deuteronomist had hoped for, or was recognized by an earlier generation of scholars dealing with the emergence of early Israel in the region.[42]

In the ancient Mediterranean world generally the landscape provided the key to the religious concerns of the locals. The distinctiveness of such natural features as springs, caves, groves, rivers and mountain tops, were all deemed to be different, and the otherness of such places constituted them as holy, suitable dwelling places of some god, nymph or spirit whose patronage it was important for humans to cultivate.[43] Among the Greeks this primitive sense of nature itself as divine was developed from the cosmological speculations of Plato and Aristotle and found its clearest expression among the Stoics.[44] Indeed there is abundant evidence that Hellenistic Judaism was able to incorporate such ideas into its own theological framework without any danger of assimilation, especially in contexts where the notion of God as creator is being developed, as in the case of Jesus' Jerusalem namesake, Jesus ben Sirach, who combines the older mythological notions of the Deep, already discussed, with the more contemporary philosophical discussions, when he writes:

> By his [God's] plan he stilled the deep and planted islands in it. Those who sail the sea tell of its dangers, and we marvel at what we hear. In it are strange and marvellous creatures, all kinds of living things and huge sea-monsters. Because of him each of his messengers succeeds and by his word all things hold together. We could say more but could never say enough. Let the final word be: He is the all [to pan estin autos]. (Sir. 43.23–27)

Jesus was unlikely to have been touched by such academic formulations, yet at a popular level this idea of the sacredness of nature was part of the religious and social koine of the East for millennia. A journey to the villages of Cæsarea Philippi involved entering a region in upper Galilee dominated by belief in the Greek god Pan, whose worship had been associated with a cave at the southern foothills of Mt. Hermon for over two centuries at least. Pan, as his Greek name indicates, had universal features, which Ben Sira may well have been alluding to in the passage just cited, suggesting that it was the Hebrew God of creation who really deserved the epithet 'the All/*Pan*', since Yahweh was the creator of heaven and earth and all that was in them. In Greek myth Pan was associated with the countryside, in particular the guardian of shepherds and flocks, and also, as the inventor of the seven-reed pipe, the patron of merry-making and the outdoor life. As such he was often associated with Dionysus, the Greek god of wine, who, like Pan could easily embody much older traits as a vegetation deity and whose cult was widely diffused in the Near East, including the surrounding region of Galilee. There may well be an allusion to the activities of the devotees of both deities in Jesus' well-known contrast between his own more joyful and open lifestyle and that of the ascetic John the Baptist: 'This generation is like children shouting at each other sitting in the market-place: "we *piped* to you and you would not *dance*; we sang dirges for you and you would not mourn." ' While John's lifestyle may have been ascetic, Jesus' was such that he could be described, probably by his enemies, as 'a *wine-drinker* and a glutton, a friend of tax-collectors and prostitutes' (Mt. 11.16–19; Lk. 7.31–35). There are echoes here of both Pan and Dionysus, and the festive merrymaking of their devotees.[45]

   In the next chapter there will be occasion to discuss more fully the cultural and religious implications of a journey in this region. Here the concern is to suggest possible associations between the Jesus tradition and the ecology of this most northerly region of the Promised Land, dominated as it was by Mt. Hermon, which reaches to over 8000 feet at his highest point. In ecological terms Hermon was the source of the Valley's most important natural resource, namely water. This fact was well known to Roman writers such as Tacitus (*Histories*, V, 6), and Pliny (*Nat. Hist.*, V, 16). In describing the Lake of Gennesareth Josephus speaks about the excellent properties of its *water*, 'sweet to the taste', excellent to drink, and pure, because of sandy beaches (*JW* 3.506). Later in the same passage he refers to the 'genial' quality of the *air* in the region (*ton aeron eukrasia*) (*JW* 3.519). This combination of water and air recalls the title of one of the most widely read books in antiquity, Hippocrates' *Airs, Waters, Places*, a work which recommended that any physician should check the quality of both the water and the air when he goes to visit a place, since these are extremely important for good health. One is tempted to ask whether Jesus' healing ministry, attested in all the gospels, might have given him a special appreciation of the climatic conditions of the Lake area, and the quality of its water, prompting a visit to its source.[46]

Josephus certainly makes the direct link with the quality of the water in the lake and Hermon as its source, noting its cool temperature: 'It becomes as cold as snow when one has exposed it to the air, as the people of the country are accustomed to do during the summer nights.' He then interrupts his description of the lake and its immediate environs to describe at some length the efforts of Herod Philip, the tetrarch of the Golan region, to ascertain the true source of the river Jordan. By a curious test he was able to demonstrate to the natives that its origin was not, as was thought by the ancients, the pool of Pan, but another spring named Phiale some distance away to the east, on the road to Trachonitis (*JW* 3.506–515). The significance of this anecdote is uncertain and one could easily read too much into it. However, one explanation could well be that in seeking a suitable water supply for nearby Cæsarea Philippi, Philip sought to convince the natives that the Jordan did not in fact originate in the pool of Pan, possibly because of their reluctance to tamper with the waters issuing from this sacred spring with its healing properties.

As in the case of Sepphoris already discussed, Jesus visits the villages of Cæsarea Philippi but not the city itself. This is consistent with Mark's view at least, that he was reluctant to become directly embroiled in the politics of urbanization and the damage that was being wrought to the fabric of village life, even when his own lifestyle and actions were a direct challenge to the values of such an ethos. His visit to the region may be understood, in part at least, as arising out of an appreciation for the recognized source of Galilee's perceived fertility. There may well have been other factors at work in Jesus' journey to the north, which will be investigated later. However, from an ecological perspective, it is important to realize that Hermon was a 'sacred mountain' for Jews as well as for pagans in the region. The fact that others who did not belong to his tradition had also found reason to name the god of this region as 'the most high and holy one'[47] need not preclude Jesus also from recognizing with the Psalmist that Hermon (together with Tabor, a sacred mountain at the other end of Galilee with earlier pagan associations also, Deut. 33.19; Hos. 5.1) 'could praise his God, the maker of heaven and earth' (Ps. 89.13), and send its 'dew to water Zion' (Ps. 133.3). Sites such as Hermon and Thabor could give rise to lively religious competition in antiquity, precisely because of their special physical appearance, but also because of the natural resource that Hermon's snows brought to Galilee.

This reading of Jesus' journey to upper Galilee in the context of the mythic understanding of the natural world and its most outstanding physical features raises the issue already touched on regarding the de-sacralization of nature in the Judeo–Christian tradition. The suggestion that Jesus too might have been attracted to the Hermon region because of its dominating physical and natural presence is not intended to imply that he was tolerant of the worship of gods other than Yahweh. Jesus was no easy syncretist, and his trust in Yahweh the creator God of heaven and earth precludes any such implication. Belief in a creator God does not mean, however, that respect for the gifts of nature was somehow diminished. As we have seen, Jesus' trust in Yahweh's graciousness was grounded in the gift of the fertility of the earth and his conviction of God's care for even the smallest and most insignificant of his creatures. The fact that his permanent retinue of followers was recruited from the Valley region put him in touch with their lifestyle in and around the lake and must have made him conscious of the blessing of water for human life. It also provided a rich field of symbolic associations for speaking about the God of Israel and his graciousness to its people. The poets of Israel, Prophets such as Jeremiah, Isaiah and Ezekiel, and the Psalmists, were deeply conscious of the blessing of rain, dew, spring and snow. Yahweh had saved the ancestors in the desert by making water gush forth from the rock, and future redemption could equally be described in terms of the gifts of abundance and fruitfulness that the gift of water in its various forms made possible. Yet there was also a real consciousness of the threat of the Deep. With such a wealth of imagery based on water it is surprising that it does not feature more prominently in Jesus' images of God's presence in the land. Yet the recognition that all life in a thirsty land was so dependent on water ensured that behind the many other images, which Jesus used for God's presence and God's activity, the reality and importance of water could never be ignored.

The parables are, perhaps, the most characteristic of the speech forms that Jesus employed, and it has long been acknowledged that they provide a rich field for investigating both Jesus' own religious imagination and the everyday world of his Galilean life. As noted in passing already, the various characters of the parables give us an insight into several different Galilean social situations, even when it is acknowledged that the realism of the stories is fictional rather than historical. None of them has a specific location, but it is surprising that, apart from the one story of the net cast into the sea (Mt. 13.47f.), all the other settings are more typical of the lower Galilean social situation than the lakeshore and its presumed activities. It is the nature parables, and the mysterious, yet benign sense of the earth, that are of most immediate interest for ecological considerations, especially in view of their links with popular wisdom and its connection with a sense of the nearness of God within the everyday patterns of life.

Part of the genius of Jesus' parable-making is his ability to take everyday experiences, such as sowing and reaping, and weave these into narratives that are at one and the same time highly realistic in terms of his hearers' world and their experiences *and* deeply resonant of Yahweh's activity on behalf of Israel as this had been described in the psalms and the prophets. For his peasant hearers their everyday work and experiences were being elevated to a symbolic level with reference to God's caring presence to Israel, as was the case also with the proverbial wisdom in the Hebrew Scriptures. The element of surprise and dislocation that many of these stories contain was intended to challenge the hearers to reconsider their understanding of God and his dealings with Israel, and to experience his presence in the world of the everyday, the world of home, village, field, sky and mountain. The parables of Jesus are such successful religious metaphors because they are the product of a religious imagination that is deeply grounded in the world of nature and the human struggle with it, and at the same time deeply rooted in the traditions of Israel which speak of God as creator of heaven and earth and all that is in them.

3

STORIES OF CONQUEST AND SETTLEMENT

Zebulon shall settle at the shore of the sea; he shall be a haven for ships and his brother shall be at Sidon. (Gen. 49.13)

The discussion of the previous chapter concentrated on how Jesus related to the natural environment of Galilee, and the indications were that his strong belief in the creator God who was the source of the fertility of the earth coloured not just the itinerant form of his ministry, but also its content. Signs of God's presence were everywhere to be discerned in the world of nature, and for someone deeply imbued with the sense of God's creative activity in the changing rhythms of the seasons, the human engagement with the landscape in farming, fishing and other activities of a peasant people spoke immediately and directly of God's care, God's promise and God's call. Yet, the impulse for this interpretation of the natural world had come from a story which not only spoke about God's universal care for all creation, but one which portrayed the special call and election of Israel. The gift of the land of Israel was a pledge of Yahweh's special love for the people of Israel. Indeed the very features of that land, its hills and valleys, its springs and rivers, could be contrasted with other lands, notably Egypt, where different ecological conditions prevailed. The natural fertility of the land of Israel was a sign of special election. For those conditions to be maintained, however, Israel had to live its life in the land as Yahweh stipulated, and that meant living separately from the nations round about, according to the dominant strand in Israel's multi-layered story, that of the Deuteronomist and the account of Israel's history that his theological viewpoint had generated.

The issue we wish to explore in this chapter, then, is how did Jesus relate to the special election of Israel as this had expressed itself in the stories of conquest and occupation of the land? Since

Galilee was part of that land and had over the centuries suffered at the hands of different invading imperial powers, it is important to enquire into the manner in which Galilee in particular was portrayed as part of the national inheritance. In the different traditions that were in circulation in the first century, and thus presumably, available to Jesus also, what aspects of Galilean participation in the project of 'all Israel' were featured and how did these impact on subsequent understanding of the region in the developing 'canonical' and dissident versions that shaped first-century attitudes to the notion of Galilean-ness? How did Galileans themselves relate to these foundational stories in the first century, and did Jesus bring any new perspectives to what they might mean for a Galilean identity, especially in the light of his creation-centred view of God and the earth, which has been suggested?

One approach to these questions has been to attempt to trace Galilee's settlement history, at least from the eighth century, in order to understand the Galilean ethnic mix of Jesus' day. In a series of important articles written between 1935 and 1954, the German scholar Albrecht Alt traced the administrative history of Galilee from the Assyrian to the Roman period (eighth to first centuries BCE), paying special attention to population shifts in the region over the centuries.[1] The outcome of the Assyrian conquest of what was then the northern kingdom of Israel, as distinct from the kingdom of Judah in the south, proved to be of pivotal importance to Alt's overall view, and debate about its impact still influences Galilean studies today. It was Alt's contention that in the first wave of the Assyrian onslaught, that of Tiglath-pileser III in 734 BCE, the general population of Galilee escaped relatively unscathed, with only the ruling elite being deported. By contrast a second attack by Shalmaneser V, some twelve years later, which concentrated on Samaria, the capital of the kingdom, resulted in a general deportation of the population and a resettlement of the area by people of a non-Israelite background. In reaching this conclusion Alt was impressed by the contrasting Biblical accounts of the two invasions (2 Kgs. 15.29, 17.5–8.24). These contrasting fortunes of the two parts of the northern kingdom laid the foundations for their separate and often acrimonious relations subsequently. The population of Galilee maintained its strong Israelite identity over the centuries and when the opportunity arose in the wake of the Hasmonean conquests of the second century BCE they gladly joined the nation of the Jews as co-religionists with their southern cousins in Judea, whereas the inhabitants of Samaria developed in a quite separate way, as the later writings, including the gospels, acknowledge.

The idea of a continued Israelite presence in Galilee has been developed in a different direction by Richard Horsley in his important study of Galilee.[2] In his view the Galileans had developed their own independent customs, practices and rituals over the centuries that were quite distinctive from those of the Judeans, who in the interim had experienced their own trauma of exile in Babylon and subsequent restoration. Over the centuries several overtures from the south were rejected. When, therefore, during the period between the collapse of the Seleucid kingdom and the rise of Rome in the eastern Mediterranean (second/first centuries BCE), the Judeans were in a position to expand their territory to the north under the native Hasmonean rulers, effectively colonizing Galilee by imposing on the natives the customs and practices of the Jerusalem temple. The fact that this was done in the name of reclaiming the national inheritance did not minimize the imposition it represented on the native Galilean Israelites. Their 'little tradition' was enveloped by the 'great tradition' emanating from Jerusalem, despite resistance, sometimes tacit, sometimes overt from the Galileans, especially when the effects were experienced at the social and political, as distinct from the religious level. It was into this undercurrent of conflict, exacerbated by the presence of Roman imperial power, that Jesus entered, when he began his ministry in Galilee, after John's arrest.

In a previous study I, too, adopted Alt's position of a continued Israelite presence in Galilee, but subsequently felt constrained to abandon it for reasons which I have developed in detail elsewhere, and which will be outlined again later in this chapter.[3] Put succinctly now, the increasing archaeological evidence from the region, based on surveys and stratified digs at various sites, does not support the idea of a continued Israelite presence in the region. In fact it points directly to a break in the settlement pattern at many sites in lower Galilee in the seventh/sixth centuries BCE with signs of an upturn in the number of settlements appearing in the Persian period, something which continued unabated to the Byzantine period. This evidence has in turn called for a re-reading of the Biblical accounts of the Assyrian conquest, in the context of what we now know from their own records of their imperialist policies more generally.[4]

These approaches to Galilean identity over a long history assume that Galilee was in fact thoroughly Israelite to begin with. However, as mentioned in the opening chapter, more recent discussion of Israelite origins would appear to question seriously that assumption. The differences between the evidence emanating from archaeological investigations on the one hand, and more critical readings of the literary accounts of the conquest and settlement, on the other, have called into question the presuppositions for such an approach. There has been a virtual paradigm shift in recent studies of the Pentateuch, with the current scholarly trend opting for a late date in the Persian period for its completion. Thus, the emphasis is less on the rediscovery of earlier traditions through source and redaction criticism, and more on the ideological perspective of the finished complex narrative. The search for the 'historical' Israel behind the texts has given way to the re-figuration of the 'constructed' Israel within the text. In other words, the accounts of the patriarchal narratives and the conquest and settlement in the land are to be read primarily as ideological statements of post-exilic Judah rather than historical reminiscences from the period of the Judges and the early monarchy. Like all such paradigm shifts there is the danger that the pendulum might swing too far in the opposite direction, and some recent rather acrimonious debates, especially to do with the origins of Israel, are symptomatic in that regard.[5] However, for present purposes of attempting to understand the 'Israel' that Jesus and his contemporaries might have envisaged on the basis of those master-narratives, there is, thankfully, no need to enter into those debates. Indeed once it is allowed that – prescinding from the issue of historical traditions from an earlier period – the Biblical narratives are in their present form a production of post-exilic Judean provenance, a reconsideration of those narratives with an eye to the issues that we know from other writings were facing the post-exilic community in Judah, can be quite revealing.

Galilee and the Twelve-Tribe League of 'All Israel'

Due to the influence of Martin Noth and Albrecht Alt, historians of early Israel have taken as axiomatic that the notion of the amphictyony, or sacred league of tribes united around a common sanctuary, known from Greece and Italy, was the best model for understanding the twelve-tribe league of early Israel. However, even before the recent swing in approaches to the Pentateuch, some scholars had begun to see the difficulties with this approach, given the fact that the model itself was based on data from a much later period and in Israel there was no one central sanctuary around which the tribes that constituted 'all Israel' were united.[6] It is, however, remarkable how consistently the number twelve is maintained, even when the names of the tribes can vary. Thus, its significance should be judged not on the basis of describing the historical reality of pre-monarchic Israel, but rather on the fact that it is symbolic of the way in which a sense of 'all Israel' was maintained. It is this function of expressing the ideal rather than the actual that makes the notion of the in-gathering of the tribes such a constant aspect of restoration thinking, not just in the *Torah* and *Nebiim*, but in a large spectrum of the writings of early Judaism (Tobit, Sirach, Psalms of Solomon, Testaments of the Twelve Patriarchs, the Qumran War Scroll, New Testament, Syrian Baruch, Fourth Ezra) as well as the Rabbinic writings.

Galilee, meaning literally 'the circle', appears in Greek as a name for the northern region of Israel relatively late in Ptolemaic administrative texts of the third century BCE. The Hebrew equivalent, *ha-galil*, occurs as a designation for smaller territories in the immediate vicinity of two centres in the north, Qadesh and Cabul (Josh. 20.7; 1 Kgs. 9.11), but not for the whole region. This is usually referred to by tribal designations, especially Zebulon and Naphtali (Isa. 8.23; 2 Kgs. 15.29), and the expression *galil ha-goyim/* 'Galilee of the gentiles' seems to refer to non-Israelite areas, eventually being applied to the pagan ethos of the whole region (1 Macc. 5.15). This consideration prompts a closer investigation of the two major texts dealing with the tribes that are embedded in the Pentateuchal narratives, Gen. 49 and Deut. 33, the so-called 'Blessings of Jacob' and 'Blessings of Moses'. A comparison of the two accounts suggests differing perspectives on Israel's identity, which have now been incorporated into the master-narrative of its origins. The settings and form of the two poetic compositions differ. Jacob's Blessings are uttered as a farewell discourse to his sons as representatives of the tribes, while the Mosaic text is in the form of a prayer to Yahweh in the context of the assembly of the united tribes before a mighty king of Jeshurun, an unusual and infrequent name for Israel (Deut. 32.15). Both texts show signs of a chequered history of composition with an intermingling of aphorisms, prayers and statements, so that the description of these two poems as 'Blessings' is scarcely appropriate.[7] While both share a view of the land's fertility, as discussed in the previous chapter, describing the territory of Joseph in particular in Eden-like terms (Gen. 49.22–26; Deut. 33.13–18), the theological perspective is very different when they are seen within their respective contexts of the books of Genesis and Deuteronomy.

The Blessings of the Tribes

The Jacob text describes the characteristics of each of the sons, and the four northern tribes are favourably portrayed, although the location of Zebulon, close to Sidon, is unusual in view of the more detailed description of its territory in the conquest narrative (Josh. 19.10–16), where it is more centrally placed in lower Galilee. It is striking that Yahweh does not appear throughout and Jacob's word is presumed to bring about the realization of the blessings or curses of the different tribes. Whereas the special role of Judah from whom 'the sceptre will not depart' (Gen. 49.10f.), is acknowledged, of particular interest in terms of the perspective of the whole book is the negative treatment of both Levi and Simeon. They are both condemned because of their violent behaviour, a clear reference to their role in the slaughter of the men of Shechem (who is treated as an individual and as a city within the narrative of Gen. 34), as revenge for the rape of Dinah, their sister. In that incident Hamor, the father of Shechem, proposed that marriages be arranged between his people and the offspring of Jacob. The terms of his offer are particularly generous: 'You shall live with us and the land will be open to you. Live and trade in it and get property in it' (Gen. 34.10). Jacob's sons agree on condition that the Shechemites undergo circumcision, which they do willingly, so that they might become 'one people' (v. 22). However, Simeon and Levi rejected the agreement and slaughtered all the males in the city in order to avenge their sister who had been dishonoured. This morally dubious act cannot be justified by the author of Genesis, and so the two tribes are cursed in Jacob's farewell (Gen. 49.5–7). Their sin was to reject the possibility of sharing the land with its inhabitants who were willing to share it with them, even to the point of undergoing the ritual of circumcision in order to achieve the unity of the two peoples. This ethno-centric behaviour by the two sons in question, despite their efforts to justify it in terms of restoring their sister's honour, runs counter to the whole thrust of the Genesis account with its open, universalist outlook, epitomized in the promise to Abraham and repeated to Isaac and Jacob, which runs as a refrain through the book: 'In thee will all the nations of the earth be blessed (or bless themselves)' (Gen. 12.2, 18.18, 22.18, 26.4 and 28.14).

Moses' prayer/address on behalf of the tribes is performed before a mighty king of Jeshurun in the context of the assembly of the united tribes. The opening provides a historical prologue recalling Sinai and God's love of his people, 'all those consecrated to him' (Deut. 33.2–5). The conclusion is addressed to the king of Jeshurun, praising the warrior god 'who rides through the heavens' to the king's help, subdued the ancient gods, drove out the enemy and ensures that Israel lives in safety in a land of 'grain and wine, where the dew drops down' (vv. 26–29). The opening emphasis on the united tribes seems at odds with what follows where a wish for Reuben's survival is uttered, and likewise a petition for Judah to 'be returned to his people' (vv. 6–7). This latter statement suggests a northern perspective, where Judah, not the northern tribes, is deemed to have gone into schism. By contrast, all the northern tribes are deemed blessed, though a note of warning is struck in the case of Zebulon (together with Issachar). (See Map 2.) They are to take charge of 'their mountain, where they offer right sacrifices' (vv. 18–19), a reference, it would seem, to the duty of removing the Canaanite worship from Mount Thabor (cf. Josh. 19.12, 22, 34), and sharing the rich produce of their territories to worship Yahweh (cf. Ps. 68.27). Both Asher and Naphtali also receive favourable mention – the former is to dip its feet in oil, and the latter is sated with blessings of Yahweh, since the Sea of Gennesareth is part of its domain (vv. 23–24), while Dan is described as 'a lion's cub, leaping from Bashan' (v. 22). The concluding description of God is thoroughly Deuteronomic in tone, with the stress on the destruction of the original inhabitants, the king's dependence on divine protection and the gift of the land to the Israelites (vv. 27–29). In direct contrast to Jacob's speech, Levi, not Judah, is now the favoured tribe. Its role is to teach the law and take charge of the cultic rituals (vv. 8–11), and hence its absence from the territorial descriptions of the tribal territories in the Deuteronomistic history to follow in Joshua.

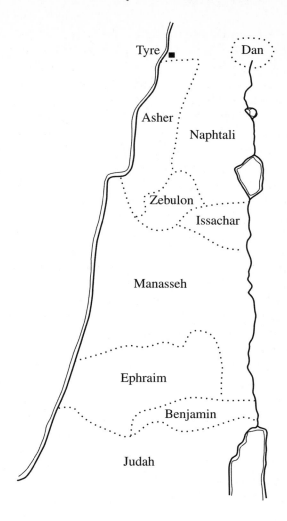

Map 2 Ideal Tribal Boundaries

Contrasting Images of 'All Israel'

Two different conceptions of both the nature of Yaweh and the symbolism of the land may be detected behind these two addresses attributed to Jacob and to Moses. On the one hand the blessings to Moses fit in well with the theocratic ideal that Yahweh owns the land and has bestowed it on Israel, but the gift is conditional on Israel's observance of the covenant law, as discussed in the previous chapter. As owner of the land, Yahweh can drive out all those other people who had inhabited it, but who have no rights there. In particular their cults have no standing before Yahweh and the Israelites must avoid any contamination by the making of idols, like the other peoples who had lived there (Deut. 4.25, 6.14, 7.4, 8.19, 11.6). The land itself is not deemed to be holy *per se*, but they are to worship Yahweh only in the place where he has chosen to make his name dwell (Deut. 12.5, 14, 16.11, 21). The name of this shrine is actually not mentioned, though of course the Jerusalem cultic community in the Persian period claimed this referred to their sanctuary. This centralization of the cult contrasts with the Genesis account where God can be encountered at various different places and under different names.[8]

Jacob's address presents a quite different understanding of the land, reflecting the overall spirit of Genesis and its universalist outlook, typified by the figures of Adam and Abraham. The sons of Jacob are promised an allotment in this land where Yahweh-Elohim plays host to many peoples and is known by different names: El, El-Olam, El-Elyon, El-Shadday. At various points all these names are identified with Yahweh, who is the one 'who brought you out from Ur of the Chaldeans' (Gen. 15.7), and who can appear to Abraham and reassure him with regard to his fulfilment of the promise at any time (Gen. 12.7, 13.14, 15.1, 17.1, 18.1, 22). Yahweh can appear at various sites in the land of Canaan where the Patriarchs build altars, thus marking out the land as holy, but not centralizing God's presence in any one place. The promise of a share in the land appears to be totally unconditional and this is reflected in the address of Jacob to his sons. Most striking is the fact that, as Norman Habel has pointed out in his highly stimulating reading of the Abraham-cycle in Genesis (Gen. 11.31–23.30), the Patriarch gains a foothold in the land, not by militarism but by negotiation and legal arrangement, in the purchase of a field from the Hittite, Ephron, as a burial site for his wife, Sarah (ch. 23).[9]

Yahweh is not a warrior God who drives out the other nations as in Deuteronomy. Instead, a long list of peoples living in the land is given in the context of the establishment of a solemn treaty with Abraham and there is no suggestion that these have either to be conquered or driven out (Gen. 15.7–21). God's intention for Abraham is stated rather cryptically: Abraham is to become a great nation, and all the nations of the earth (*eretz*) shall bless themselves by him' (18.18). Ethnic harmony in a shared land, rather than ethnic cleansing is what is envisaged. Abraham has good relations with all the peoples in the land – which is repeatedly described as 'the land of Canaan'. This includes Israel's dreaded enemies, the Philistines, whose king, Abimelech, shows outstanding generosity to Abraham by offering him a place of residence in his land 'wherever you please' (Gen. 20.16). It is because of this tolerant and pacific perspective of the book as a whole that Levi, who is lionized by Moses in the Deuteronomic account of the blessings, is, together with Simeon, condemned because of their violent act of revenge against the men of Shechem, as previously discussed.

Perhaps the most significant aspect of Abraham's career from the perspective of Jesus' ministry is that, even though he acquires property, Abraham's is an essentially itinerant lifestyle, as he continues to journey through the land as a *ger*, or resident alien (Gen. 20.1, 21.3, 23.4). He is invited to travel through its length and breadth: 'all the land within sight, towards the north and the south, towards the east and the west' (Gen. 13.14–17). This notice will find a much more detailed elaboration at a later period in the *Genesis Apocryphon* from Qumran. There, Abraham in a night vision is represented as travelling from the Great Sea to the Euphrates in the east, and from the Taurus mountains in the north to the Red Sea and the Gihon River in the south, before returning to make an altar to 'the God most high' (*El Elyon*), having been joined by three Amorite brothers who were 'his friends'.[10]

These two contrasting accounts of how 'all Israel' is to be constructed correspond to two different tendencies of the Second Temple period, as far as Judah's life was concerned. The conditional nature of the gift of the land gave rise to an ethno-centric attitude towards non-Israelites in general and the avoidance of outside cultural influences, whereas the inclusive and more tolerant outlook of the Genesis account reflects the cosmopolitan environment that was generated by the Persian and Greek empires in that period. However, in the final editing of the Pentateuch this more open view was to an extent co-opted as a preface or pre-history to the dominant Deuteronomic and priestly strands. The God of the burning bush who brought them into the land was repeatedly identified with the God of Abraham, Isaac and Jacob (Exod. 3.15; Deut. 26.4–10; Josh. 24.2–13). Yet, the fact that two different perspectives on the tribal federation are tolerated and loosely fused in this way, suggests that no unitary view of what constituted 'all Israel' had been able to impose itself fully. The process of defining that entity was still being negotiated when the Pentateuch reached its final stage of composition. Persia, Greece and Rome successively replaced Egypt, Assyria and Babylon in providing the parameters and policies within which the ideal of 'all Israel' had to find some expression. The twelve-tribe ideal provided a symbol of lost unity from the past in the foundational narratives of the Pentateuch. How this ideal could be realized was still to be decided, however.

Galilee and the Conquest and Settlement Narratives

If Yahweh owns the land, then he alone is responsible for deciding who will dwell there, according to the point of view of Deuteronomy, a perspective that is maintained in the account known as the Deuteronomistic History (Joshua to 2 Kings). The narratives of the conquest and settlement of the tribes are of special interest to this study, with the focus in particular on how the northern tribes fared, since these should point to the problems being encountered in the post-exilic period and the configurations of the future that were being envisaged. Yahweh's role as conqueror is reflected in the 'holy war' that he wages on behalf of Israel, as reported in the first half of the book of Joshua (Josh. 1–12), whereas in the second half, dealing with the settlement (Josh. 13–24), the tribes are expected to claim their allotted land. Not all are equally successful, and Joshua chides them at a general assembly at Shiloh: 'How long will you be slack in going in and taking possession of the land that the Lord, the God of your ancestors has given you?' (Josh. 18.1–3). The book ends with another assembly of all Israel, this time at Shechem, warning the Israelites that they will only live securely in the land if they put away foreign gods (Josh. 24.20, 23, 27). In contrast to this account of the conquest and settlement, that of Judges paints a more realistic picture of the difficulties which the Israelites encountered and the continued struggle with the Canaanite inhabitants of the land (Judg. 1–2, 5). A brief consideration of each of these issues separately will assist in the discussion of the problems facing Jewish identity in Galilee of Jesus' day.

Failures of the Tribes

A detailed description of the tribal boundaries and the principal towns in each territory is given in Joshua chs. 13 to 20. The overall intention of these descriptions, which no doubt drew on existing administrative districts and their centres, probably dating from the period of the united monarchy (cf. 2 Sam. 24.1–9; 1 Kgs. 4.7–19), was to reaffirm the idea of the total conquest and the unity of all Israel within its allotted territory of the land of Canaan. Among the descriptions of the tribal allotments, that of Judah receives the most extensive treatment, as one would expect from a document written from a southern perspective. It is particularly noteworthy that Judah is represented as having conquered the Philistine plain, so that its western boundary was that of the Great Sea, that is, the Mediterranean (Josh. 15.1–12). This is clearly an idealized picture since it represents a territory greater than that ever claimed for David or Solomon, even though the Great Sea is mentioned more than once elsewhere as the western limits of the ideal Israel. Two aspects of the treatment of the northern tribes are significant. On the one hand there is a detailed description of the border between the territory of Asher and the Phoenician territories of Tyre and Sidon (Josh. 19.28–30), and on the other hand a strip of territory in the north running from Sidon to the foothills of Hermon is listed among 'the territories yet to be subdued' (Josh. 13.1–7, especially vv. 4–5). (See Map 3.)

As already mentioned, two descriptions of the borders of the land of Canaan at its most extensive are given quite independently of the tribal boundaries. In the north this boundary is described as running from the Great Sea to Mt. Hor, and from there to the Pass of Hamath, and the boundary will end at Zedad (Num. 34.7–9; Ezek. 47.15). The line of this boundary corresponds well with the more detailed description of the northern limits of the 'remaining land' and the peoples not yet driven out, in the account of the territories yet to be subdued (Josh. 13.4–5; cf. Josh. 11.8; Judg. 3.3). Without entering into a discussion of the detailed topography of these passages, it is clear that what is envisaged is a boundary that includes the valley of the Litani river as it flows south from Lebanon, turning west to enter the sea between Sidon and Tyre.[11]

This strip of unconquered territory in the north should have been occupied by one of the northern tribes, ideally the tribe of Dan, which was allotted the territory around Hermon after it had failed to establish itself in the south according to Judg. 1.34–35, but no such extension of its borders is suggested.[12] Another possibility for claiming this territory for the Israelites would have been the tribe of Naphtali. Curiously, however, there is no mention of a northern

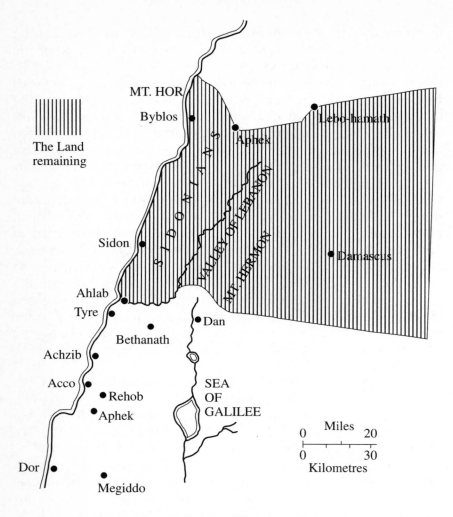

Map 3   The Land Remaining in the North

border for this tribe, even though a detailed description is given for all the other sides (Josh. 19.32–39), and several settlements that one might have expected to be mentioned are missing from the list of the tribal towns. These are intriguing omissions from the description of the territory of Naphtali and its towns in Joshua. Irrespective of which tribe – Dan or Naphthali – is intended, the implications from a southern perspective seem to be that, unlike Judah, the Galilean tribes had not only failed to occupy the full territory allotted to them, but they had even failed to establish any boundary between themselves and other ethnic groups in the region.

The situation on the western side of the northern tribal territories differed from that on the northern front. A detailed description is given of the boundary between the tribe of Asher and the Phoenician cities (Josh. 19.29–30). Interestingly, there is no mention of the Great Sea here, even though elsewhere it is given as the western boundary of the inherited land of Canaan, as we have just seen. While the matter is debated, the likelihood is that neither Tyre nor Sidon were ever within the territory of Asher, but were certainly considered to be part of the land of Canaan, and therefore belonged to the category of 'the land remaining'.[13] Why then the detailed account of the border between Asher and this region, in contrast to the case of Naphtali just discussed? The answer would seem to be that this particular border remained a highly sensitive issue throughout Jewish history, as we shall see below. This continued focus of attention throughout the centuries suggests that there was greater pressure, and therefore, greater concern to maintain ethnic separation in this region than in the Hermon area, irrespective of what ideal images of the land might dictate. The implications of this suggestion for Jesus' journeys in the region will call for further discussion.

Canaanite Cities in the Allotted Land

If, then, the issue of 'the land that remains' in Joshua can be plausibly understood as a criticism from a Judean point of view of the failure of tribes in the north to maintain the absolute borders of the land as Yahweh had established them, the account in Judges gives even greater prominence to the fear of cultural contamination in the north.[14] Though the account interrupts the narrative of the conquest, the overall effect is to suggest a more realistic, history-like version of the problems encountered by the Israelites. In the case of Judah, for example, in contrast to the claim in Joshua that the western boundary extended to the Great Sea, its failure to drive out the Philistines from the plain is acknowledged, though attributed to their superior military skill with the war chariot. Yet, 'the Lord was with Judah' in taking the hill country to the south (Judg. 1.8–21, especially v. 19). Of the four northern tribes, Asher comes in for the most serious criticism, for failing to drive out the inhabitants of a long list of important places. As in the case of the description of the boundary of Asher previously discussed, this tribe seems to have come in for special attention, suggesting difficulties in maintaining a separate identity in the region. This would also explain the censure which the tribe, together with the tribe of Dan, receives in the Song of Deborrah for its failure to respond to a call to arms against the Canaanite king of Hazor, Jabin. Both tribes seem to have found the benefits of maritime activity too alluring, thereby implying close contacts with the sea-faring Phoenicians (Judg. 5.17). By contrast, both Zebulon and Naphtali are praised for their alacrity to engage the enemy, providing leaders in the battle (Judg. 5.14, 18). Yet both tribes are named among those who failed to drive out fully the Canaanites from their territories, more or less following a fixed formula, suggesting that those Canaanites who did stay were reduced to forced labour (Judg. 1.30, 33).

Jesus and Israelite Galilee

Three interrelated issues emerging from these considerations of the problems encountered by the northern tribes appear to be crucial in terms of Judean concerns about Galilee later. These are: the extent of the Israelite territory in the north and its relations with non-Israelite peoples; the threat of continued Canaanite presence in the tribal territories, and the allure of trading links with the Phoenicians. It is only with the rise of the Hasmoneans as a native political force from the mid-second century BCE that it is possible to see how the Israelite ideology of the allotted land and its settlement began to manifest itself clearly. The political situation in the previous centuries, at first under the Persians and afterwards the Greeks, did not give any room for Judean self-determination to express itself. However, the break-up of the Seleucid kingdom in Syria provided such an opportunity and the Judeans had to hand the accounts of the ancestral territory and could draw on them in bolstering their right to reclaim it. The author of First Maccabees expresses the ideology of this position clearly in ascribing the following claim to Simon, the third of the Maccabean brothers:

> We have neither taken foreign lands nor seized foreign property, but only the inheritance of our fathers, which had at one time been unjustly taken by our enemies. Now that we have the opportunity we are firmly holding the inheritance of our fathers. (1 Macc. 15.33)

Even though Hasmonean rule lasted for less than 100 years, a desire for Jewish independence from foreign domination was awakened which would ultimately lead to two bloody and disastrous confrontations with Roman imperial power, the revolts of 66–7 and 132–35 CE. Debates with regard to national identity intensified, as is evident from the literature of the period, especially the question of a national territory.[15] Various and contrasting strands of opinion with regard to how Israel should conduct itself among the nations, now became more strident, it would seem. The narrative of Israel's origins played a role in these debates, something that is reflected in the rewriting of some aspects of that history in such books as Jubilees, The Testaments of the Twelve Patriarchs and the Genesis Apocryphon, for example. Signs of a developing sectarianism have been detected already in the Persian period, and it is no accident that once the possibility for self-determination arose these quickly emerge in full light of day, with mention of the Pharisees, the Sadducees and Essenes for the first time in our sources (*JA* 13.171–173). It is within this matrix of debate and dissonance that marked Second Temple Judaism of the Roman period that we must locate the Jesus-movement with its distinctive position with regard to the great issues of the day, based on its founder's understanding and retrieval of certain aspects of the national inheritance.

Jesus and the Land Remaining

In the previous chapter Jesus' visit to the upper Galilee region was examined in the light of the ecological importance of Hermon for all of Galilee. There were other, more tangibly historical reasons why he might have wanted to visit this region also. As part of the Anti-Lebanon range, Hermon falls well within the borders of the greater Israel as envisaged in various Biblical descriptions of the ideal boundaries of the land. (In addition to Num. and Ezck. already cited, cf 1 Kgs. 8.65; 1 Chron. 13.5; 2 Chron. 7.8; Amos 6.14.) As a prophet interested in Israel's restoration, it would have been natural for him to journey, Abraham-like, through the Promised Land. Did he share Abraham's views on relations with other people in the land?

When the possibility of a journey by Jesus to the north is discussed, it is usually in relation to his going to a gentile territory. Scholars are reluctant to attribute such a move to the historical Jesus, however, preferring to discuss the information in relation to Mark's interest in linking the gentile mission of his own day with Jesus.[16]

There are, however, good reasons why somebody, operating within the parameters of Jewish identity concerns might want to travel to the region. We know that there were Jews living in Cæsarea Philippi and in Syria more generally, on the eve of the first revolt, who, if Josephus is to be believed, were interested in receiving oil that had been produced within the borders of Eretz Israel, as these were known to them at the time (*Life*, 74–75; *JW* 2.592). On the basis of Jesus' aligning himself with John the Baptist in keeping his distance from 'royal palaces' and those who live in them (Mt. 11.15), it is highly unlikely that he would have deviated from this practice on a visit to upper Galilee. Jewish villages in the region would have been a different matter, however. Mark is meticulous in suggesting that Jesus operated within the orbit of the cities of the region – 'the borders of Tyre', 'the territory of Gadara', 'the midst of the Dekapolis' and 'the villages of Cæsarea Philippi' – but in none of the cities in question. In attributing these 'framework' references to Markan redaction, little attention is given to their accurate awareness of local administrative arrangements or the urban–rural tensions they suggest.[17] If Mark were interested in projecting the Pauline mission to gentiles on to Jesus, one might have expected that he would have represented him as visiting the urban centres, and not the rural villages.

In addition to Josephus, there is other literary evidence of Jews living in the region. Several Rabbinic debates discuss the issue of tithing obligations on produce that had been grown in Syria. 'Whoever acquires land in Syria is like one who acquires it in the outskirts of Jerusalem' (M. Hall 4.1), is the principle that was enunciated in accepting gifts from Syria in contrast with other parts of the Diaspora. For purposes of observing the *halakah*, Syria was regarded as part of the land of Israel, something that Josephus also seems to hint at when he speaks of the mixing of the two peoples because of the proximity of their countries (*JW* 7.43).[18] Clearly, the discrepancy between the actual and the ideal borders of the land was a live one in the first century CE, especially when the land bordered Syria.

Of even more immediate interest in view of the Biblical focus on the border between the territory of Asher and Tyre is a list of places in Rabbinic writings dating from the second century CE at the earliest, which is known as the 'Baraita of the Borders'. This list shows that the Rabbis were particularly interested in establishing exact boundaries of the land for purpose of religious observances, with special attention being given to that particular border. No border towns are listed for the Banias/Cæsarea Philippi region, and one village from the Pass of Ayun, a site well north of Cæsarea in the Litani valley, is among those that is inhabited by people 'who came up from Babylon', i.e. by observant Jews.[19] By contrast several places in the territory of Tyre are listed as 'forbidden villages', meaning that according to the Rabbis' judgement, they lay outside the holy land for purposes of halachic observances. (See Map 4.) It is difficult to know whether these lists refer to actual historical situations, or whether they reflect Rabbinic idealization of the land. If this latter were the case, we would expect that there would have been no mention of the territory of Tyre, but rather that the whole area as far as the Mediterranean would have been deemed to belong to the Land of Israel in accordance with the Biblical warrants already discussed.

Irrespective of the historical intention of these lists, the incident reported by Josephus concerning the Jews of Cæsarea Philippi suggests that the matter of correct borders was of concern to some Jews living in the region of Cæsarea in the first century. The fact that the Rabbis continued to debate the matter subsequently shows that it was of particular concern within one interpretation of what constituted 'all Israel'. There is nothing historically implausible, therefore, in suggesting that a journey of Jesus to the region could well have been based on his concern 'for these lost sheep of the house of Israel', while operating with a different perspective on what constituted the ideal Israel. People living in border areas might well have felt themselves marginalized, even excluded, in the light of one prevailing understanding of what constituted Jewishness. From Jesus' point of view they did live within the borders of Israel as this was ideally understood, and they too should be reassured that they were invited to participate in the new 'family' which he was gathering for the banquet with Abraham, Isaac and Jacob.

Two writers from the early Hasmonean period can illustrate how these different views of restoration expressed themselves on the territorial dimension of the restored Israel at a moment of crisis, caused by Antiochus Epiphanes' attempt at transformation of the Yahweh cult in Jerusalem into that of Zeus. First Maccabees is written in heroic style to honour the achievement of the Maccabean brothers in laying the foundations of an independent Jewish state. The geography of the various campaigns are of special interest, since they reflect a mixture of the ideal and the pragmatic in dealing with

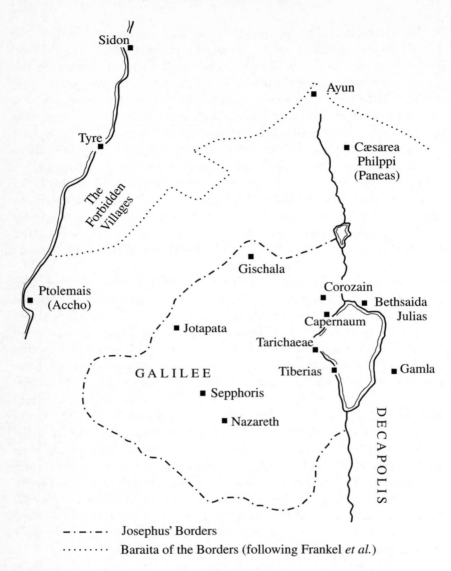

Map 4   **Roman Period Borders of Galilee**

the north, as part of the inherited land. In the first of two excursions against the Seleucid enemy, Jonathan defeated Demetrius II at the plain of Hazor, routing him as far as the stronghold of Qadesh (1 Macc. 11.63–74), which means that the episode occurred well within the political bounds of Galilee of later time. On the second occasion, however, Jonathan proceeded to block Demetrius at Hamath, situated on the ideal border according to all the accounts, and then wheeled his army around and went as far as Damascus, 'going through the whole province'. What the northern tribes had failed to accomplish, Jonathan, like a new Joshua, was achieving by military prowess in the name of reclaiming the allotted land.

Fragments of Eupolemus' account of 'the Kings of Israel' have been preserved by the Christian writer Eusebius, allowing us to discern elements of the 'greater Israel' ideology at work in his account also. The perspective is based on the royal ideology of David's and Solomon's reigns as depicted in 2 Samuel and I Kings.[20] Describing David's conquests, the list of subjugated peoples includes Assyrians in Galadene (Gilead), Syrians dwelling in the region of the Euphrates, Itureans, Idumeans, Nabateans and the otherwise unknown Nabdaeans. In addition Souron, the king of Tyre was forced to pay tribute, and a treaty of friendship was established with Vaphres, the king of Egypt. As a result, Solomon, David's son, could demand assistance from the kings of Tyre and Egypt in building the Jerusalem temple of 'the great god, who made heaven and earth'. This deliberate revision of the Biblical account, though couched partly in terms of the prevailing Hellenistic culture, is based on Jewish restoration hopes. The temple is being built to honour 'the great god' (*theos megistos*), the same designation as that of the inscription found on Mount Hermon, yet the Israelite belief in God's creative power is affirmed. The provisioning of the foreign workmen is to be done by the 'twelve tribes of the Jews' (not Israel), one tribe for each month, who can also be designated in terms of the different regions of the enlarged land – Galilee, Samaria, Moab, Ammon and Gilead. There is no mention of the 'land remaining' but there can be little doubting the source of the author's thinking is that of the greater Israel, extending to the Euphrates. The fact that the list of conquered peoples includes some of Judah's neighbours in the second century – Itureans, Idumeans and Nabateans – suggests that Eupolemus, too, holds the hope that Israel can once again rule the nations in an enlarged land.

These samples of writers close to the Maccabean period indicate that the notion of 'the land remaining' was highly pertinent to the thinking and ideological legitimation of the Hasmonean expansion, whether this be based on the conquest narrative of Judges or the royal ideology of the Davidic monarchy. The tension between the ideal and the actual, which that axial period of Israel's history

encountered, continued into the Roman period, as is clear from
Josephus' various writings. He too has an expansive view of Israel's
land in his description of the original allotment (*JA* 1.134–142, 185,
2.194–195, 4.300). At the same time he is only too well aware of the
actual borders of the Galilee to which he was appointed as governor
on behalf of the revolutionary council in 66 CE, as well as the hostile
presence that lurked outside those borders, especially in the
surrounding cities (*JW* 2.452–480, 3.35–38). By his day Israel's
territorial ambitions were centred on obtaining control of the
territories that had become thoroughly Judaised over the two
centuries since the Hasmoneans had expanded the borders of the
allotted land, north and south. Due to the changed political climate
arising from Rome's advance in the east, these territories were only a
fraction of what might have been included on the basis of the
conquest and settlement narratives. The hopes of Israel based on the
territorial aspirations to a greater territory had to find other
expressions than the militarism of the Maccabees, if they were to
be meaningful. Both Jesus and the Rabbis, despite their very
different perspectives, had discovered other ways of exploiting the
territorial symbolism of restoration, the one by including the
territorially marginalized Jews in his invitation to the banquet, and
the other by extending the boundaries of the land, not for military
conquest, but for halachic observance.

Welcome for Canaanites?

Evidence for the population of Galilee in the Persian and early
Greek periods is scant, but going on the few available scraps it would
seem that 'Galilee of the Gentiles' was not a misnomer. A
predominantly gentile presence in Galilee would explain the
motivation and manner of the Hasmonean expansion, as described
in the heroic literary tone of First Maccabees, and Josephus' further
embellishment. The details of the conquest are somewhat obscure,
not least the fact that Aristobulus I, who is credited with its
Judaization, reigned for just one year (104/3 BCE). His father, John
Hyrcanus, the son of the third Maccabean brother, Simon, began the
campaign in the north, quite late in his reign (111/10 BCE). His first
target seems to have been the Samaritan temple on Mt. Gerizim (*JA*
13.255), an act that replicates that of Josiah, the reforming king of
Judah some 400 years earlier. He demolished the high places of
Bethel and elsewhere in Samaria, destroying the altars that were used

in the worship of Baal, the Canaanite god, slaughtering their priests and burning their bones to ashes (2 Kgs. 23.15–20). The similarities between the two events are not lost on Josephus, the Jerusalemite priest-author with his strong anti-Samaritan bias (*JA* 13.255f.).

Subsequently, the campaigns of John took him to the Greek cities of Samaria and Scythopolis, the former being razed to the ground and the latter taken by Hyrcanus' sons, who ravaged the whole plain of Jezreel as far north as Mt. Carmel (*JA* 13.280f.). At the same time the Idumeans in the south, an Arab people who had infiltrated from the territory of Edom in trans-Jordan, were forcibly circumcised (*JA* 13.258). Josephus does not report any concerted campaign in Galilee proper, but it is clear that both he and his source, First Maccabees, assumed that this territory also belonged to the Israelite inheritance. His account of how Aristobulus, one of John Hyrcanus' sons, had obtained additional territory for the Judeans and 'brought over a portion of the Iturean nation, whom he joined to them by the bond of circumcision' (*JA* 13.318f.), is particularly important, if highly problematic. Josephus' source for this information is a Roman writer, Timagenes, as cited by Strabo, thus suggesting that he himself has no direct information about the matter. The account has given rise to a lively discussion, especially in view of the fact that the influential modern historian of the period, Emil Schürer, concluded that the Iturean territory conquered by Aristobulus was identical with Galilee, 'or the greater part of it', thereby giving rise to the widespread view of the Galileans as converted Itureans.[21] It is difficult to avoid the suspicion that Josephus has simply produced an account for the Galileans' conversion to match that of the Idumeans in the south, especially since, unlike the Idumeans, Galileans are never once subsequently labelled as half-Jews, and furthermore, the archaeological evidence for an Iturean presence in Galilee is singularly lacking.[22]

Despite these misgivings, the account is illustrative of the underlying ideology of the Maccabean period as this continued to be current in certain Jerusalem circles of Jesus' day. Like the Idumeans to the south, the Itureans of the north had one of only two options – either join themselves to the Jewish people by the rite of circumcision or depart from the territory. It is interesting to note that the two peoples in question, the Itureans and the Idumeans, are of Arabic background, who, unlike the other 'nations round about', notably the Philistines, were deemed to be related to Israel through the brothers Jacob and Ishmael, sons of Abraham. This attitude,

reflects some very positive treatment of the Arabs, as children of
Ishmael in other literature of the Hasmonean period, most notably,
the Book of Jubilees.[23] However, from the perspective of the
ideology of conquest on which Josephus' account is based, there is
no place for non-Jews in Galilee. Nor is there any sign of a tolerant
attitude, similar to that depicted in Genesis, towards others living in
the land. Instead, the picture drawn reflects the warrior God of
Deuteronomy who drives out the other nations, not the 'host' God
of Genesis who generously includes all surrounding peoples living
together peacefully in the land.

The archaeological data support the overall tenor of the literary
evidence. An important cult-site situated on the border between
upper and lower Galilee in the Meiron massif, aptly named *Har
Mispey Yamim,* since one can see both the Great Sea and the Sea of
Galilee from this point, was abandoned in the second century BCE,
and never again occupied.[24] On the basis of the finds it was an
important site, a 'high place' where both Egyptian and Phoenician
deities were worshipped. While there is no literary record of the
destruction of the site, the likely date of its abandonment suggest that
it, as well as other cult sites such as Thabor and Carmel in lower
Galilee, were all victims of the Hasmonean 'cleansing' of the region.
Evidence also suggests population shifts in the same period, and the
changes in the coin profile from Phoenician city coin types to
Hasmonean bronzes, proclaiming the 'assembly of the Jews' are clear
indicators of a settlement from the south.[25] The process continued at
other sites also, and the number of places where these Hasmonean
coins appear at bedrock suggest many new foundations over the
following 100 years.[26]

By the first century CE the successors of these Hasmonean settlers
constituted the bulk of Galilean Jews, even if other elements, Jewish
and non-Jewish, had entered the mix as a result of the conquests and
rule of Herod the Great and his son, Antipas. It is important to
acknowledge, therefore, contrary to several modern claims about
Galilean opposition to Jerusalem, that there was a strong attachment
to the mother-city, its temple and customs, among Galilean Jews of
Jesus' day. The archaeological investigation of Roman-period
Sepphoris, as well as other sites in Galilee, has produced compelling
evidence of Jewish observance in domestic settings at these centres,
based on the frequency of similar evidence from Judea and
Jerusalem.[27] This would explain the continued interest in Galilee
by the Jerusalem religious authorities, such as the scribes whom

Mark tells us had come from Jerusalem to discredit Jesus' healing ministry in the Galilean villages (Mk. 3.31, 7.1). It should also be remembered that Jesus himself, if not a Judean, had come under influences emanating from that quarter during his sojourn with John in the desert. He too, could be counted as bringing a southern perspective into Galilee, therefore.

It is significant that in addition to the silence of the gospels about a visit by Jesus to the Herodian centres of Sepphoris and Tiberias, there is also no mention of visits to such places as Jotapata and Gamla on his journeys through Galilee. These are locations where evidence for observance of Jewish dietary laws and ritual purity by some, at least of their residents, has been unearthed in the recent archaeological investigations of the sites.[28] Both places were also centres of strong Jewish resistance to Roman militarism some 30 years after Jesus' ministry, unlike Sepphoris, which had opted for peace with Rome. One could easily read far too much into such silence, yet gospel evidence of conflicts with the Pharisees over issues of Sabbath observance, purity and dietary regulations – all topics to do with the maintenance of Jewish ethnic separation – might explain the matter, despite the scepticism of modern scholars about dating these conflicts to Jesus' ministry.[29] Thus, when one holds up a map of Jesus' movements in Galilee, against the template of a more detailed description of the region indicating known places of Jewish observance, he is more frequently to be found in the environs of, if not actually within, pagan cities, than he is in recognizably Jewish locations. According to Josephus, the Pharisees were particularly popular with the townspeople, a piece of information that might suggest the need to differentiate in Galilee as elsewhere between various types of settlement and those who inhabited them (*JA* 18.15). Later Jewish sources point to a more varied array of types of settlement than is covered by the terms 'city', 'town' and 'village'. If there were Pharisees in Galilee the more likely locations in which to find them would be either in the Herodian cities or in medium-sized places such as Jotapata, Gamla, Gischala, Meiron and Khirbet Shema – all sites in which evidence of a more observant form of Jewish identity have been uncovered for the first century – and not in the small rural hamlets dotted throughout the countryside.

It has been suggested above that there is no good reason to claim that Jesus' movements in the region of the pagan cities in the circle of Galilee, meant that he had inaugurated the gentile mission. Jews, we saw, lived in those regions and contact with these might well have been the objective of such visits. Was this because Jesus felt they were in more serious danger of assimilation to pagan ways, or because he himself was less threatened by contacts with the pagan world than were the more observant Jews of the Galilean towns who were meticulous in maintaining visible signs of Jewish religious and ethnic identity? These are interesting questions, more easy to pose than to answer, and they will recur in the next chapter also. An examination of Jesus' sayings does not yield too much evidence of, or concern about gentiles. Their participation in the eschatological banquet with the Patriarchs is spoken about, more as a threat to 'this generation', meaning the Jews of his own day, than as good news for non-Jews, it would appear (Mt. 8.10–12; Lk. 13.28–29). However, mention of the Partriarchs here – Abraham, Isaac and Jacob – as well as reference to the points of the compass from whence people are to come, brings to mind Abraham's vision of the land stretching out in all directions and the promise to him that his seed would be countless and that all the nations of the earth would bless themselves by him. According to the Genesis Apocryphon, after he had returned from his travels he dined with his Midianite brothers. Perhaps this is the best clue we can garner for Jesus' own attitude to gentiles at this juncture. In that case it would not seem too far-fetched to suggest that he must have shared some of Abraham's attitudes, more so than if he were operating out of the legacy of the conquest tradition, with its attitude of suspicion and hostility to pagans living in the land.

On the Borders of Tyre

> Well ours is not a maritime country; neither commerce nor the intercourse which it promotes with the outside world has any attraction for us. Our cities are built inland, remote from the sea; and we devote ourselves to the cultivation of the productive country with which we are blessed. (Josephus, *Against Apion*, 1.60)

This rather tongue-in cheek description of Israel's location, lacking direct access to the Mediterranean especially in the north, was undoubtedly formulated with one eye on the Phoenician neigh-bours, whose sea-faring exploits had made the cities of Tyre and Sidon the envy of the ancient world. Josephus, one suspects, understood the pressures on Asher and Dan to enjoy the fruits of the sea rather than engage in a war against the Canaanites. Indeed one can detect a sense of grudging admiration for the opulence of Tyre in particular, in the many prophetic oracles addressed against that city (Isa. 23; Ezck. 26–29; Jer. 25.22; Amos 1.9–10; Joel 4.4–8; Zech. 9.2–3). Unlike Egypt, Bablylon or Assyria, Tyre and Sidon had never posed a serious dynastic threat to Israel. It was their opulence and the perceived pride that went with it that is most abhorred in the prophetic oracles. Yet there was also an awareness of the importance of these cities and their needs for Israelite and Judean commercial life. The prophet Ezekiel juxtaposes an oracle of woe against Tyre (ch. 26) with a lamentation for its fall (ch. 27) in view of its once-proud position among the nations, acknowledging also the contribution of both Israel and Judah to its success as providers of corn, wax, honey, tallow and balm (v. 17).

In the Hellenistic and Roman periods the attraction of having such a powerful neighbour close by gave rise to quite an ambivalent relationship. Inscriptional and literary evidence suggests strong commercial links in early Hellenistic times with such centres as Marisa, the capital of Idumea and Samaria (*JA* 11.344, 12.257f.). Association with Tyre was strong also among the Jerusalem elite of this period, who were in favour of the Hellenization of their cult. An overly separatist attitude, it was claimed, precluded sharing in the benefits of the increased trade of the Hellenistic age (1 Macc. 1.11). They arranged for a collection to be made for the games in honour of Herakles – the Greek equivalent of the Tyrian god Melqart – but the envoys who brought the money to Tyre baulked at the idea of using it for sacrifice to the pagan god, arranging for its use for other purposes (2 Macc. 4.18–20).

Even more surprising still is the fact that the Tyrian half-sheqel was deemed in later Rabbinic texts to be 'the coin of the sanctuary' which every male Jew was expected to pay annually for the upkeep of the Jerusalem sanctuary. There is no evidence that this practice troubled pious Jews, despite the fact that the coin bore the images of Herakles/Melqart, the patron god of the city, and that of Zeus, unless Jesus' action in the temple were to be understood as such a protest. However, this seems unlikely, as will be discussed in a later chapter. According to one account of John of Gischala's greed in buying up all the oil of the region, he was able to pay for it in 'Tyrian money' (*Life*, 72f.). Such attitudes among those who in theory at least practised an aniconic form of worship are difficult to understand. The most plausible explanation is that of all the different currencies in antiquity, that of Tyre was the most prized because it maintained its weight over several centuries and was not therefore subject to deflation. Good money was no respector of cultural boundaries in antiquity, as also today, it would seem.[30]

These scattered indications suggest that despite the ideological differences between Israel and Tyre, expressed in relation to the extent of the former's allotted territory, commercial exchanges between the two regions were not entirely precluded. Nevertheless, it is clear that relations varied at different periods. One must ask how typical was John of Gischala, especially at a time when the Jewish community in Tyre, as elsewhere in the surrounding cities, was under extreme pressure from the gentile populations there. In John's case, not merely is he alleged to have used Tyrian money, his personal army included fugitives from Tyre, also. The hostility between Qadesh and the Galileans, which Josephus claims once belonged to Galilee (*JA* 5.63), is best explained in the light of the recent discoveries of the remains of an important administrative archive from the Greek period at the site. The discovery of more than 2000 seals suggests that Qadesh was a substantial Tyrian outpost in terms of tax and other revenues in the area.[31] Behind Josephus' casual remark lurks a longer history of disputed territory, brigandage and occasional occupation, but this type of relationship may well have been the result of border difficulties, and untypical in terms of broader dealings with the coastal cities.

More secure results regarding commercial exchanges may be obtained from recent archaeological evidence, based on pottery and coins, especially since it seems possible to establish a definite pattern. The preponderance of Tyrian coins at sites not only in upper Galilee, close to the Tyrian hinterland, but also in lower Galilee, must mean that commercial activity did continue there, even allowing for such distorting factors as the use of Tyrian money for the temple offerings among the Jews and the fact that the Tyrian mint may have produced more coins than any other in the region. The extent of this trade has been variously estimated by different scholars, but the recognition that the largest percentage of coins are bronze, seems to suggest that the trade was not as extensive as is sometimes claimed.[32]

Interesting variations emerge when comparisons are made between different sites, however. Thus, Jotapata, an important centre of Jewish resistance in the first century CE, as previously mentioned, was situated not far from the borders of Ptolemais, the closest of the Phoenician cities to lower Galilee. There was a marked drop in the number of Phoenician city coins from the mid-second century BCE, a trend that corresponded with other changes at the site, coinciding, it would seem, with the Hasmonean re-claiming of Galilee. At Gamla on the other hand, situated east of the Jordan, but equally nationalistic in the first century, coins from the Tyrian mint continued to be used right through the period.[33] Proximity to the perceived threat of cultural contamination may have been a factor in this varied pattern. On that hypothesis, the example of Asher's succumbing to the allurements of the sea might well have provided observant Judeans living in Jotapata, with reasons to regard the Phoenician cities as a 'dangerous' environment, thus cutting off all commercial contacts.

Provenience studies, which can trace ceramic remains back to their place of production, have become increasingly important as indicators of trading links, both internal and external. This applies both to household wares and to containers of products of oil, wine and salted fish for import and export. There were two important centres of ceramic production within Galilee – Kfar Hanania and Shikhin – both servicing the domestic market for household wares, including storage jars. There is some evidence also of export of this ware to non-Jewish sites in the Golan over a time-span from the Hellenistic to the Byzantine period, thereby indicating a developing Galilean economy to meet the demands of a growing population.[34] The fact that these wares were also deemed highly suitable to the requirements of the purity laws according to Talmudic sources must surely have been a factor in their continued success. This observation on the development of an indigenous Galilean ceramics industry to meet the demands of local religious requirements would seem to be borne out by the findings of an important survey of another type of ceramic ware, described as 'Phoenician semi-fine ware' with a likely provenance in Tyre.[35] This collection of household jars, juglets and amphora, as well as ointment pots and unguentaria is particularly significant in that it can be dated to the period of Judean expansion into Galilee and its consolidation there. Traces of the ware have been found at sites all around the perimeter of Galilee, but not in the interior, thus confirming the conservative attitudes of Galileans with regard to imports from Phoenicia in the Hasmonean period.

Changes in commercial activities, especially in relation to modes of production and distribution, bring about changes in values also. It was this aspect, not the exchange itself, that was most threatening to a religious environment that was separatist and conservative in its attitude. The accounts of the tribal settlements suggested that from the beginning the northern tribes were most at risk from this point of view, with Asher and Dan coming in for special notice. There can be little doubt that the underlying tensions were the result of the extraordinary successes of the Phoenician trading empire and the demands for goods and services that this brought to the hinterland. The strong ethno-centric view expressed by Josephus with regard to Israel's 'turning its back' on the sea, can be seen for what it was, namely, apologetic rhetoric for the benefit of Greco-Roman readers. Other more religiously concerned individuals such as the second-century Rabbis sought different ways to protect Israel's purity by defining carefully the borders between the territory of Tyre and the land of Israel, and listing certain villages that lay outside that line as 'doubtful' in terms of purity maintenance.[36] In developing the port of Cæsarea Maritima, south of Galilee, Herod the Great sought a piece of the action on the Mediterranean in order to fund his many projects at home and overseas. Under his son, Antipas, Galilee was not immune to these changes to the infrastructure and the opportunities that they offered were a serious threat to the traditional values that the people of Jotapata, for example, had espoused in shunning commercial contacts with the Phoenicians. As was suggested in the previous chapter, these changes posed a serious threat to the ecological conditions of Galilee, but they impacted on the social and religious situation also which Jesus sought to address.

Jesus' alternative lifestyle, allied to his challenge to the value-system of the rich, meant that he was unimpressed by the wealth of the Phoenicians. Yet, unlike the Israelite prophets who had repeatedly called for judgement on the nations, including Tyre and Sidon, Jesus' warning of coming judgement is directed instead to Galilean towns. Corazin, Bethsaida and Capernaum are unfavourably compared to Tyre and Sidon, who, had they experienced the favours of these places, would, like Niniveh, (where a Galilean-born prophet, Jonah, had preached)[37] have done penance in sackcloth and ashes. For a Galilean audience such comparisons were extraordinary given the size and importance of the Phoenician cities and their reputation within the Israelite tradition. The intention was to shame the Galilean towns. Nevertheless, behind the rhetoric is a veiled recognition that such places too have a place in God's plan, something that it would be difficult for those who adhered to the Deuteronomic idea of the nations to accept.

Jesus, we are told by Mark, went to the region of Tyre, presumably for similar reasons to those which had brought him to the villages of Cæsarea Philippi. There were, as was seen above, Jews living beyond the boundaries recognized by political and religious practicalities of the day, but according to the idealogy of the ideal land, it was the Mediterranean that was regarded as the true limit of the allotted land. There is no suggestion that Jesus was interested in making territorial claims, however. His choice of the Twelve did not envisage a historical return of the tribes, necessitating a re-apportioning of the tribal territories as Ezekiel had suggested, to the actual exclusion of any place on his map for either Tyre or Sidon (Ezck. 47.13–23, especially v. 20). It is in the region of Tyre that Mark locates the story of Jesus' encounter with the woman who was Syro-Phoenician by birth, but 'a Greek', signifying presumably, somebody who religiously was 'pagan' and culturally Hellenized, but also a person of a high social status. The historicity of the account has been challenged by many scholars, most recently by John Meier on the basis that it is 'so shot through' with early Christian mission theology, that he deems it to be the product of the first-generation Christians.[38]

This judgement merely begs another question, however. One would still want to enquire about Jesus' own likely attitude to the presence of gentiles in his new family, and the manner in which his Galilean border encounters with gentiles might have coloured his views, or at lest provoked his thinking on the subject. In the next chapter this issue arises in regard to the pilgrimage of the nations to Zion, yet here it is appropriate to recall that the Jew/gentile opposition occurred in contexts other than the religious sphere, even in Palestine. Thus, for example, Josephus sees his own role as a historian to inform his readers, 'the Greeks', about the privileges which the Jews of Asia had traditionally been granted by various rulers, even supporting their way of honouring God, in order that he might 'reconcile the other nations to us, and to remove the causes for hatred that have taken root among thoughtless people among us as well as among them' (JA 16.175).[39]

The issue of reconciling Jew and Greek was a commonplace in the East, because of the long-standing hostilities that existed on both sides, even, or perhaps more especially, in Palestine. It seems inevitable, therefore, that the problem was faced by Jesus also, once it is accepted that he did move outside the borders of political Galilee into the territories of the surrounding Greek cities.[40] Since Jesus' view of Israel's restoration was not one of territorial conquest or expulsion of non-Jews from traditional tribal territories, then we must surely allow him to have been as concerned about the issue as was Josephus, within, of course, the parameters of his self-ascribed role, which was not the same as that of the Jerusalem-born statesman/apologist. Other prophetic voices before Jesus had also addressed the issue of reconciliation with the gentiles within the overall divine plan, without thereby diluting Israel's sense of its special election. *Pace* Meier and others, the early Christian missionary pattern of 'Jew first then the Greek' was not invented by the first-century Christian missionaries, even though it is variously used by them in terms of their own debates and dilemmas, especially by Paul and Luke. The strong local colouring of the story of the Syro-Phoenician woman whom Jesus is reported to have encountered in the region of Tyre suggests that, if the incident is not historical, it is in all probability Palestinian, and addresses an issue that Jesus too must have been faced with in his own life in that region.[41] The manner of his response, if not the precise wording, is unlikely to have been very different from that which is reported by Mark, or his source. He did, after all, speak about loving the enemy, and there was no shortage of those on either side in the Galilee of Jesus.

All three topics that had arisen in the conquest and settlement narratives of the Pentateuch – the land remaining, the Canaanites dwelling in the land and the allurements of the Phoenician cities – were extremely actual in Roman Galilee. In dealing with those issues as they presented themselves in Galilee, patterns of response inspired by the conquest narratives were readily discernible, as various ideas of and attitudes towards restoration competed with each other within Jewish Galilee. We have sought to read aspects of the Jesus-story as reported in the gospels in the light of those issues, often relying on the criterion of contextual plausibility in evaluating the likely historicity of the patterns, if not the details suggested by the gospel story. There are many uncertainties, and one is often forced to deal in generalities, given the highly selective nature of the sources, especially the gospels. It would appear, however, that approaching the Jesus-story from the perspective of a contextual reading against the backdrop of the Biblical narratives does open up new vistas on his life and ministry, especially highlighting the points where his attitudes differ markedly from those of his contemporaries. As in all such discussions, it is easier to identify the choices which he did *not* make from the inherited traditions than to be positive about those that did inspire him. Nevertheless, the image of Abraham travelling through a land inhabited by various ethnic groups, including traditional enemies of historical Israel, and encountering the God who directs his travels at many places within the land, does have quite striking resonance with the Jesus-story at several points. While the special place of Israel is indeed affirmed, especially through the account of Jacob's blessing of the tribes, the fact that two of those are roundly condemned for their behaviour, even when they acted in the name of restoring honour, shows that election involves responsibility for others and that violation of the laws of hospitality was indeed a very serious matter.

4

ZION BECKONS

All call Zion mother, since all were born in her. (Ps. 87.5)
Jerusalem, Jerusalem ... How often would I have gathered your
children, as a hen gathers her brood under her wing and you would not.
(Mt. 23.37; Lk. 13.34)

The evangelist Luke was not just a historian, he was also a literary
artist, creating many memorable scenes in his re-telling of the Jesus-
story for Theophilus. His account of Jesus' visit to Nazareth at the
beginning of the public ministry is one such, full of colour and
suspense (Lk. 4.16–30). Jesus seems to take the initiative in standing
up to read; the book is handed to him, but he decides what passage
will be read; as he resumes his seat there is a palpable sense of
expectation: 'the eyes of all in the synagogue were strained on him'.
There seems little doubt that Luke has constructed this scene as a
programmatic introduction to the public ministry of Jesus, but from
the perspective of this study, the choice of Isaiah as the most
appropriate text to introduce Jesus' ministry poses the more
intriguing question: How did Jesus read Isaiah?

The short answer to that question is that Jesus read the prophetic
text, prophetically.[1] As Luke presents it, Jesus is citing not just one
passage from Isaiah about 'the acceptable year of the Lord' (Isa. 61.1–
2), but also another one dealing with relief for the blind, the lame
and the deaf (Isa. 35.3–6). The same combination of Isaianic
references occurs in the earlier (than Luke) Q version of Jesus'
response to the messengers from John, querying whether he was 'the
one who is to come' (Mt. 11.4–6; Lk. 7.23–24): 'Go and relate to
John what you have heard and seen: the blind see, the lame walk, the
deaf hear, the dead rise again and the poor have the gospel preached
to them.' Most intriguingly, a recently published fragment from
Qumran (4Q 521) offers a close parallel to Jesus' response, based
clearly on the same Isaian passages, and including also the reference
to the dead being raised, something that is not actually found in
Isaiah, but is associated with Elijah in Jewish lore. Furthermore, the

Qumran fragment introduces the passage with the statement: 'Heaven and earth will listen to his messiah', giving the whole passage the same messianic flavour as did John's question to Jesus in Q.[2] It would seem that Luke has not only painted an exciting scene from inside the Nazareth synagogue, but he has also opened the window on a world of the messianic appropriation of Isaiah in circles with which John and Jesus had affinities, if not direct associations.

Following this 'inspired' lead, this chapter will involve a fairly lengthy detour through the book of Isaiah with a special focus on his theology of Zion, before returning to the question of Jesus' actual indebtedness to the prophet with regard to this topic. Isaiah is above all a prophet both of and for Jerusalem, the chief, but not the only architect of its mythicization. Having concentrated on Jesus' preoccupation with the borders of the land in the previous chapter, attention is now turned to his relations with the centre. On a first reading, the epigraph of this chapter – Jesus' so-called 'lament for Jerusalem' – suggests a genuine sadness on his part for his failure to convince Jerusalem about his message. It even presupposes that Jesus actually visited the holy city many times, thus reflecting the Johannine rather than the Synoptic outline of his public ministry. The lament is found in two different contexts in Matthew's and Luke's gospels (Mt. 23.37–39; Lk. 13.34–35). Since most students of Q regard the Lukan order as the more primitive, this saying is deemed to declare judgement on the city rather than offer a promise of future redemption, as its formulation in Matthew suggests.[3] It reflects, it is claimed, a 'cognitive map' that is hostile to Jerusalem on the part of the Q community, at whose core is a group of early Christian prophets operating in Galilee after the death of Jesus and before the destruction of Jerusalem in 70 CE.[4]

However, even if one were to agree with this judgement, it need not mean that Jesus himself shared this view. Q, it is claimed, is a literary work with its own perspective, and its ideas cannot automatically be attributed to Jesus, even when the authenticity of the saying itself is not seriously questioned. Nevertheless, there has been a tendency in some recent studies of Jesus to distance him also from Jerusalem and its institutions. The stress on Galilee alone as the theatre for Jesus' public ministry in some recent accounts is based on the assumption of a deep-seated opposition between Galilee and Judea/Jerusalem, resulting from a previous history of tensions between the two regions. However, in the light of the discussion in the previous chapter regarding the Judeans of Galilee, this assumption is not well founded. Crossan's reasons for distancing Jesus from Jerusalem are slightly different, though elsewhere he does seem to share the notion of Galilee/Jerusalem opposition. With regard to Jesus' visit to Jerusalem he writes:

> I am not sure that poor Galilean peasants went up and down regularly to the Temple feasts. I think it quite possible that Jesus went to Jerusalem only once and that the spiritual and economic egalitarianism he preached in Galilee exploded in indignation at the Temple as the seat and symbol of all that was non-egalitarian, patronal and even oppressive on both the religious and political level.[5]

What seems to be missing from this view, however, is any reflection on the possible symbolic importance of Jerusalem for a Galilean peasant. Why did Jesus feel constrained to go to Jerusalem, if only to vent his anger there? What hopes did he entertain for Jerusalem and how important were those hopes to his own project as it unfolded in Galilee?

A full answer to those questions would call for a complete study on its own.[6] For that reason it is planned to focus, after a brief historical introduction, on the manner in which the theme of Zion is developed in the book of Isaiah, since, as will emerge, it is central to all three major sections of that composite work. Though the book must have arrived at its present form only as late as the Persian period, it contains material dating to the eighth century BCE, the period of the historical Isaiah. Thus it should be possible to trace the manner in which the mythicization of Zion developed over the centuries and the ways in which related topics became associated with it.

Jerusalem as Centre

The central importance of Jerusalem within the Israelite and Judean narrative was due to its choice by David as his base of operation once he conquered the fortress of Zion (2 Sm. 5.6–12). Subsequently, Solomon made it the centre of his imperial ambitions, completing the work of his father by building a temple to Yahweh, who now became the patron God of the city and the king (1 Kgs. 3–10). According to the royal ideology behind this narrative, Solomon's wealth and his wisdom went hand in hand. Eventually his empire embraced not just the tribal lands of Israel, but all of 'Transeuphratene', i.e. the whole region west of the Euphrates river to the Mediterranean (1 Kgs. 4.20–25). Jerusalem with its temple was the capital and centre of this great achievement. Solomon's wisdom embraced all knowledge, so that men from all nations came to hear his wisdom and he received gifts from all the kings of the world (1 Kgs. 5.9–14). His was a 'Golden Age' literally and metaphorically, but it was not destined to last.[7]

Solomon's fall from grace by worshipping foreign gods is the immediate setting and cause for the break-up of David's kingdom. When the author of 1 and 2 Kings comes to pass judgement of the fall of both Israel and Judah his verdict is exactly similar to that which brought about the break-up of Solomon's kingdom:

> 'They and their kings worshipped other gods; they followed the practices of the nations that Yahweh had dispossessed for them . . . . They set up pillars and sacred poles on every high hill and every spreading tree. They sacrificed there after the manner of the nations . . . They worshipped the whole array of heaven and they served Baal.'

Thus Yahweh rejected 'the whole race of Israel' (2 Kgs. 17.19–23). The deportation to Assyria and the deportation to Babylon a century and a half later were, for this author, rooted in the same act of disobedience, expressed in terms of worship of foreign gods.

Yet despite this negative judgement the same author(s) have included in the promise to David on which so much of the hopes for the future would be built, the promise of restoration of the dispersed: 'I will provide a place for my people, Israel; I shall plant them there and they shall dwell in that place and they shall never be disturbed again . . . Yahweh will make you great; Yahweh will make you a house' (2 Sm. 7.4–16). When this promise to David is read in the context of the history as a whole, it is clear that it was not directed to Judah and Jerusalem only. David's house was to include the north as well, since the establishment of the kingship was intended to provide stability in face of the attacks and allurement of surrounding nations, and in this respect the northern tribes were even more vulnerable than Judah. The fact that in the post-exilic period the promise to David became identified with the promise to Zion (Ps. 132, for example) should not obscure this important fact that the fate of both Israel (northern kingdom) and Judah (southern

kingdom) were bound together in the hopes associated with David
and his house according to the Deuteronomistic historian.

The severe criticism to which the kings had been subjected by this
writer meant that another focus for the hopes of the future was
required, especially in the exilic and post-exilic periods. The
celebration of Yahweh's kingship in the cult provided the
foundation for further development of a more lasting kind. Psalm
132, recalling David's transfer of the ark to Jerusalem, announces the
fact that Yahweh has chosen Zion as his dwelling place. Thus, the
fortress which David had captured and made the centre of his
operations, and which Solomon had made his imperial capital, was
gradually transformed into a symbol of Yahweh's abiding presence.
Jerusalem was changed from a royal city into a cult city, to use
Martin Noth's terminology, and in the process the role of the
monarchy as the bearer of Israel's hopes was considerably reduced.[8]
Zion and its people could equally be bearers of the promise. While
the temple was the recognized place of the divine presence, the
sanctity and holiness associated with the temple extended outward to
the city as a whole, and it is around the name of Zion that such ideas
would develop.

The Psalms were particularly significant in developing and
disseminating these ideas about the centrality of Zion in view of
common people's undoubted familiarity with them through the
various rituals, domestic and communal. The fact that the Psalter is
deemed to express a consistent theological point of view from the
post-exilic period, is also helpful in tracing aspects of the Zion motif
as it developed over time.[9] One cluster of psalms (Pss. 46–48)
consists of a short poem celebrating the kingship of Yahweh over all
the earth, where, significantly he is described as 'the God of
Abraham, before whom the princes of the people gather' (Ps. 47, cf.
v. 9). It is bracketed by Ps. 46, speaking of the holy city in cosmic
terms as an unshakable fortress, because 'God is within', and Ps. 48,
hailing the wonders of Zion, impregnable against the attacks of
various kings because 'God is in the temple' (Ps. 48). Here
Sennacherib's failure to capture the city in 701 BCE has stirred the
imagination of the poets of Israel, and the redemption from the
impending disaster is attributed to Yahweh's presence and his
lordship over the whole earth, not to the Davidic promises. Other
'songs of Zion' (cf. Ps. 137.3) celebrate various aspects of Yahweh's
reassuring presence and its attractiveness to the nations also (Pss. 76,
102).

Isaiah and Zion

These motifs from the Psalter find more developed expression in the Book of Isaiah, which was one of the most popular books in the Qumran library on the basis of the number of manuscripts represented in the collection as well as commentaries on various sections.[10] It is important to recall that for over 100 years modern scholarship has dealt with the book of Isaiah as three quite distinct compositions – First Isaiah (chs. 1–39), Second Isaiah (chs. 40–55) and Third Isaiah (chs. 56–66) – dating from the pre-exilic, exilic and post-exilic periods. First-century Jews were not privy to such insights. Whoever added the final inclusion of 66.17–24 to match 1.27–31 clearly considered the whole to have a unity of sorts, but this does not preclude 'a cumulative process of reinterpretation and re-application', both within individual sections and between sections. Ironically, Isaian studies are today going through the same 'paradigm shift' as Pentateuchal studies, namely, the desire to read the book as a whole as representative of a single voice and having a consistent plot, despite what source and redaction criticism has taught us.[11] In tracing the different themes it will be necessary to maintain a balance between both approaches, particularly since we are interested in discerning possible developments and changes of perspective.[12]

Three interrelated aspects of the Zion tradition in Isaiah are highly significant for purposes of identifying those dimensions of the received tradition which seem to have influenced Jesus' understanding of his ministry. These are: 1) the pilgrimage of the nations and the restoration of Israel; 2) the symbol Zion and its application over time; and 3) the 'servant community' of Zion. We shall trace Isaiah's contribution to the understanding of each of these.

The Nations and the Restoration of Israel

Isaiah's description of the 'pilgrimage' of the nations to Zion (2.2–4) gives a triumphant and 'universalistic' perspective to the book from the outset. Their desire to hear the word (*dabar*) of the Lord emanating from Jerusalem and the instruction (*torah*) that proceeds from that source is surprising and unexpected. The recognition of Yahweh's wisdom by the nations is in stark contrast to the reality of Judah and Jerusalem as the historical Isaiah uttered his oracles, with the Assyrian army of Sennacherib at the gates of the city. The suggestion that the nations will beat their sword into ploughshares is deeply ironic, therefore, but it offers an alternative vision of Israel's relationship with the nations to the usual one of aggressive militarism, as Israel had experienced it in its history. It is definitely a vision for the future – 'in the days to come' – but it prompts an urgent plea from the prophet: 'O House of Jacob [a designation that is used throughout for the people Israel, e.g. 46.3, 48.1, 58.1] come let us walk in the light of the Lord' (2.5). Later, in the second section of the book, it will be the task of the Servant (*Ebed*) of Yahweh not only 'to raise up the tribes of Jacob and restore "the survivors" of Israel' but also to be a light for the nations, so that Yahweh's salvation 'might reach the end of the earth' (49.6). Thus Israel's fate and that of the nations are intimately connected from the outset, and the image of 'light' plays an important role throughout the book as expressive of Yahweh's presence in the world, since as the creator God, Yahweh is the source of light for all (42.16, 45.7, 51.4, 60.3).

Restoration of the tribes is not very central to Isaiah's ideas of the future, something that makes the reference to Galilee and the Galilean tribes (8.23) all the more significant. Galileans of the first century could be assured that their territory too shared in the blessings to come, even when the main locative focus of the book is, as we shall see, on Jerusalem. This reference is one of two allusions to the Davidic promises in the opening section of the book. In the first instance (8.23–9.6) the deportation of the northern tribes is recalled in a prose introduction to a poem celebrating the birth of a child whose reign will bring extensive sovereignty and peace to David's house. Two separate campaigns seem to be envisaged in the introductory oracle, one of them being clearly that of Tiglath-pileser III, with the mention of the 'bringing low' of the land of Zebulon and the land of Naphtali (2 Kgs. 15, 29). It is not absolutely clear whether 'the way of the sea, the land across the Jordan, Galilee of the Gentiles' in the second part of the statement refers to the same tribal territories or to different regions along the coastal plain and in Transjordan.[13] In that event the consolation offered to the north – both to Israel and to its surrounding territories – which is once again expressed through the image of light, is based on the birth of the true son of David. This figure is given a series of names, describing the qualities of the future ideal ruler, the most important of which is 'prince of peace', while significantly, in view of past failures, that of king is missing.

The second reference to the restoration of the northern tribes follows a similar pattern in Isa. 11.1–9. This poem celebrates a future ruler of the 'stock of Jesse', David's father. The spirit of Yahweh will endow this ideal ruler not with military prowess, but with the gifts of understanding and wisdom. Truth and peace will reign through the establishment of justice for the poor and the humble, while the powerful and greedy will be restrained. There is a subtle parallelism between the harmony that is established in the human world and the animal kingdom, as the powerful and the predatory will be transformed.[14] This poem with its cosmic overtones becomes the trigger for another one (vv. 10–16) celebrating the healing of the rift between Ephraim and Judah, who will no longer be jealous of each other (cf. 9.21). The Galilean tribes are not mentioned explicitly here as in 8.23, but the scope of the poem is broader than the healing of a particular rift between Jerusalem and Samaria, since it refers to the repatriation of the 'residue' (she'ar) of Israel from all the nations.

The restoration of peace and justice in Israel would be a signal to the nations to return the 'residue' of the people, and the same image is employed in the second part of the book also for the restoration of the exiles (11.10–11, 49.22).[15] In this instance, however, the peoples will carry the sons and daughters home. This introduces a rather different tone to the repatriation theme, one that treats the peoples, even Cyrus, as Israel's servants. The Persian ruler is (ironically?) described as Yahweh's anointed (45.1, 13), and foreign kings and queens will be reduced to the roles of foster fathers and nursing mothers (49.23). This tone becomes even more strident and triumphalistic in the concluding section of the book, especially in chs. 60 to 62, where the role of the nations in the restoration of the dispersed Israelites is portrayed as Yahweh avenging past injustices by the nations and their rulers. The joyous atmosphere of the opening oracle has disappeared and the foreigners are press-ganged to build up the walls of Jerusalem, hand over their wealth to the city, with their kings taking part in a triumphal procession (60.6–11, 61.6).

These sentiments are described by Blenkinsopp as 'perhaps, understandable as "fantasies of the oppressed" ', but a far cry from a genuine religious universalism as this finds expression elsewhere in the book (e.g. 2.2–4, 19.24–25).[16] They are in his view the opinions of one voice among several that can be heard within the book, especially in the concluding part, with differing opinions as to who should be included in the new Israel under discussion. The original image of the nations coming to 'the house of the God of Jacob' in

Zion begins to be realized with the declaration (attributed to Jesus in Mk. 11.17): 'My house will be a house of prayer for all the nations' (Isa. 56.7). This statement comes in the opening oracle of the third part of the book (56.1–8), and is, therefore, usually dated to the period of the return from the Babylonian captivity. Foreigners/ *allogenoi* and eunuchs 'who observe the Sabbath and cling to my covenant' will be given an everlasting name in God's house, more than the sons and daughters, and their sacrifices will be welcome on the altar. Zion is not just a place of illumination for the nations as described in the opening oracle, it also provides a 'house of prayer' for some, even when this would mean ignoring the legal regulations concerning those who were allowed to participate in the cult (Deut. 23.3–9). Such people belong to the extended family that Yahweh will join to the returning exiles in accordance with the promises to the patriarchs:

> One man will say, 'I belong to Yahweh',
> Another will call himself by Jacob's name.
> On his hand another will write Yahweh,
> And be surnamed Israel. (Isa. 44.1–5)[17]

The conditions for this welcome for the nations must be read in the context of the book as a whole, which envisages the nations waiting for *torah* also (2.3, 42.4), a light which the servant will eventually bring to them (51.4). Even in 56.1–8 there is no reference to circumcision, the food laws or other concerns of the purity regulations. Apart from the general stipulation of maintaining justice and observing what is right, only observance of the Sabbath is singled out as essential for Yahweh's welcome to those who seek to cling to him. This choice of what is paramount to Israel's God might appear unusual, until the fact of the creator God resting on the seventh day after completing all his work is recalled (Gen. 2.3f.). It is this same creator God that is the ultimate warrant for Isaiah's picture of future salvation (Isa. 43.16–21). The 'redeemer of Israel' is the one who has 'created the heavens and rolled them out' and given shape to the earth, and life to the creatures that move in it (Isa. 42.5). When this God rests, therefore, both Israel *and* the nations must rest also, thus acknowledging his lordship over the whole creation.

'Clinging to the covenant' should also be read within the wider context of Yahweh's creation and new creation. The apocalyptic vision of destruction in ch. 24 describes the conditions of the earth in terms reminiscent of the flood: 'A curse consumes the earth and few are left ... The sluice gates above are opened and the foundations of the earth rock' (vv. 1–4, 19–21). This universal devastation, which includes Jerusalem also (vv. 7–18), will come about because 'they have transgressed the law, violated the precept, broken the everlasting covenant' (vv. 5–6). The covenant that the nations are expected to observe, therefore, is not that of Sinai, but that which Yahweh made with Noah and the post-deluvian population of the earth (Gen. 9.9). It is that covenant that has been violated in the Isaian perspective, giving rise to the threat of repeating the devastation of the past.[18]

As the book develops, then, it is possible to trace a progression in terms of the nations sharing in the salvation to come with the restoration of Israel. The image of the joyful pilgrimage of the nations to Zion of the opening of the book, gives way in the second part to a heightened expectation of Israel's return from exile. This will be achieved through a mighty deed of Yahweh, the creator God whose servant will bring light to the nations from a restored and purified Zion. In the third and final section the hope for the nations reaches a partial climax through the acceptance on the holy mountain of all who cling to the covenant, including foreigners and eunuchs, by allowing them a full share in the temple worship. Interspersed with this portrayal is another voice or voices, which do not share this vision of a universal covenant and a shared house. The pain and anguish of exile is till too raw for such an openness to the nations to find universal acceptance. It is one of the remarkable features of the book that the author(s) found space for the different perspectives. The book's closing includes a reassurance that as part of the 'new creation' Yahweh will send messengers to the coastlands far away 'who have not heard of my fame or seen my glory'. These strangers will bring as their offerings repatriated Israelites. Even some of those who come will become priests and Levites so that 'from new moon to new moon and from Sabbath to Sabbath, "all flesh" will come to worship in my presence' (Isa. 66.18–21).[19]

Mother Zion

The locative focus of the book of Isaiah is on Jerusalem, understandably so, given the circumstances of the historical Isaiah, who, as a Jerusalemite, was deeply involved in the politics of the city during the period of Assyrian invasion of Judea, especially after the fall of the northern kingdom (734–701 BCE). However, it is as Zion that the holy city is most often spoken of throughout the book, though the two names can be interchanged (40.9, 41.27, 52.1). The two opening chapters provide a vibrant contrast between a present desolated Zion, left 'like a lean-to in a vineyard' and resembling Sodom and Gomorrah, and Zion of 'the days to come', when the nations will arrive with joy to be instructed in the ways of the Lord: 'For from Zion instruction [*torah*] will proceed, and the word [*dabar*] of the Lord from Jerusalem' (Isa. 2.2–4). Zion's condition of ruin and decay is the direct result of the moral and religious failures of its elite citizens. Religious observance that lacks genuine ethical concern is condemned unreservedly (1.12–15), and they will be ashamed of their involvement in strange religious practices (1.29). Zion can only be redeemed when justice reigns and the wicked receive their due punishment.

The first major section (chs. 1–39), has as its main focus the historical Isaiah's involvement in Judean politics from the reign of Ahaz (chs. 6–10) to that of Hezekiah, a period of 30 years (chs. 36–39). In the case of Ahaz, the prophet's warning to trust in Yahweh's presence with Israel rather than on political alliances falls on deaf ears. The moral decay continues and the wealthy women of Jerusalem persist in their haughty behaviour while the widows are still left to mourn (3.16–4.1). However, even then, future redemption is in view and Jerusalem 'will be called holy'. Yahweh's protection will be with them by day and by night, since the entire site of Zion and its assemblies will be covered with a cloud by day and a brightly burning fire by night (4.2–4). Hezekiah, too, is given a sign that Sennacherib, who in 701 was marshalling his troops to invade the city, would never enter, and that the people of Jerusalem could begin again to till their crops as before. Unlike Ahaz, who had ignored a similar sign (7.14–16), Hezekiah, a person of trusting faith in Yahweh, heeds Isaiah's word, and indeed the city is delivered from the Assyrian threat.

In between these two political episodes involving Isaiah and his appeal to the Zion tradition, the oracles against various peoples who are seen as Israel's enemies from the time before and after the exile are the main feature (chs. 13–27). The message seems to be that despite their power and arrogance they will all be brought low by Yahweh's superior might. The devastation of the whole earth because of the violation of the covenant with Noah is merely a prelude to Yahweh's inauguration of his reign in Mt. Zion and Jerusalem, climaxing in the great banquet of rich food prepared for all people on this mountain, because he will destroy there the mantle in which all people are wrapped (24.21–25.8).

In the second section of the book (chs. 40–55) the focus is not on the eschatological Zion to come but on the present one and its tribulations, reflecting the condition of the exiles in Babylonia and their intense longing to return to Jerusalem. The eschatological pilgrimage of the nations to Zion is now subordinated to the return of the exiles, as Yahweh is about to do 'a new thing' (43.18). The role of the nations is to accompany them and assist them in their return. The prophet is called on to announce the joyful news to Zion/Jerusalem that her God is present, pointing no doubt to the restoration of the temple that had been destroyed. In the absence of any real leader in Zion/Jerusalem to respond to the good news, Cyrus is chosen as the one who will execute the return (41.27, 44.26–28). The reader is invited to imagine the exiles preparing for the return, and in reversal of the capture and exile, now it is the survivors of the nations who are coming in chains (45.14, 20) or as escorts and slaves (49.22–23). Zion had begun to doubt that the return was really happening, but she is invited to look and see the returning hordes (45.14–22). As the location of the reader shifts from Babylon to Jerusalem, the locative dimension of Zion gives way to the personal. Yahweh, as a good feeding mother, will not abandon his child (49.15).[20] The exilic experience is like a divorce from a faithless bride, except that no bill was ever written and so the parting is not definitive (50.1). Soon the shout goes up: Yahweh will remove the cup of bitterness and call on Jerusalem to prepare herself like a bride. Zion is no longer the captive daughter, and she is informed that her God is king (51.17–52.12).

Clearly, the exilic experience raised serious questions for both exiles and those left in the land regarding Israel's identity and future. The situation called for a new interpretation of old symbols. The focus now was on Israel, since the advent of the Persian empire and Cyrus' more liberal regime with captive people, meant that Israel was given the space to re-invent itself in and around the temple in Jerusalem. The promise to David was no longer significant or useful. It did not speak to the situation of the post-exilic community, whereas that of Zion did. The Davidic kingship could be replaced by the kingship of Yahweh, and Zion would be his bride. Very soon, however, this message of good news for Zion was to seem illusory as the restored community was torn by various divisions, disappointments and uncertainties. The symbol Zion was once again up for negotiation and various interpretations would be forthcoming.

The final section of the book (chs. 56–66) is built around a core of chs. 60–62 which are addressed to the whole group, with no internal divisions in evidence. The portrayal of Zion in these chapters is both a reprise and a development of the image as it functioned in chs. 40–55. The tone is one of joy and delight at the unexpected reversal of fortune for Zion. Many of the associated motifs already encountered are here repeated and embellished: violence is absent and peace and integrity reign (60.18); the light that emanated from Zion is now given cosmic proportions – the sun shall never set nor the moon wane – because Yahweh is the everlasting light. In particular the motif of the nations accompanying the returnees is expanded: not merely do they act as escorts, they bring their wealth also to adorn not just the city, but the temple (60.7, 9, 13). The personification as a woman is also enhanced. Yahweh is like a young man taking his bride in marriage, and Zion is given new names – 'My Delight' and 'the Wedded One' – symbolizing the union (62.4–5).

Yet the fact that this paean of delight is interrupted by the voice of an individual prophet, claiming to have been anointed by Yahweh and to be endowed with his spirit, is both unexpected and ominous (61.1–9). It suggests that the picture of Zion being drawn here is both an idealization and a projection in the face of very real social evils of the day (cf. Neh. 5.1–11). Despite the high hopes of the returning exiles very little has changed. Captives have to be set free, the poor need to hear genuine good news and the acceptable year of the Lord can also be a year of vengeance. The hopes associated with the glorious and triumphant Zion have not been translated into a genuine social and ethical reform in Judah. Simply repeating the ideology that served the situation of exile as counter-propaganda to that of the neo-Babylonian empire will do little to achieve a new sense of Israel in a post-exilic context as part of the Persian province 'Beyond the River'. Deprived of such props from the past as a native monarchy and a state-supported temple, there was need for some new symbolic universe to emerge that would give direction for the future. How might the Zion symbol be refashioned to function meaningfully in this new situation?

It has already been pointed out that the opening oracle of this section of the book (56.1–8) had suggested a situation in which membership of the cultic community was being opened up. Foreigners and eunuchs 'who clung to Yahweh' could participate fully and their offerings could be more acceptable to Yahweh than those of sons and daughters. Further, the temple is described as a house of prayer, hinting at least of a sense that ritual activity devoid of ethical seriousness was useless in the eyes of Yahweh. Could the Zion symbol be transformed to support such radical innovations and their challenge to the dominant ideology?

The highly coloured closing eschatological chapters (65 and 66) provide a positive answer to this question. Here a clear separation emerges between 'those who did not seek Yahweh', the stubborn and rebellious people who practised syncretistic cults (65.1–7) and the remnant, the new wine, who are described as Yahweh's servants, the people whom he has created from Jacob. They will be heirs to his mountains and feed their flocks in the Plain of Sharon (65.9–10). There shall be no more mourning, as the former things will not be remembered. Yahweh is about to create a new heaven and a new earth, and create Jerusalem as a joy, and its people as a delight (65.17–18).

Appropriately, a final poem (66.5–16) – addressed to 'those who shake at Yahweh's word' – celebrates the miraculous birth that Mother Zion has achieved without labour, the work of Yahweh's glory. Those who approached her can rejoice and be filled with blessings from her consoling breasts, 'like nurslings fondled on her lap' (66.13). Those who hate and exclude Yahweh's servants will be put to shame. The voice of judgement as well as of blessing can emanate from the temple (66.6). Despite the miraculous birth that signals the new creation, there is still more to come. 'Can a land come to birth in a single day? Can a nation be born all at once?' (66.8). The book concludes with Yahweh promising to come and gather the nations of every tongue, so that they can come and witness his glory in Jerusalem. Yahweh's final word is one of eschatological reassurance: As the new heavens and the new earth will endure so will the worship of 'all flesh, your posterity' continue to honour Yahweh in Zion (66.18–23).

The Servant Community of Zion

Zion emerges as a contested symbol in post-restoration Judah, therefore, as various religious attitudes begin to come into view through the prism of the text. Of particular importance is the group who are described as 'my servants' since they are closely related to, if not identified with another group described as those 'who tremble at my word' (65.15, 66.5). Initially, the designation 'my servants' applies to all Yahweh-worshippers (55.6, 63.17), but just like the Zion symbol, this description is also applied to a particular group who have won Yahweh's favour because of their loyalty to him in the closing chapters (65.8–15, 66.14). In these contexts, Yahweh's servants stand over against those who have forsaken him and neglected his holy mountain for various syncretistic religious practices (65.1–7, 11–12). The former will be rewarded by Yahweh for their loyalty, while the others will be punished in a scene of eschatological reversal of fortunes. The imagery of feasting and celebration recalls the eschatological banquet that Yahweh has prepared for all nations on his holy mountain (25.6–8).

However, such a perspective does not exclude an actual situation of social oppression within the restored community, especially in view of the task enjoined on the prophetic figure namely, to preach good news to the poor by calling for Jubilee enactments of release of captives and freedom for prisoners (61.1–4).[21] Situations of social inequality and disregard for the needy, as described in the opening chapter of the book, are the seed-bed for scenarios of eschatological reversal:

> My servants shall eat, but you will go hungry;
> My servants will drink, but you will go thirsty;
> My servants will rejoice, but you will be put to shame.
> My servants will exult with gladness, but you will cry out for sadness.
> (Isa. 65.13–14)

The key to understanding the divisions that have occurred and the conflicting views of the Zion symbol is provided by the immediately following oracle, dealing with a group who are described as 'those who tremble at Yahweh's word' (66. 2, 5). The passage opens with Yahweh declaring what appears to be a criticism of the whole temple-rebuilding project: 'Heaven is my throne, the earth my footstool. What kind of house could you build for me?' This is followed by a declaration that Yahweh's favour rests with 'the poor, the afflicted in spirit and those who *tremble at his word*' (66.1–2) (*emphasis added*). Next comes a statement of rejection by Yahweh of those temple authorities who are engaging in various syncretistic practices (66.3–4). Finally, the tremblers are addressed directly with a word of Yahweh. They are described as hated by their brothers, cast out (banished) for the sake of Yahweh's name and taunted by their opponents who ask why God will not vindicate their claims by immediately 'revealing his glory' to their advantage (66.5). Clearly, a situation of serious conflict has arisen with not just a war of words taking place but an action of formal expulsion by those in authority. The passage ends with a reassurance to 'the tremblers' that they will indeed be vindicated, as Yahweh is already speaking his judgement against the authorities from within the temple.

Who are the tremblers and how might they be related to the servants of the Lord? The description 'tremblers' (*harredim*) suggests an expression of strong religious emotion, with actual physical manifestations, as the history of such groups as Quakers, Shakers and Ultra-Orthodox Jews of later times indicates.[22] They are identified in the text with the poor and those broken in spirit, as opposed to those who are in a position to expel them from the cultic community. This action would have brought about social deprivation, since under the Persians the laws of the Jewish temple community were recognized for state purposes also. This provides the background to the 'status reversal' oracle dealing with the servants, cited above (65.13–14). On a deeper level it would seem that at issue was the true significance of the temple, on which so much emphasis was being placed because of the status and benefits it would have conferred on certain elements of the community. Yahweh was not against the temple – he utters his judgements from there (66.6) – but he does question an over-reliance on it, devoid of moral seriousness. Heaven is his throne and the earth his footstool, all are reminded, by the one who dwells in an exalted place (57.15). While some relied on the temple, the tremblers are expelled because of their adherence to his name. The development of a name-theology for Yahweh in the Second Temple period marked the beginning of a more transcendental understanding of his true nature, and this may well have had implications for the expulsion of the servant/tremblers.[23]

With these various associations it is possible to link the tremblers to the servants more convincingly, but also to clarify further the source of their dispute with the temple authorities. In the opening oracle of this third section of the book, already discussed, the foreigner was in dread of being cut off from Yahweh's people and the eunuch deemed himself accursed in the absence of any offspring (56.1–8, cf. v. 3). Both are reassured that those among them who 'cling to Yahweh', 'who are his servants' and 'who love his name' will themselves receive an everlasting name, and be welcome in 'his house of prayer' which is open to 'all nations'. The description 'tremblers' does not occur here, but the affective language of 'loving' and 'clinging' points to an emotional attachment and suggests close links, if not identity between the two groups. More significantly still, their full admission to the temple community in defiance or abrogation of the temple rules, was a daring act that did not appeal to any existing authority for its warrant. It is Yahweh who speaks here, thus betokening the prophetic rather than the institutional voice. In this perspective the temple worship is not an instrument of strict social and ethnic control but of inclusion of 'outsiders' who wish to join the Yahweh-worshippers. The designation of the place as a 'house of prayer' further suggests a broader understanding of worship and a search for alternative forms of piety, as dissatisfaction with cultic ostentation devoid of ethical responsibility is a constant feature of the prophetic message, and is well represented in this final section of the book also (58.1–14).[24]

Behind the 'servants of the Lord' of this section stands the figure of 'the servant of the Lord' of chs. 40 to 55. In chs. 40 to 48, the figure, though always mentioned in the singular (*Ebed*), would appear to have a collective reference as Jacob/Israel (41.8–9, 44.1–2, 45.4 and 48.20). It is only at 49.1–6 that the servant speaks as an individual in his own name, describing the two-fold charge he has received from Yahweh – to Israel and to the nations – and later his voice is deemed authoritative for others in discerning the 'way of the Lord' (50.10–11). The 'suffering servant' figure (52.13–53.12) does not speak personally but Yahweh reassures him that he will be vindicated and raised high at the beginning and end of the passage. An anonymous 'we', who are clearly followers of the servant and see him as their representative before God, tell his story of suffering and rejection and his ultimate vindication, not least in the procurement of 'offspring who shall prolong his days'.

Thus, both as a missionary of Yahweh and as one who is rejected but vindicated, the servant becomes a model for others who see themselves following in his footsteps, and whose story as it unfolds in the final chapters of the book is patterned on that of this mysterious figure. In particular the prophetic figure who claims to have been anointed by the Spirit and who speaks the Jubilee-message of justice for the poor (Isa. 61.1–2) is, both by the manner of his investiture and the description of his message, the authentic continuation of the earlier servant's voice. This same prophetic voice was to be heard more than once subsequently in Israel's history, as its use in both Qumran and early Christianity, illustrates.

Jesus and Zion. An Isaian Perspective

It would be interesting to trace these different fault lines as they have surfaced in the final section of Isaiah, especially in view of the fact that it has been claimed that those 'who tremble at the word of Yahweh' reflect the beginning of a sect-like movement, traces of which are to be found in other writings from the Persian period (Mal. 3.13–21; Ez. 9.4, 10.3). There is further evidence from other literature of the Greek and Roman periods that Isaiah's hopes for Zion played an important role in various circles of Second Temple Judaism (Sir. 36.16; Tob. 13.11, 21; Ps. of Sol. 11.2; 11Q Ps. of Zion, line 14). The focus of this chapter, however, is to explore the possibility that Jesus' attitude to Zion and its associated traditions were indeed influenced by Isaiah, as Luke's idealized picture had suggested. That focus was further sharpened by Crossan's suggestion that Jesus was a Galilean who, on the occasion of his one visit to Jerusalem, had exploded in anger at his experience in the temple. The alternative being suggested here is that, as a Jewish Galilean prophet with deeply held convictions, Jesus had shown continuing and real concern for the central role that Jerusalem was expected to play within the perspective of restoration hopes, especially as these had been articulated by Isaiah. It remains to establish the broad basis for that claim in light of the foregoing discussion.

Jesus and the Nations

In the previous chapter this topic was touched on in the context of Jesus' journeys outside the boundaries of political Galilee of his day. It will be recalled that when viewed from a perspective of the symbolism of 'the land remaining', those journeys need not be interpreted as a decision to admit gentiles now. They were perfectly understandable within the parameters of the 'greater Israel' and its restoration hopes. At the same time Jesus' movements in these 'outer' border regions of an essentially Jewish Galilee pointed to his greater sense of freedom with regard to contact with non-Jews than that displayed by some at least of his Galilean co-religionists. Their ideas about the need to remain separate from gentiles can be inferred from their observance of such identity markers as abstinence from pig meat, use of stone vessels and practice of purity immersions in domestic settings. While Jesus may have shown a vigorous awareness of the distinction between Jews and non-Jews in his encounter with the Syro-Phoenician woman, it was felt that on the balance of probabilities, his overall philosophy of 'love your enemies' would have inclined him to avoid ethno-phobic attitudes towards the traditional enemies of Israel living in that region. What, if any, new perspective might Jesus' putative reading of Isaiah have brought to his attitudes as he operated in a Galilee that was surrounded by gentiles?

Clearly, Isaiah's reference to the land of Zebulon and the land of Naphtali would have attracted the special attention of any Galilean reader/hearer, but especially somebody who felt endowed with a prophetic spirit and working in the very region covered by the oracle. Were he to have understood the other geographic references – 'the way of the sea', 'the land beyond the Jordan' and 'Galilee of the gentiles' – as describing different areas to that of traditional Israelite tribal lands of lower Galilee, Jesus could well have taken this oracle to refer to both Jewish and non-Jewish areas of the greater region. The territory covered by the oracle would then have represented in microcosm the twofold mission of the servant as this was described on the macro-level in Isa. 49.6. In that event Jesus' journeys to outlying areas was not solely because they were part of the land remaining and because the lost sheep of the house of Israel needed to be gathered. From the perspective of the servant's mission there was nothing to preclude a ministry to both Israel and the nations when representatives of both were encountered in the same region. According to Isa. 8.23, the gentile inhabitants of those regions could well be understood as 'those who walked in darkness'. Jesus' going to them would then be for the purpose of bringing a 'great light' as the servant was expected to do (49.6, 51.5). Furthermore, the promise of salvation for the north was connected with someone whose name was 'Prince of Peace' and who would bring about an end to strife and bloodshed (Isa. 9.4–6). Insofar as he may have thought of himself as in some sense embodying such a role, he would have conceived his task as bringing to an end the hostile relations between Jews and non-Jews, which were current in Galilee as elsewhere in Palestine in the first century CE. Bringing light to those in darkness would, in Isaian terms, have also meant an awareness that these people were awaiting for Yahweh's *Torah* also (42.4), and that they would regard it as light for their lives. In practical terms what might this have meant?

As a Jewish prophetic figure, endowed with the spirit, could Jesus, in accordance with Isa. 56.1–8, have possibly dared to suggest that foreigners and eunuchs would be welcome to participate fully in the Jerusalem cult, despite their lack of qualification according to the prevailing legal view? An inscription from Herod's temple to the effect that any gentile who went beyond a certain point would be subject to the death penalty, indicates that while gentiles did in fact visit the temple, their rights of access were strictly curtailed. Some further information from Josephus suggests a considerable degree of sensitivity about uncircumcised people living in Jewish towns even in Galilee (*Life*, 113). In the light of this evidence the absence of any mention of circumcision in the recorded sayings of Jesus is as surprising as is its absence in Isa. 56.1–8. Does silence in either or both cases mean that it is taken for granted as a precondition for full admission, or was it deemed to be irrelevant? By the first century there was a recognized process in place for non-Jews to undergo circumcision and become proselytes, but could admission of non-Jews to the cultic community be contemplated without such a full conversion?[25] Or are we to suppose that a prophetic figure could claim a personal authority to dispense with such halachic regulations entirely, and yet expect a following? The fact that the early church continued to discuss this matter, as we learn from the Pauline letters, suggests that Jesus did not express himself definitively on the question of the conditions for the admission of gentiles to his movement. Indeed the evidence of Jesus engaging directly with non-Jews is scanty, yet nobody objected to a gentile mission, when in fact it began. After sifting the evidence, perhaps the best conclusion is that of E. P. Sanders when he writes: 'The overwhelming impression is that Jesus started a movement which *came to see the gentile mission as a logical extension of itself*' (his italics).[26] The more likely scenario by which Jesus could have contemplated a situation of Jew and non-Jew coming together in a common worship would have been to await the imminent eschatological gathering of the nations, which God would shortly bring about as the completion of what had already been inaugurated in and through his own ministry.

Such a consideration only made the in-gathering of Israel all the more pressing. The seemingly brusque response to the Syro-Phoenician woman might after all have been good news for her and her people's long-term interest. This was the point where the Twelve's symbolic role had to be activated with an urgent mission to the towns of Galilee, even though we are given little information as to the geographical range or the particular audience for such a sending. While there is some evidence from later Jewish writings of a belief that the ten tribes were awaiting in isolation from wicked gentiles for the final summons to return to God's eschatological banquet (IV Ezra 13.39–50; II Baruch 62.5, 77.19, 78.1–82.9), the probabilities are that Jesus and his group thought much more locally. At any event such a miraculous return would have to be God's doing, and these texts envisage the destruction of the nations, not their return to Zion. The task for the Jesus-group was to convince those who were within their compass that now was the time, and that the signs accompanying Jesus' ministry indicated that God's final intervention was already taking place. While the Jesus tradition is ambivalent about Samaria (Mt. 10.23, 15.24), it too would have had to be visited according to the Isaian script, since the old animosity between Ephraim and Judah would have had to be overcome (Isa. 11. 13f.; cf. Gen. 13.14–15).

However Jesus might have envisaged the repatriation of the survivors of Israel, he certainly does not seem to have shared the idea, so strongly represented in Isaiah, that the role of the gentiles in the great eschatological drama about to unfold, was to accompany them on their journey, acting as chaperones, back-carriers and camel drivers. Jesus was not an uncritical reader of his own tradition. He would seem to have deliberately reversed the roles suggested by these repatriation texts. For Isaiah (Isa. 43.5–7, 49.12) as well as for other Jewish writers in the Second Temple period also (e.g. Zech. 8.7–8; Baruch 4.4; Pss. of Sol. 11.2; 1 Enoch 57.1) the cardinal points of the compass, or their equivalent (e.g. Assyria and Egypt), refer to the exiles returning to Zion, but it is less clear who Jesus has in mind when he speaks of many coming from east and west to join in the banquet with the Patriarchs (Mt. 8.11; Lk. 13.28–29).

While several commentators are quite definite that it is not gentiles but the Jewish survivors from the Diaspora that are intended here, that conclusion is in my view not wholly convincing.[27] The banquet motif links the saying with the parable of the banquet (Mt. 22.1–14; Lk. 14.16–24; cf. Gos. of Thom. 64), where complete 'outsiders' become replacements for those who had been invited, but who had refused. Isaiah's eschatological banquet is 'for all peoples', as 'the covering cast over all peoples' is removed (Isa. 25.6–8). The presence of Abraham at the banquet could scarcely be construed as signifying anything other than a gathering from many nations. If the saying is intended to shame or provoke the addressees to reconsider their decision, then a gentile rather than a Jewish group would be more appropriate, and furthermore, in line with the 'shocking' character of Jesus' speech. Significantly, no location is given for this great festal gathering, though Isaiah had clearly located it on 'this mountain' meaning Mt. Zion (Isa. 24.23, 25.6). Could this omission and reversal of the expected guests be deliberate? Did Jesus really exclude Zion from its eschatological role or was he challenging prevailing views as to how this image of universal salvation was to come about?

Jesus and Zion

The one attributed saying of Jesus which mentions Jerusalem has been used as the epigraph to this chapter: 'Jerusalem, Jerusalem, ... How often would I have gathered your children as a hen gathers her brood under her wings, and you were not willing?' (Mt. 23, 37–39; Lk. 13, 33–35). The same image of the hen gathering her brood, possibly influenced by Jesus' saying, occurs in another first century CE document, where it is combined with images of God as father, mother and nurse to express God's care and affection for Israel (2 Esdras 1, 28–34). On Jesus' lips it suggests that he wished to play a similar role, but Jerusalem's refusal to accept the prophet's call would inevitably lead to rejection and judgement. When the historical Isaiah suffered a similar fate his language became colourful and harsh. The daughters of Zion will be disgraced; instead of the luxurious life-style they will be reduced to mourning widows (Isa. 3, 16–26). Lady Zion is no longer mother but mistress. Jesus, however does not use such imagery. His words of judgment are tinged with sadness and warning of impending destruction.

Nor does the reference to the constant stoning of prophets and killing those who were sent to it have an Isaian ring. As a Jerusalemite, the historical Isaiah must have had a high social standing, given his involvement with the politics of the day. While his challenge to Jerusalem's elite were stinging in their tone, there is no suggestion that his life was in danger because of his verbal attacks. Jesus' saying reflects more the ethos of the country prophets who feel drawn to the centre of their own tradition, literally and metaphorically. The inevitable clash of perspectives between the guardians of the institution and the charismatic 'outsider' means that the institution will always seek to protect the status quo, either by vilification, threat, or in extreme cases, death. In this regard the biography of Jeremiah would seem to be a closer parallel. His life was certainly threatened by his daring challenge to the temple and the city. As a native of Anatoth in the tribal territory of Benjamin, he, rather than Isaiah, would be the prototype of the country prophet being persecuted once he dared to challenges the centre (Jer. 18.18– 23, 26.1–24).

In addition to Jesus of Nazareth, another interesting example of this pattern from the first century is his namesake, Jesus, son of Ananias. Shortly before the first revolt against Rome this 'rude peasant from the country' engaged in a constant public lament for the city, the people and the temple. He intensified his efforts on the occasion of the festivals and was eventually arrested by the authorities and questioned as to his motives. However, he refused to give any answer so that he was declared to be a maniac. On release he continued the exercise and eventually fell victim to an enemy ballista and died as he continued to utter his sad and ominous dirge (*JW* 6.300–310). There are striking similarities between this account and those of Jesus of Nazareth, not least their silence when questioned – a tactic that in modern parlance might be described as 'refusing to recognize the court'.

This aspect of the prophet's behaviour is reminiscent of the suffering servant described by Isaiah: 'He was oppressed, and he was afflicted, yet he did not open his mouth; like a lamb that is led to the slaughter, and like a sheep that before its shearers is silent, so he did not open his mouth' (Isa. 53.7). The silence of the prophets should not be interpreted as stubbornness or resignation, but as exasperation at their audience's refusal to listen to the prophetic message, and a recognition that they and their oppressors are operating from totally different perspectives that preclude any understanding. Although the sufferings of Isaiah's servant-prophet are not explicitly linked to Jerusalem, the fact that the remarkably vivid account of his sufferings is wedged between two different hymns celebrating Jerusalem's anticipated redemption makes an obvious link between the career of the prophet and the fate of the city. We might well ask what prompted the author of this section of Isaiah to introduce this apparently discordant note at this point. The first of the poems celebrating Jerusalem (Isa. 52.1–2, 7–12) evokes a sense of unadulterated joy for the 'captive daughter of Zion' as Yahweh leads the exiles back carrying the sacred vessels of the temple. They are not to leave Babylon as fugitives after the manner of their ancestors leaving Egypt, but are to proceed in triumphant procession. The second hymn (Isa. 54) has a slightly more sober tone, contrasting the previous barren condition of Jerusalem with her future fertility. Yahweh did forsake her for a period, but now in his great love he has taken pity on her. Thus the fate of the city and the fate of the servant previously brought low, but now exalted by Yahweh, turn out to be identical.

One might well enquire about the influence on Jesus of Nazareth or Jesus son of Ananaias of this sequence in terms of their perception of the Jerusalem populace of their day and their own relationship with the city. We know nothing more about Jesus, son of Ananias, other than Josephus' brief account. In the recorded sayings of Jesus we do catch faint echoes of how he might have viewed his own destiny in Jerusalem. These echoes are virtually drowned out by the amount of post-factum detail that the various expressions of his foreboding about what lay ahead in Jerusalem, now contain, prompting modern scholars to regard them as prophecies after the event (Mk. 8, 31; 9.30–32; 10, 32–34). However, such sweeping judgements may be somewhat hasty, provided one accepts that Jesus was acquainted with the figure of Isaiah's 'suffering servant', the biography of Jeremiah and other prophets, as well as the fate of his mentor John. Nevertheless, the pull of Jerusalem was irresistible for the Galilean prophet, not because he wished to share in the great triumph of Zion's exaltation over her enemies, but rather because he wanted to challenge her to view the relationship with the gentiles differently.

The opening of Jesus' lament for Jerusalem – 'How often?' – hints at a far greater preoccupation with the city than just one casual visit would suggest. Here the Johannine framework of a three-year public ministry and several visits to Jerusalem including a ministry in Judea also, sounds far more realistic, despite the fact that in its present form the Fourth Gospel has exploited the symbolism of those visits for its own theological purposes. Be that as it may, Jesus must have known the fate that was in store for him eventually, and either we accept that he carried on recklessly and without any reflection or that he had sought to understand his impulse in the light of his own confident faith that had been nourished, we must suppose, by the inherited traditions of his own people.

Jesus never appeals directly to Zion as the symbol of either his present engagement or his future hopes, though the expectation of a new temple is attributed to him at his trial. His reticence about Zion should not be interpreted as lack of interest in that symbolic world, however. The silence with regard to the name Zion may well be due to the manner in which other groups had exploited the motif and the different ideologies that had become attached to it in the Greek and Roman periods. Ever since the profanation of the temple by Antiochus Epiphanes in the mid-second century BCE, Mount Zion had been turned into a fortress as well as a holy place.[28]

In Jesus' day, Herod the Great had built the Arx Antonia, a fortress that housed a Roman garrison. A restored and highly embellished temple building dominated the Jerusalem skyline. Both symbols of Roman imperial presence and Herodian propaganda (*JA* 15.380–387). Resistance to such foreign exploitation of the religious centre hardened into a militant nationalism. In the first revolt against Rome the rebel forces had made the temple mount the location of their final stand, leading eventually to its destruction by Titus and his army (*JW* 6.250–280). Similar feelings were current in Galilee also. Just 30 years after Jesus' death, the Jewish citizens of Gamla had a coins struck locally whose legend runs: 'For the freedom of Zion, Jerusalem the holy'.[29] Such ideas were surely current in Jesus' day also. Galilean Jewish villagers sought to retrieve their Maccabean/ Hasmonean past as a way of resisting the Romanization of their world by the Herodian rulers, typified by such centres as Sepphoris and Tiberias, and resented the encroachment on their traditional way of life.

Jesus had rejected both the Herodian cities and the Hasmonean-style militarism based on the holy war ideology. His was a more open perspective on Jewish ethnic identity. If Zion was to be a meaningful symbol for him and his movement it would have to strike a different note to either fortress Zion or triumphant Zion. It needed to be able to include the interests of those on the margins, both the socially marginalized among his Jewish co-religionists with whom his healing charisma had brought him into contact, and the geographically marginal such as the Syro-Phoenicians and others from 'the nations round about' whom he must have encountered on his sojourns in the outskirts of Jewish Galilee of his day.

Jesus' Disciples as the Servant Community

In Isaiah, we have suggested, Zion was a contested symbol, claimed by those who controlled the cult, despite their own aberrant ways, and those who regarded themselves as the 'servants of Yahweh'. Despite their religious ostrascization and social deprivation these latter could still consider themselves as being invited to the great banquet. Behind this group stood the figure of the servant-prophet who had been given a mission that kept both Israel and the nations within its horizons, while at the same time posing a challenge to the triumphalism of those who appealed to a version of the Zion symbol that cast the nations in the role of servants and slaves. For this group, a humbled Zion, like the humbled servant, offered the best possibilities of a genuinely inclusive universalism. The catalyst for this different understanding of what Mother Zion could mean was a changed understanding of Yahweh and the nature of his demands. The 'servants of Yahweh' group certainly did not espouse a notion of tolerant syncretism in which Yahweh would merely be one of the many different names for God. Ironically, that was the position of the dominant group, while at the same time exploiting the Zion symbol to regard the nations as their servants. For the 'servants of Yahweh', on the other hand, Yahweh *alone* was God, but this one God was concerned for all because he had created all. He should not be used for ethnically exclusive or socially selective purposes. Isaiah's Yahweh and Jesus' God is no tribal warrior, but one whose 'eternal covenant' was with all the children of Noah, as well as with the earth.

In discussing Jesus' attitude towards the earth and towards the land in the two previous chapters it was suggested that his interest was in the creator God rather than in the God of Sinai and the Exodus, and that his lifestyle was based more on the story of Abraham than on that of Moses. These emphases are very much in line with Isaiah's trajectory also and reflect the outlook which supports the servant's mission and values. When Isaiah describes the returnees as 'the survivors of Israel', implying that only a remnant will return, this group are repeatedly described as a 'seed' that will eventually produce a great horde of people. While the promise to Abraham and the fruitfulness of his seed in the barren womb of Sarah lies behind these declarations of an abundant offspring,[30] in Isaiah the image of the seed also relates to the prophetic word that continues to be fruitful (Isa. 55.10–11). This is the meaning of the promise that the servant-prophet will be able to prolong his days through his posterity (literally his seed/*zera'* (53.10). Thus, the group who are designated '[my] servants [of the Lord]', and who, as was pointed out earlier, regard themselves as his followers in replicating his lifestyle and values, can also arrogate to themselves the status of the true remnant. In Blenkinsopp's estimation, this is the most radical idea introduced by the great early prophets and is further exploited by Isaiah, in that he rejects the notion that 'the ideal Israel is identical with its current political embodiment'.[31] Thus it is not intended as a lifeline but as an instrument of social and religious criticism in the present as well as a pledge of future fulfilment of the promises.

This profile of the identity and role of 'the servants of Yahweh' provides a highly important analogue for Jesus and his group, and may well have functioned as an inspiration for his project. The shared social values are the most obvious connection, surely. The beatitudes are cut from the same cloth as Yahweh's oracle to the temple authorities, declaring that it was the poor and those who are broken in spirit and not they, who will eat, drink and rejoice. This declaration must have come as just as great a shock, as did Jesus' declaration that the blessed are the poor, the hungry and those who mourn (Isa. 65.13–14; Lk. 6.20–21). Behind both statements lurks the present of actual social deprivation because of the greed of elites, but also a future sharing in the eschatological banquet. They are also inspired by the Jubilee announcement of 'good news for the poor' which was proclaimed both by the anointed figure of Isa. 61.1–2 and by Jesus, whereas in 4Q 521, it is God himself, not his messiah, that makes the announcement.

Not that Jesus' core group were themselves poor. However, they were invited to abandon all and imitate Jesus' lifestyle who had 'nowhere to lay his head' (Mt. 8.20; Lk. 9.58). Jesus' radical abandoning of the values of home, family and possessions and his expectation that his followers would do likewise was, we have maintained earlier, based on the Jubilee values of total trust in Yahweh's gifts of food, shelter and the necessities of life. Without a context in which prophetic signs act as radical expressions of social critique, such a manifesto could only be regarded as irresponsible. While the Jubilee enactments may never actually have been put into practice, they represented a strand of radical thinking in Israel, by espousing a reversal of the normal pattern of relationships by which humans engage with the earth and with one another. They call for a recognition of total dependence on God and a confidence to trust in God's benevolent care for all his creation. It is interesting that it was prophetic voices, not priestly legislators (the original context of the Jubilee legislation, Lev. 25), who seem to have been most impressed with what the idea of the Jubilee signified. Thus, the prophetic figure in Isaiah that continued the servant-prophet's challenge to the Zion ideology drew on aspects of the Jubilee in order to point up the social inequalities of the time, which were clearly being ignored in the euphoria of the triumphant return from exile (Isa. 61.1–4). Likewise, Jesus employed it on his return to lower Galilee, faced with the situation of real human need in the midst of plenty that had resulted from Herodian policies in the region.

Did the Jesus-movement share with the Isaian servant-group a sense of being the remnant as understood in the prophetic book also? One interesting pointer that has not been sufficiently explored is the importance of the image of the seed for both groups. Isaiah's 'servants of the Lord' see themselves as the first manifestation of the servant-prophet's seed or offspring. Jesus does not employ this image for his own followers, but he does use it in the nature parables as an image of the kingdom of God producing an abundant and miraculous harvest, of which they are to be the harvesters (Mt. 9.37, Lk. 10.2). The kingdom is the most inclusive symbol employed by Jesus, prompted in part at least by its association with Zion and Yahweh's universal kingship. Here it is important to make the connections between the kingdom, the patriarchs, Abraham, Isaac and Jacob, and the universal character of the eschatological banquet in Jesus' view, as previously discussed. Excluded from that gathering are those who elsewhere are described as 'this generation' – a code word in the Jesus tradition for his contemporaries who did not accept him or his prophetic words and who, therefore, are destined for judgement (Mt. 11.16; Lk. 7.31; Mt. 12.41; Lk. 11.29; Mt. 23.36; Lk. 11.50).[32]

From that perspective, Jesus' group does function as a voice of judgement against this generation, giving rise to its sense of outrage that it may not participate in Yahweh's blessings unless it listens to the prophetic challenge that is now being presented to it. The fact that Jesus' group had at its core the symbolic Twelve only exacerbated the situation for those co-religionists who did not share his sense of openness, nor his eschatological vision. Theoretically, the Twelve could suggest that Jesus was espousing a territorial restoration, but as we have seen from the Genesis account, the image could function in a context other than that of tribal conquest. In the Jesus tradition while the Twelve have a symbolic role to play in the present, the tribes are consigned to a future eschatological setting (Mt. 19.28; Lk. 22.30). The Queen of the South (Sheba) coming to hear Solomon's wisdom, and the Ninevites repenting at Jonah's preaching are adduced as evidence of 'outsiders' seeking wisdom and taking the prophetic warning seriously (Mt. 12.40–42; Lk. 11.30–32). The clear implication of these examples from the past suggest that those who are seeking a sign from Jesus in regard to the authenticity of his message do not understand the universal scope of their own tradition. Wisdom is available to all and repentance is a possibility for non-Jews. Insiders who espouse an ethno-phobic point of view involving total separation clearly cannot share in the eschatological banquet which Jesus envisages. The appeal to Jonah seems particularly apt as an analogue for Jesus' activity, since there was a tradition that he too was a Galilean prophet.[33]

While there is no mention of gentiles actually joining the Jesus-movement during his own lifetime, Elijah-like, he does befriend those who seek his help in their needs – the Syro-Phoenician woman's daughter (even when that story is making a separate point), the Roman centurion's child and the Gadarene demoniac. The issue of Jesus declaring that foreigners and eunuchs could fully participate in the cultic community has already been touched upon, and the suggestion was that prudence might have suggested waiting for the eschatological future. However, the present was in a sense anticipating that future in Jesus' view, and there would be nothing to preclude his befriending them, Elijah-like, in a Galilean setting as distinct from the Jerusalem cultic setting.

The meaning of the phrase 'those who make themselves eunuchs for the kingdom' (Mt. 19.12) has been disputed, referring either literally to those who have voluntarily undergone castration for ascetical reasons, or figuratively to those who practice sexual abstinence for a higher cause. Recently, Moxnes has pointed to the important social impact of the expression in redefining contempor-ary ideas of male sexuality.[34] While agreeing that the saying does indeed challenge male stereotypes in the ancient world about the connection between masculinity and the production of offspring, thereby reducing the female to a passive receptacle for the male semen, the religious implications of the saying are important also. We have seen already that the biological understanding of seed as offspring, stemming from the story of Abraham and Sarah, shaded both easily and naturally in Isaiah into the notion of the prophet's word generating offspring. Jesus, it would seem, shared that understanding of his own words in relation to his disciples. In answering the prophetic call he himself had abandoned the normal male roles of father, husband and provider, and he invited others to follow him in this radical challenge to normative male roles. In terms of those norms he was declaring himself and his followers as eunuchs, a shameful, not an honourable condition. If one were to see Jesus' attitude as grounded in the servant community's daring declaration that eunuchs as well as foreigners were welcome to Yahweh's house, then the social implications of Jesus' own daring lifestyle and his saying on eunuchs had theological consequences also. Yahweh could never again be called on to legitimate male, patriarchal values. Surely, that consideration adds further background to the inclusion of women also in the circle around the historical Jesus.

These initial impressions of the possible influence of certain aspects of the Zion tradition as elaborated by Isaiah on Jesus' own self-understanding and that of his group of permanent followers open up intriguing possibilities. Some further aspects will be explored in the two remaining chapters, including also the circumstances that lead to his death. It has become obvious that Jesus was no slavish follower of his tradition, not even Isaiah, with whom he had a special affinity. He was a critical reader, not critical, however, in the sense of a modern reading, but in relation to the social situation of his own time and place and the manner in which the inherited religious tradition might be brought to bear on those conditions. Joining a long line of critical prophetic voices from the past in situations that were not dissimilar to the ones he was experiencing, he too felt called to address his own contemporaries with a prophetic challenge to a world of imperial domination and the threat of religious collaboration with the forces that had continued to keep Israel in bondage.

5

CONFRONTING THE CHALLENGES
OF EMPIRE

Whose image and inscription is this? (Mk. 12.16)

The characterization of Cyrus, the Persian ruler, as Yahweh's 'anointed' (Is. 41.15–45.15) points unmistakably to a loss of confidence in the Davidic monarchy and the promises attached to it that had been accentuated by the Babylonian exile. It was also a defiant statement of belief in Yahweh to claim that Persian imperial rule was attributable to his power and subject to his intentions. This was a bold rhetorical strategy by the prophetic author of this section of Isaiah, writing from the perspective of the province of Yehud, consisting of a 'temple state' of no more than 30 miles radius around Jerusalem. It constituted just a tiny segment within the Persian satrapy of Ebernari (literally, 'Beyond the River'), a vast territory which stretched from the Euphrates to the Mediterranean according to the Greek historian, Herodotus (*Histories* III, 89–97).

Such confidence in Yahweh had its origins in the belief that he had driven the nations out of Canaan in order to provide Israel with a promised land. However, the historical Isaiah had developed the universal scope of Yahweh's power in another direction with his admonition to the Judean kings, Ahaz and Hezekiah, to trust in Yahweh rather than in any political alliance in the arena of international politics that Assyrian imperialist ambitions of the eighth century BCE had generated. Isaiah's message had been simple, if a little disconcerting, as the sound of marching troops could be heard advancing on Jerusalem (Isa. 10.28–34). The net outcome of these interventions in international politics was to introduce important changes in Israel's theological understanding as reflected within the Isaianic corpus. Instead of calling for a holy war against the enemy it was possible to conceive of universal peace or *shalom*, embracing the nations, who would transform their swords into ploughshares. While the future ruler described in chapters 9 and 11 is from the Davidic house, he is not given the title king. Instead one of his titles will be 'Prince of Peace' and his reign will see universal harmony of mythic proportions (Isa. 9.5, 11.6–8). Despite these idyllic vignettes, the theme of a Davidic ruler disappears thereafter, to be replaced by that of Yahweh as king, who, however, retains his warrior image, thus emphasizing his power over the nations to do his bidding. Even the great king, Cyrus, is reduced to such a role, as are also the other nations in achieving the repatriation of the exiles discussed in the previous chapter.

In Isaiah, especially in the second part of the book (Isa. 41.21, 43.15, 44.6, 52.7), the acknowledgement of Yahweh's kingship has a cultic tone, echoing strongly the so-called Kingship of Yahweh psalms (Pss. 47, 93, 95–99). In these the emphasis is on such themes as his majesty or glory as the source of his power in the world, the forces that he can muster to do his will and his sovereign rule on behalf of his own people.[1] It is in Jerusalem that Yahweh declares his kingship and from there that he manifests it to the nations: 'The moon will be put to shame and the sun abashed when Yahweh Sabaoth inaugurates his reign on Mt. Zion and in Jerusalem, revealing his glory in the presence of the elders' (Isa. 24.23; cf. 29.6). As the mirror image of the great king of the Babylonian and Persian empires, Yahweh sits enthroned in his splendour surrounded by his court. The frequent (more than 70 times) use of the epithet 'Sabaoth' (hosts) has associations with the ark of the covenant in the Jerusalem temple, where the nations as well as Israel can worship Yahweh.[2] Yet he can also use his power to wreak vengeance on his enemies among the nations as he sees fit (Isa. 13–23, 51, 59.15–19, 63.1–6).

This process of transforming Yahweh from national deity to cosmic Lord was undoubtedly influenced by various Near Eastern myths such as the Enuma Elish epic, which had a wide currency in the ancient world. Asshur, Marduk and Ahura Mazda functioned as legitimating deities for the rulers of the Assyrians, the Babylonians and the Persians, the three imperial powers that Israel had encountered. Judah could have no such imperial ambitions, however, and Yahweh's role is one of eschatological vindication of her true, if somewhat utopian position among the nations 'in the days to come' or 'on that day'.

The social context for developing this image of Yahweh as a counter to the gods of the nations – 'who are no gods' – is that of

imperial devastation of the land of Israel. The Assyrian expansion in
the north had set the benchmark for all subsequent invasions of the
region because of its strategic importance for any ruler from the
interior who might aspire to control the fertile crescent as far as the
Mediterranean. Whereas previously powerful rulers in the region
had made vassal treaties with conquered nations, with the Assyrians
the machinery of empire involved not just political subjugation but
domination of every aspect of the life of the vanquished. Territories
were divided up and their administration entrusted to foreign scribes
whose responsibility it was to develop a system of control and
management of the resources, guaranteeing a flow of goods to the
centre. Military outposts were established to ensure that the rule of
law was maintained and safe passage guaranteed. Land, the most
important resource in agrarian empires, was confiscated and
parcelled out to loyal supporters of the regime such as veterans of
the imperial armies, thus destroying older settlements. Native
peoples were removed and used to serve elsewhere by providing
cheap labour as required in building projects or as agricultural serfs or
slaves.

The Assyrian royal records as well as the archaeological evidence
from the north covering the period of the eighth to the fifth
centuries, show all the signs of such a process, with the beginnings of
a recovery only in the Persian period.[3] By comparison, the Judean
countryside seems to have fared somewhat better under the
Babylonians, even though the fate of the north was still vividly
remembered there (Isa. 8.23). Recent studies have challenged 'the
myth of the empty land' with regard to Judah, suggesting that there
was less disruption of the native population than that which had
occurred in the north.[4] However, passages such as Isa. 62.1–6, when
read against the background of the social situation described in Neh.
5.1–11, suggest strongly that despite the exuberance at the prospect
of the return to Zion of Isaiah 40–55, the Persian period restoration
did not achieve social justice in Judah either.

It has recently been argued that 'as a result of the enduring
tendency of the imperial rulers of the eastern Mediterranean in this
period to rule partly autonomous regions through local agents, a
Jewish society gradually coalesced in Palestine', leading to the
emergence of an integrating ideology around the belief in one God
who resided in the Jerusalem temple and who had expressed his will
in the *Torah*. This simple ideological outline provided, it is claimed,
a coherent framework for a Jewish society to emerge and function

throughout the Second Temple period, even if this society was loosely centralized and frayed at the edges.[5] On the whole, I am in agreement with this picture, even though it goes against the grain of much contemporary discussion of the radical sectarian tendencies of Second Temple Judaism, fuelled in particular by the discovery of the Dead Sea Scrolls.

What is missing from this analysis, however, is a recognition of the different social and political effects of the imperial interventions at different levels of this society. Real tensions had arisen between the myth and its guardians – the priests and the scribal elites in Jerusalem – and the social conditions of ordinary people struggling to maintain connections with the centre, despite its increasing distance from them and their concerns. This sense of alienation was brought about by those imperial masters, however tolerant they might appear to have been as in the case of the Persians who had allowed the Jews to return and rebuild their temple. Once the guardians of the myth and its institutions were expected to be the 'local agents' of distant imperial rulers, serious problems would inevitably arise for the effective functioning of the myth as the constitution of an independent Jewish community. Thus the price of return and restoration, Persian-style, was to create various fault lines within Judean society which are reflected in the literature of the period, including the final edition of the national epic the Pentateuch and the companion volume the Prophets. This has become evident even in this study with probes into the conquest narratives and the Zion tradition, indicating different attitudes towards the land and the temple reflected in the final texts. The Greek period allows us to see the ways in which some of these differences began to express themselves socially and religiously, thus providing the ethos in which the Jesus-movement would emerge in Galilee, just one of several expressions of the myth of Yahweh's kingship as a response to imperial pressures.

Judean Response to Greek and Roman Imperialism

The rise of Alexander the Great with his successful designs on the Persian empire in the fourth century BC presented a new challenge for the Jewish community, both in Palestine and in the increasingly diverse Diaspora, but especially in Egypt. Previously the imperial

masters had come from the east but now they were from the
opposite point of the compass, bringing a different ideology and
world-view to that of Semitic cousins.[6] While Alexander's empire
was short lived, his military conquests which took him to the borders
of India, allied to his and his Ptolemaic and Seleucid successors'
policy of establishing Greek-style cities throughout the whole
region, were to prove decisive for the cultural and social history for a
millennium at least. Rome's role, once it began to expand eastwards
from the first century BCE, was mainly one of providing an
administrative and legal framework as far as the Euphrates for the
Hellenized east. It was only with the rise of Islam in the seventh
century CE that a new cultural and spiritual force entered that region,
sweeping all before it.

The focus here is to outline briefly the ways in which Jewish
identity in Palestine was affected by these changes and the manner in
which the inherited tradition was retrieved in dealing with the new
imperial forces determining Jewish life. Previously we have touched
on this issue in discussing Jesus' handling of the territorial dimension
of Jewish ethnicity in Galilee and in profiling his particular
understanding of the Zion tradition. In this chapter, however, the
interest is on the manner in which imperialist values from the
Assyrians to the Herodians had continued to shape the Galilee of
Jesus' day, and how he responded to that situation. Or to put the
matter in terms of the discussion of the meaning of place in the
opening chapter, how did Jesus envisage an alternative Galilee to the
imperialist version which he encountered, and how did he utilize his
own tradition in developing that alternative view?

Opposing the Great King

In order to address this question adequately it is first necessary to
examine the different responses to imperial domination that surfaced
in the first serious threat to Jewish identity, the so-called Hellenistic-
reform of Antiochus Epiphanes in the mid-second century BCE. This
crisis saw the flowering of Jewish apocalyptic writing with the
emergence of the Book of Daniel. In its present form (as distinct
from earlier redactions) this book has been confidently dated to the
immediate setting of Antiochus' reign and the attempt to transform
the cult of Yahweh in Jerusalem into that of Zeus.[7] The origins of
apocalyptic as an independent genre and a distinctive world-view
within the Second Temple period is a much-debated topic which

need not concern us here, other than to state that irrespective of the issue of outside influences, it can reasonably be described as a critical reception of some aspects of the prophetic message, though this is now cast in a different mould and within a different world-view. In this regard the links between Isaiah and Daniel are of particular interest to the argument of this study. In the previous chapter it was claimed that the profile of 'the servants of Yahweh' group as this emerged from Isa. 40–66 provided a highly plausible analogue for the Jesus-movement, and the kingship of Yahweh idea as outlined above is clearly the foundation stone on which the apocalyptic imagination could build alternative world-views.

In order to explore that topic properly, however, it is first necessary to establish the ways in which an apocalyptic world-view provided several different options to Jews when confronted with the threat of imperial domination in the Hellenistic and Roman periods. For our purposes the analysis provided by John Collins based on a long and detailed engagement with this material provides a welcome pathway through what can sometimes appear as a dangerous jungle. He distinguishes three different forms of millennial (apocalyptic) expectations in the context of those who are impelled by the utopian dream of a better world. These are the triumphalism of imperial power regarded as the fulfilment of history; the deferred eschatology of those hoping for an eventual utopia, but who are prepared to accept the current status quo; and thirdly, the revolutionary expectation of an imminent and radical change. The triumphalist version of the millennial dream is particularly associated with imperial politics and, as we shall see shortly, the advent of the reign of Augustus provides an excellent example of this thinking with the official propaganda that a new age had in fact dawned. The deferred eschatology could be associated with Josephus' views of history, on the one hand seeking to affirm the continued rule of Rome as the result of providence, while at the same time leaving the future in the hands of God.[8]

It is the third form that is of special interest in terms of Jesus and his movement as well as for other expressions of Jewish protest in this period. Daniel ch. 7 is the classic statement of this radical interpretation of history. While the schema of four world empires, each succeeding one another had been utilized by the author to suggest deferred judgement on the Babylonian king (2.38), in chapter 7 it is developed quite differently to refer to the imminent demise of the persecutor, Antiochus (vv. 8–9, 11–12, 23–25). His evil rule will be replaced by that of 'one like a human being' ('son of man', vv. 13–14), which is later identified with 'the kingdom of the holy ones of the Most High' (vv. 26–27). Two centuries later the anonymous author of IV Ezra, writing in the Roman period, was able to use the schema to similar effect, explaining that the fourth kingdom mentioned by Daniel was the Roman eagle, thus announcing the imminent fall of Rome in the immediate aftermath of the destruction of the Jerusalem temple in 70 CE (IV Ezra 12.32–33). Thus, within apocalyptic circles images could be reused to function in different political situations, once circumstances of oppression and persecution similar to the original situation were perceived to be present. It will be interesting to examine the extent to which this might also be true of Jesus and his movement earlier in the first century, especially in view of the obvious connection with Daniel that the use of the Son of Man image in the gospels underlines.[9]

The image of the four kingdoms, represented by four beasts, is not explicitly used in the New Testament, but the frequent reference to the victorious Son of Man suggests a shared horizon concerning the demise of the wicked empire. In Daniel the fourth beast is doomed for destruction because Daniel's vision indicates that 'the Ancient of Days' has already passed judgement and has conferred universal kingship on 'one like a human being' (literally, 'son of man'), an enigmatic image until it is explained later in the vision to Daniel that it applies to 'the saints of the Most High,' thus suggesting a collective understanding of the replacement for the wicked king. In the context of this vision the replacement of the wicked ruler who sought 'to change times and laws' for those 'who were in his power for a time' (v. 25), was intended as a message of hope to all who had suffered for their loyalty in the persecution which Antiochus' decree had instigated. However, the language and images employed have a deep and universal application, thereby ensuring that the message would continue to resonate powerfully in other contexts also. Even the name for God is unfamiliar and the oscillation between the 'one like a human being' and 'the holy ones of the Most High' calls for special insight to understand its true referent and its application to the actual situation. The monsters arising from the deep at the beginning of the chapter evoke the return of the creation to chaos, only to be confronted not by God himself, who is enthroned in heavenly splendour with his court, but by his agent(s) who has been endowed with universal royal power, so that 'all peoples, nations and tongues shall serve him', thus ensuring the final victory over evil.[10]

This first vision of Daniel stands at the mid-point between 'the court tales' of chs. 1 to 6 and the further visions of victory to come in chs. 8 to 12. There are literary and thematic links with both sections, and so the inaugural throne-vision must be understood within the context of the whole book. Chapters 1 to 6 in their present form serve to illustrate Daniel's superior wisdom to that of the court seers, a gift which he attributes to God in his prayer:

> 'May the name of God be blessed for ever and ever, since wisdom and understanding are his alone. His to control the procession of times and seasons ... to confer wisdom to the wise and knowledge to those with the understanding to discern; his to uncover depths and mysteries, to know what lies in darkness'. (Dan. 2.20–23)

On the basis of this prayer, Daniel's wisdom is much broader than that associated with the power to interpret dreams, since it encompasses an ability to understand the divine plan which is hidden to all except God. In the opening scene Daniel and his companions are introduced as 'proficient (*maskil*) in all wisdom', the Hebrew term implying 'instructed' or 'learned' (Dan. 1.4,17). The term recurs towards the end of the book (Dan. 11.33–35) with reference to a special group who have instructed the many (*rabbim*) and have themselves suffered, some of their members having actually perished. However, in the final victory of the saints they will be granted a special honour, 'shining like the stars for ever' (Dan. 12.3).[11] Clearly the author's intention is to present Daniel as the prototype of this group both in his fidelity to God, even when threatened with dangers, and in the reward of having received special insight into the present crisis and its outcome.

The Wise Ones

Apart from the figure of Daniel, the description of the group as a whole is not highly developed, and we must infer their role from the few hints that are given. They perform a teaching role, seeking to help the masses to understand and lead them to righteousness. In the context this description implies, presumably, that they sought to dissuade the common people from assimilating to foreign ways. It suggests that they constituted a group who, at the height of the crisis generated by Antiochus, had stood firm in their faithfulness to

Jewish observance, accepting persecution and death freely without much support from others of their co-religionists. This profile would separate them from both the Maccabean freedom fighters and the *Hasidim*, a separate group also mentioned in the sources for this period (1 Macc. 2.42, 7.12–13; 2 Macc. 14.6). Their role is not clearly defined either, other than that, unlike the *maskilim*, they seem to have supported the militarism of the Maccabees.[12]

Most interesting is the fact that the description of the *maskilim*, brief though it is, has clear echoes of the suffering servant of Isaiah 53. He, like they, will give instruction (*maskil*, Isa. 52.13), he suffers without resistance, but his death will lead the many (*rabim*) to righteousness (Isa. 53.11; cf. Dan. 12.3), and in the end he is vindicated by God.[13] In the previous chapter it was suggested that the servant-group, which took its origins from the servant figure, provided an interesting analogue to the Jesus-group in challenging a triumphalistic understanding of Zion. The similar role played by the *maskilim* group in Daniel provides an important further pointer in the search for a more adequate understanding of Jesus and his followers, therefore. While the servant-group emerged in a context of conflict within the restored temple community, the *maskilim* group came to light in the white heat of the struggle for ethnic survival, as an external imperialist force sought to impose its views as to which God should be worshipped in Jerusalem. The strategies adopted by both groups can help to illuminate the Jesus-movement in both its Galilean and its Jerusalem phases by providing a broader context for understanding its challenge to imperial values in Galilee and Zionist ideology in Jerusalem.

Pharisees, Sadducees and Essenes

Daniel ch. 7 is only one example of apocalyptic resistance to naked imperial power that sought not just to subjugate the Jewish people but also to dismantle their mythic world-view. Other responses to that particular crisis can be documented from the sources of the period. The quietism of Daniel can be contrasted with the heroic militancy of Judah the Maccabee and his brothers (1 Macc.), or the recognition of the importance of martyrdom, while also endorsing Judas and his campaign of holy war (2 Macc. 8.3, 10.29–31). Further along that same trajectory of martyrdom is the figure of Taxo in the Testament of Moses, a document of uncertain date, but which clearly has the events of the Antiochian crisis in view. Here martyrdom is freely undertaken, not just submitted to, but with a view to arousing God's vengeance to destroy the enemy.[14]

To these responses, which can be situated in the immediate context of the crisis, can be added those of the different 'philosophies' – Essenes, Pharisees, Sadducees – which emerged within the newly formed Hasmonean state once the threat of Antiochus had been finally averted. Each of these must have developed its own strategy for dealing with the presence of empire also, even if we are not in a position to reconstruct all the details.

Of the three, we are best served in regard to the Essenes, provided one assumes with most modern scholars that, with the discovery of the Qumran scrolls, we are in possession of some of the group's own writings and can extrapolate their eschatological views as to how they viewed the *kittim*. This term, which in the Bible had referred to foreigners, especially island peoples, is applied to the Romans in several Qumran texts (1QpesHab. 2.12, 14; 4QpesIs. 3.7; 4Qpes-Nahum 1.3). The war-scroll (1QM) carries the title, 'the war of the sons of light against the sons of darkness'. This work is a curious mixture of Hellenistic military strategy and highly mythological notions of cosmic struggle. The focus of the work, however, is no longer on the national struggle of Israel against its enemies, but espouses instead a cosmic dualism similar to that of the Zoroastrian religion from Persia in terms of the conflict between good and evil.[15] Yet the dangers of attempting to develop a single consistent point of view from this collection of writings which spans 200 years of the group's history can be seen by other texts such as 4Q 521 which expresses a longing of those 'who are seeking the Lord in his service' for a messiah who 'will honour the devout ... freeing prisoners, giving sight to the blind, straightening out the twisted. He will heal the badly wounded, give lavishly to the needy, lead back the exiled and enrich the hungry.' Other fragments suggest a more apocalyptic notion of the great God waging the decisive battle against the nations and ensuring peace for his people (4Q 246). While dating these fragments securely or eliciting a consistent point of view from them is extremely difficult, it can nevertheless be suggested that the reign of Herod the Great might well have generated an outburst of messianic speculation in the pious circles reflected in these texts with various aspects of Isaiah's multi-faceted eschatology generating renewed speculation and hopes.[16]

Herod's intolerance and suspicion of any opposition meant that neither the Pharisees nor the Sadducees, both of whom had been at the centre of political life in the Hasmonean kingdom, were in any position to adopt a critical stance with regard to his or his Roman patron's role in Judean life. We are particularly poorly informed about the Sadducees, but on the supposition that they were associated with the Hasmonean elite, Herod's purge of this group at the beginning of his reign must have effectively put an end to any political involvement for the Sadducees subsequently (*JA* 15.5f.). The information about their rejection of any notion of life after death, shared by both Josephus and the New Testament (*JA* 18.16; Mk. 12.18; Acts 23.8), can be taken as shorthand for their rejection of any apocalyptic understanding of history. Their political views would, therefore, have been conservative, seeking to maintain whatever privileges they might have gained as part of a temple-based aristocracy, and with little interest in challenging Roman imperialist values, many of which they would have shared as an aristocratic elite.

The Pharisees were a separate issue, and their changing role is suggested, if somewhat overstated, by the title of Jacob Neusner's study, *From Politics to Piety*. Their origins are obscure, though their belief in life after death (*JA* 18.14) suggests that they shared an apocalyptic world-view, and this must have also determined their political stance, indicating possibly a background among the Hasidim of Maccabean times. As a group with a political role, they first appear in the reign of John Hyrcanus, a first-generation native ruler, after the formation of an independent Jewish state. In that instance the king is portrayed as being highly respectful of the group's opinion on how he might live a life pleasing to God, thus anticipating Josephus' frequent characterization of them as 'being the most accurate interpreters of our laws' (*JA* 13.288–298). One of the Pharisees challenged his right to be high-priest, thereby initiating a serious rift between the group and the ruling Hasmoneans. During the long reign of John's son and successor, Alexander Jannaeus (103–76 BCE) they suffered with other Jews who challenged his right to the high-priesthood, and undoubtedly there were Pharisees among the 800 whom he had crucified during his reign (*JA* 13.431).

The Psalms of Solomon dating from the mid-first century BCE may well give the best indication of Pharisaic attitudes to imperialism, as Roman power was beginning to manifest itself in the east with the campaigns of Pompey the Great in the Mediterranean region. Ps. 17 in particular is not merely a condemnation of the Hasmoneans for unlawfully usurping the throne of David, but also a call for a just king to arise who would drive the foreigner from Jerusalem. Here at least one is hearing the voice of a militant messianism longing for the ideal Davidic ruler.[17] Once Herod had been declared 'king of the Jews' in 40 BCE these hopes must have gone underground to a large extent. Even though Pharisees continue to be actively involved in the affairs of state. Their refusal to take an oath of allegiance to Herod early in his reign goes unpunished, because of his respect for one of the most influential of their number Pollion (*JA* 15.368–372). No reason is given for their refusal, which could have been for religious grounds because of Herod's close association with the Romans. Yet we do hear from Josephus of their influence at the court through their association with some of the leading women, but in a subversive rather than a supportive role (*JA* 17.41–51). Summing up the evidence as a whole then, it does seem that by the first century the Pharisees, having originated as a radical party of opposition within an apocalyptically inspired world-view, had settled for a 'retainer' role as political operators, content to function within the existing system rather than lead a religiously motivated revolution. In terms of Collins' classification, theirs was a 'deferred' eschatology, and as in the case of Josephus also, this seems to have been acknowledged by the Romans in the settlement which they made with the Pharisaic scribe, Johannan ben Zakkai and his school, after the first revolt. Those among the Pharisees who still harboured religiously inspired views of a revolutionary nature had to seek alternative outlets, as we shall presently see.[18]

Jesus and Roman Imperial Values in Galilee

When Jesus came into Galilee he was re-entering a region where the signs of Roman propaganda were beginning to dot a landscape that was no stranger to imperial powers. Not many Galileans were likely to have read the Augustan poets celebrating the dawn of a new age as described by Virgil and Horace. The refurbished Sepphoris and the newly founded Tiberias were relatively modest in terms of their architectural splendour by comparison with other provincial sites, even in Palestine. Yet there can be little doubt that in their own way they were intended to honour the imperial patrons of the Herodians. Bethsaida, with its new name Julias, had been given a Roman colouring also, but not much of the architectural evidence for this has so far come to light. Galilean pilgrims would have encountered at first hand some of Herod the Great's building projects in Jerusalem, as Mark suggests, when telling of the expression of wonder by Jesus' followers on seeing the temple building (Mk. 13.2). Temples to Roma and Augustus were erected in prominent positions at various centres – Samaria, whose new name Sebaste was Greek for Augustus, Cæsarea on the coast and Paneas, also renamed as Cæsarea Philippi at the foot of Mt. Hermon in the north. There could be little doubt, even for Galilean peasants that a new age had dawned, the last age, according to the Cumae's Sibyl, in which Romans believed that 'their empire would know no bounds, nor periods, dominion without end' (Virgil *Eclogues* 4; *Aenead* 1.278–279).

Even though the effects of this propaganda on the lives of ordinary Jewish peasants were mediated through Herodian rule, they had a serious impact on the economic, social and ecological life in Galilee, as previously discussed. The building projects of Herod Antipas in Galilee were inevitably a drain on the resources of the region, material as well as human.[19] More significant than the buildings, however, was the introduction of a new element into the population who are encountered occasionally in the gospels as the Herodians. These represented new elite and retainer classes, replacing the old Hasmoneans who had resisted Herod and had paid the price eventually. The new cities, even when the majority of their inhabitants were Jewish, were alien to and parasitical on the surrounding territory.[20] An urban culture introduced new types into the population, scribal administrators, military personnel, and others in various retainer roles, acting on behalf of the ruling elite and the native aristocracy. It also made new demands for goods and services – thereby, however, increasing the burden of taxation on the peasantry. This pressure from the top inevitably led to an increase in the levels of poverty, and the slide from landowner to tenant farmer to day labourers, to beggars, all characters we hear of in Jesus' parables, was inexorable. As always in such situations it is the poor who are most vulnerable, exposed to the effects of disease and dispossession. These conditions are the breeding ground for violent outbursts of hostility and pillaging, and it is no surprise to find that one of the effects of the Herodian rule was the increase of what has been described as 'social banditry'. This phenomenon has been defined as pre-political and rural-based, arising in conditions of major upset in the social equilibrium, when the official instruments of control are weak and unable to act swiftly and decisively, and its applicability to first-century Galilean conditions seems in general appropriate.[21]

In previous chapters Jesus' attitude to the domination of his own people has been touched on in discussing the likely impact of the conquest and Zion traditions on his ministry in Galilee. It was suggested that while his choice of the Twelve as the symbolic core of his permanent retinue demonstrated his concern for the restoration of Israel, he showed no interest in a territorial understanding of the twelve-tribe symbol. His movements in the adjoining regions of Galilee could possibly reflect an awareness of the notion of a greater Israel as 'the land remaining' but his attitudes towards people of other ethnic backgrounds, slim though the evidence is, could not be interpreted in the light of the conquest narratives which called for their removal, conversion or annihilation, as the Maccabean heroes had attempted. If the suggestion is correct that his image of God was inspired more by the Genesis than the Exodus account, then we must ascribe to him a broader horizon for understanding Israel's role among the nations than one of hostility, leading to an aggressive militancy in reclaiming Israel's political freedom. Likewise, it appeared that while showing a genuine concern for Jerusalem, Jesus refused to endorse the triumphant Zion ideology which viewed the nations as Israel's servants, and which was to provide a rallying call for some of Jesus' near-contemporaries in their struggle against Roman imperialism.

The likelihood of Jesus being actively involved in a Zealot-style revolt against Rome – a claim that has had a remarkably long shelf life in the study of the historical Jesus[22] – seems highly improbable, on the basis of this understanding. More recent scholarship has seriously questioned the notion of a Zealot party, to be identified with Josephus' Fourth Philosophy (*JA* 18.4–10 and 23–25), and existing from the imposition of direct Roman rule in Judea after the deposition of Herod's son, Archelaus, in 6 AD. It has been noted that Josephus himself never makes that connection, reserving the name Zealot for the group of lesser priests who instigated the revolt in 66 CE by refusing to offer the loyal sacrifices on behalf of Rome (*JW* 2.409–410).[23] The claim that the Fourth Philosophy, with its radical position of refusing to pay taxes to Caesar or to call any person 'Lord' except God, had been founded by a Galilean, Judas, easily gave rise to the notion that Galilee of Jesus' day was a hot-bed of organized revolutionary activists. This impression was further reinforced by Josephus' description of the Galileans as courageous in resisting foreign enemies and independent-minded, a description that was intended to impress Roman readers of his achievements as governor in Galilee at the outbreak of the revolt (*JW* 2.41f.). With such a background it was possible to develop a profile of Jesus and his movement as typifying the Zealot ideology of Galilee, traces of which, it was claimed, can still be detected in the gospels, despite the best efforts of the evangelists to suppress any such information in the interest of the movement's survival in the Roman world. A more critical reading of Josephus has brought about the collapse of the Zealot-hypothesis and the notion of a Galilee seething with revolutionary fervour.[24] Thus the figure of Jesus as a Zealot has given way to other ideas about the revolutionary character of his movement in conditions of undoubted social unrest.

Jesus and the Kingdom of God

There is virtual unanimous agreement that central to Jesus' proclamation was the notion of the kingdom of God, the political implications of which must be recognized in the light of its usage in contemporary literature, Jewish and pagan.[25] Not everyone, however, is prepared, to accept that apocalyptic writings provide the proper setting for understanding Jesus' use of the image. Thus, Crossan stresses the revolutionary nature of Cynicism not just as a moral protest against Greco-Roman values but as an attack on civilization itself insofar as it espouses an introversionist attitude to the world, which is deemed evil, according to a typology of religiously based protest movements, proposed by cultural anthropologist, Bryan Wilson.[26] This emphasis prepares the ground for Crossan's portrayal of a Cynic-like Jesus who is seen as having engaged in a similar form of social protest in the third section of his major study. Crossan does examine the various forms of Jewish protest against Roman rule, which could be deemed to be apocalyptically (or millennially, in Wilson's terminology) motivated. However, in discussing Jesus' attitude to the kingdom of God, he opts for a sapiential rather than an apocalyptic understanding of Jesus' preaching of the kingdom of God. The model of kingly rule that Jesus espouses in his parables and his aphorisms is a 'here and now Kingdom of the nobodies and the destitute ... a kingdom performed (through magic and meal) rather than just proclaimed'. In other words, Crossan sees Jesus' vision as inspired, not by millennial dreams but by Cynic notions that the wise person is king insofar as they remain detached and free from any outside influences that might control their lives. To the extent that such ideas give rise to a movement that is deeply counter-cultural they pose a serious threat to society itself.[27]

Richard Horsley takes a very different position in developing his portrayal of a revolutionary Jesus in several of his writings.[28] He challenges what he describes as synthetic and theologically driven notions of apocalyptic that describe 'end-time' scenarios or cosmic catastrophes, and focuses instead on the symbolic nature of apocalyptic language within specific social and historical circumstances. Jesus' ministry must be understood within the context of the 'spiral of violence' that dominated first-century Judean society as a result of the presence of imperial structures and their repressive attitudes towards the little tradition of the Jewish peasantry. The symbol of the kingdom of God as employed by Jesus signified God's victory over the evil forces, a conception that was shared with standard Jewish apocalyptic expectations. The poor and the oppressed would be vindicated, the wicked and unjust punished and a new Israel constituted, in which egalitarian social relations would be operative and the institutions of oppression, both Roman and Jewish, would come under God's judgement. Whereas Crossan draws on the cross-cultural models of Bryan Wilson, Horsley uses a social theory of conflict in order to expose the structural sources of alienation in terms of control of the resources by the elite in Roman Palestine, thus giving rise to deep-seated resentment and social unrest.

This account is more convincing in its broad outline than that of Crossan, whose decision to opt for a sapiential, as opposed to an apocalyptic understanding of the kingdom, seems somewhat arbitrary. As is clear from recently published wisdom texts from Qumran, these are not antithetically opposed world-views as seems to be presumed by those who seek to remove all apocalyptic colouring from Jesus' teaching and ministry.[29] Nor is the revolutionary potential of the Cynic hypothesis among Galilean peasants very convincing, any more than is the suggestion of a Cynic-like Jesus, whose motivation is only marginally, if at all, inspired by radical strands of his own Jewish tradition.[30] While differing on many detailed aspects, I share Horsley's depiction of Judean society as conflictual. Yet there are problems about applying a contemporary Marxist-inspired model to ancient societies, especially when a purely materialist analysis ignores the role of

religious belief in discussions of the social and economic causes of
exploitation. The argument of this study is that Jesus' primary
motivation was based on his understanding of Israel's God as the
creator God, and that this perspective determines the manner in
which he appropriates certain aspects of his tradition, in contrast to
various other strands of Jewish thinking in his day.

These two examples of recent discussions of Jesus' revolutionary
attitudes arising from their understanding of the kingdom of God
could be easily multiplied.[31] They serve to illustrate the point that,
while there is general acceptance that the theme is central to Jesus'
preaching, there is no agreement on the specific contours of the
expression as used by him. Part of the difficulty is that the nominal
form 'the *kingdom* of God' or its near equivalents are rare in the
Hebrew Scriptures, whereas the active, verbal form of God as king,
ruling not just Israel but the whole of creation is widespread, but
particularly prominent in the Psalms and Isaiah, as we have seen.
Though the notion of Yahweh's kingship was embedded in the
covenant idea within the context of royal treaties with vassal states of
the Ancient Near East, its coming to prominence coincided with a
loss of confidence in the Israelite monarchy and the domination of
Judah by various empires with their ideologies of universal kingship.
These political implications were carried over and found new
elaboration in the apocalyptic literature of resistance in the Second
Temple period. In the Book of Daniel God's universal lordship has
both cosmic and political reference. It provides reassurance that
while earthly kings such as Darius may rule temporarily, the
universal rule of Yahweh will prevail (chs. 1–6). At the same time
the fact that God's rule will soon be handed over to 'saints of the
most high' offers hope and consolation to those living and dead who
have experienced the horrors of Antiochus' persecution (chs. 7–12).

It would be a misjudgement of the way in which the myth of
Yahweh's universal kingship functions if one were to attempt to
separate these two different referents as though they applied to two
distinct events, one immediate and one in the unspecified future. It
is an essential aspect of the functioning of a myth that the universal
and cosmic dimensions of the divine rule be reaffirmed. A particular
feature of the genre, and of apocalyptic thinking generally, is a thirst
for total presence, so that 'all' is one of 'the great governing
apocalyptic words'.[32] This demands that the story becomes the story
of 'all the kingdoms of the world' and not just a particular local
incident. The concentration of 'the plot' is on the end of the story

when the total victory over the evil forces takes place through a complete reversal of the present situation. It is this universal perspective that makes an apocalyptic interpretation of the present both relevant and reassuring in the midst of a current crisis.

This understanding of the nature of apocalyptic and its literary expressions may not please either the theologian attempting to develop a doctrine of 'the last things' or the literalist keen to translate apocalyptic symbolism into a map of world history. Both approaches are attempts to impose our mental maps of time and space on to those of first-century Mediterranean people, including Jews. Bruce Malina has warned against such anachronistic reading on the basis of anthropological studies. Peasant societies, such as that reflected in many of Jesus' sayings, are orientated to the present and the past, but have little sense of future, long-term goals, he suggests in his provocative essay.[33] Thus statements which to our ears may appear to be referring to some future event (cosmic or otherwise) may well have much greater concern about the present than we can readily grasp. The same applies to our understanding of spatial references in apocalyptic literature. The realms of angels, human and demons belong in the same cosmic space, even when they operate on different tiers, and as John Collins reminds us, the Jews who had been persecuted for their faith by Antiochus would have been more than pleased to hear that a heavenly host was fighting on their behalf, since 'the heavenly counterparts were not only real, but vital to human destiny'.[34] When Jesus declares that he 'saw Satan falling like lightening from heaven' (Lk. 10.18), we can capture something of the way in which he too shared in this apocalyptic world-view and recognize the source of his reassurance that he was endowed with a heavenly power to cast out demons (Mt. 12.28; Lk. 11.18).

Apocalyptic Imagination and a Values' Revolution

The inconclusive discussion in recent scholarship as to whether Jesus' thinking about the kingdom was sapiential or apocalyptic, present or future, may be irrelevant in the light of these considerations. The question concerning Jesus' use of the phrase 'the kingdom of God' needs to be posed differently. How did an apocalyptic imagination assist him in constructing a new under-standing of the kingdom in the light of his Galilean experiences, and how did that exercise help him to interpret the present differently? Previously it was suggested that Jesus' move from the desert to lower

Galilee might assist in explaining the difference of emphasis between him and the Baptist with regard to their respective understanding of the present, based on the different ecological conditions. However, that suggestion did not exclude the exploitation by imperial agents of the rich resources of that environment for their own needs. The fact that Jesus' lifestyle was accompanied by a call for total trust in Yahweh, the creator God, as this was expressed in the Jubilee and Sabbath year legislation, no matter how utopian such a call might have appeared, indicates just how incensed he was by the situation that he encountered. It was these conditions, so alien to the Biblical ideals of a restored Israel, that acted as the catalyst for his apocalyptic imagination to challenge the existing unjust structures, not by the traditional means of a militant resistance, but by a new and creative interpretation of the kingdom of God. At least this is the proposal that must now be tested in the light of the evidence available.

For John the image of the axe placed at the root of the tree, implying imminent judgement, would appear to have been central, though his concern for justice to one another, as mentioned by Josephus, should not be ignored (*JA* 18.117), an aspect of his ministry that is spelled out by Luke also (Lk. 3.10–14). According to Josephus, Herod Antipas decided to have John removed because of the danger of a social revolution among the people, thus suggesting a greater political focus to his ministry than the gospel portrait implies. It also suggests that there is nothing incompatible between a world-view that expects God's imminent judgement and a concern for right living in the present. Recent discussion of the Wisdom writings from Qumran Cave 4, especially 4Q 416–418, shows how naturally and freely Jewish thinking in the circles within which both John and Jesus moved could combine a sapiential and an apocalyptic understanding of life. The instruction in this document is not sectarian, since the addressees are clearly people of affairs engaged in everyday pursuits involving financial, social and familial relations. As well as instructions of a conventional wisdom style similar to those found in writings such as Sirach, apocalyptic admonitions about rewards and punishments are drawn on to emphasize the importance of the advice being given. At the same time the person being instructed is repeatedly told to study the 'mystery that is to come' (*raz nihyeh*) so that he may 'understand all the ways of truth and contemplate all the roots of iniquity. And you will know what is bitter for a man and what is sweet for his fellow.'[35] There are clear echoes here of the apocalyptic scenario of good and evil, rewards and punishments. The word for mystery is a Persian loan-word *raz*, and it occurs in Daniel with reference to the hidden knowledge of the divine plan that Daniel is privy to because of his pious lifestyle, which included prayer and ascetic practice of fasting. Study and contemplation of the divine plan are the way to a deeper wisdom that will bring reassurance of the ultimate victory of the creator God, Lord of the universe. Thus, prayer and politics go hand in hand for those endowed with the apocalyptic imagination, and in this regard, it would seem, John the Baptist was no exception.

As far as Jesus was concerned, his move to Galilee meant a change of environment and a different strategy, yet he did not abandon the values and beliefs which he brought from his desert experience with John. In this respect students of the historical Jesus have given too little attention to the importance of prayer in the unfolding of his ministry, especially in view of the emphasis on contemplation and reflection for the seer/wise person within both the wisdom and apocalyptic traditions, allied to his acetic lifestyle that eschewed the comforts of home, family and possessions. Indeed the locations suggested by the evangelists for Jesus' prayer indicate that the 'desert' setting was an important feature of his practice.[36] His hymn of thanksgiving is a recognition of the gift of understanding that has been given to his followers: 'I praise you, Father, Lord of heaven and earth because you have hidden these things from the wise and understanding and revealed them to babes' (Mt. 11.25f.; Lk. 10.21).

The social standing of Jesus-followers was similar to that of the person being addressed in 4Q 416–418. Repeatedly he is reminded that he is poor, yet this does not excuse him from the search for knowledge. Honouring of parents even in one's poverty involves recognition of the fact that it was they 'who uncovered the ear to the mystery that is to come', thus underlining the kinship context of Jewish education. For Jesus also, wisdom and understanding of the mystery is not the preserve of upper-class scribes or the well educated, but it can be mediated in and through the everyday circumstances of home and village life. For him poverty is no obstacle to an understanding of the kingdom's mystery, but the emphasis is on the gift-nature of the wisdom, thus subverting the elite notions of scribal wisdom being the preserve of those who have the time for leisure (Sir. 38.24–39.5). The Qumran Wisdom text suggests that being poor frees one from desire for more so that the true source of wealth can be recognized:

You are poor. Do not desire something beyond your share, and do
not be confused by it, lest you displace your boundary. But if they
cause you to dwell in splendour, walk in it, and by the mystery that is
to be/come study its origins. And then you will know what is allotted
to it and in righteousness you will walk. For God will cause to shine
his (blank) on all your ways.

The thematic similarities with Jesus' sayings are easily recognizable,
yet the Qumran Wisdom text suggests an acceptance of one's lot,
whether it be in poverty or in wealth. Missing is the radical sense of
changed values that Jesus' teaching represents – poverty is not just a
good teacher of the way things are, it is blessedness itself; the first
shall be last and the last shall be first!

As in the case of John, Josephus is an interesting outside witness to
the parameters of Jesus' ministry: 'At this time there appeared Jesus, a
wise man. For he was a doer of startling deeds, a teacher of people
who receive the truth gladly' (*JA* 18.63–64).[37] If his deeds could be
described as *paradoxa*, 'surprising' or 'startling', his speech patterns
were equally enigmatic. Images of the kingdom were drawn from
the everyday experiences of his audiences, yet the message is not
obvious – it is hidden, calling for insight in order to be properly
grasped. 'Nothing is hidden except to be revealed' is a statement that
is characteristic of his approach. The hidden meaning of the world
had already been disclosed in the creation, yet the idea of newness to
come was at once in continuity with and yet different from what
could now be experienced. The metaphorical mode was appropriate
to express the continuities and discontinuities involved: the kingdom
of heaven is *like*, not *identical with* present realities, because the
creator God is the author of both. His speech was pithy and
proverbial, best described by the Hebrew word *mashal*, a term, the
meaning of which ranged from riddle to short story or parable. Yet
for Jesus these sayings and stories were pointers to the hidden nature
of the kingdom that he proclaimed, a hiddenness that was in stark
contrast to the pomp and ceremonial display of power that was an
essential feature of Roman rule in its Herodian manifestation.

The image of the seed growing mysteriously was an excellent
metaphor for the process that was already in motion, information
about which he shared with his followers. From his perspective the
raz nihyeh, 'the mystery to come', could be shared with those who
followed his way, 'to you has been given the mystery of the
kingdom of God' (Mk. 4.10), but yet the exact contours of that

kingdom, like those of the creator God, were hidden and mysterious, but also very real. What could be discerned was the proper course of action in the present, based on the recognition that Satan had fallen from heaven, implying that the cosmic struggle involving 'the kingdom of the holy ones' was already decided. The way of wisdom provided one element of an appropriate response in the present, since God's wisdom could be discerned from his creation. Yet the radical element of newness was provided by the apocalyptic belief that a fundamental change was occurring now in and through his own actions, one that was radically opposed to that being proclaimed by Roman propaganda.

Confronting Roman Power

There are very few sayings of Jesus which directly address the Roman presence. The saying 'Render to Caesar what is Caesar's and to God what is God's' (Mk. 12.17) occurs in a Judean, not a Galilean setting, yet no doubt it is indicative of his overall view of Roman power and Roman demands. Its enigmatic meaning has baffled commentators. In addition to the three synoptic witnesses, versions of the saying occur also in the Gospel of Thomas and Papyrus Egerton 2, suggesting that it was quite important to early Christians of various backgrounds. Critically, it provides a fitting climax to a controversy story in which opponents of Jesus seek to entrap him. Those who pose the question about paying taxes to Caesar are the Pharisees and Herodians, for both of whom, as supporters of the administration, this was not likely to have been an issue. The word used for tribute, *kensos*, appears to be a loan-word from the Latin *census*, recalling the census held by the Romans which gave rise to a tax revolt in Judea following the imposition of direct Roman rule in 6 CE. Posing the question in this way, therefore, was an attempt to place Jesus on the horns of a dilemma: either he accepts Roman rule and its right to impose a tribute, or he will be exposed as a supporter of Judas the Galilean and his radical rejection of Rome, as described by Josephus (*JW* 2.118; *JA* 18.4). By calling for the coin of tribute, Jesus changed the whole issue from one of tribute to one of images, a highly sensitive topic in all branches of Judaism, even in the first century, with its strong aniconic belief, based on the decalogue.[38]

Many different nuances have been read into Jesus' reply by different interpreters, ancient and modern, ranging from a call to respect both civil and religious authority to downright support for the radical position of his fellow-Galilean, Judas of Gamla.[39] Any definitive decision on the political implications of the remark must depend on Jesus' overall attitude to Roman rule in Palestine, and hence it is necessary to spread the net more widely in order to discern insofar as possible his stance. Three related issues emerge as worthy of further exploration:

Jesus and Herodian Centres: To begin with, it is worth enquiring further into Jesus' possible motives for avoiding the two Herodian foundations in Galilee, Sepphoris and Tiberias, while conducting a healing and teaching ministry in the neighbouring villages.[40] The omission is all the more surprising in view of his willingness to travel outside the immediate confines of Jewish Galilee. The fact that both became important Jewish centres later suggests that these were never pagan cities in the full sense of that term, even if there was some gentile presence in the population from the outset. As was noted earlier, there is archaeological evidence from Sepphoris of observant Jews living in an important residential area of the city in the early Roman period. Even though the Herodian palace in Tiberias did violate the aniconic law it was torn down by radical elements in the city's population, aided by some Galileans from the countryside (*Life*, 65). Jesus' avoidance of these cities cannot therefore be attributed to their pagan ethos. It could of course have been for strategic reasons, especially in view of the fate of his mentor, John the Baptist, at the hands of Antipas in Perea. However, the fact is that there is no suggestion that Jesus was a fugitive, and he could have easily been captured in Galilee had the occasion arisen at any time in his public ministry and had the administration so wished.

The avoidance is, therefore, best explained as principled, based on Jesus' views of the values represented by these cities and his own call to minister to those who had become the victims of their elitist lifestyle. A critical attitude to urban life and its values had surfaced already in pious Jewish circles at the time of the Maccabean revolt (1 Macc. 2.29), and this found expression subsequently among those of the Essene movement who opted for the desert life. Both John the Baptist and Jesus must be seen to belong broadly to this same ascetic tradition, so that when Jesus came into Galilee and began an active ministry, his focus continued to be on the countryside, rather than on the urban life, with the exception of Jerusalem, as we shall discuss in the next chapter.

It is in his encomium of John the Baptist that one can best observe this attitude coming to expression. A threefold rhetorical question is posed by the formula 'What did you go out to the desert to see?' Three different options are posed: a reed shaken by the wind, a man dressed in fine garments and a prophet. The expectation of the questioner is of a 'no' to the first two comparisons and a ringing 'yes' to the third. It has been argued that the reed shaken by the wind has a veiled reference to Herod Antipas, because of the emblem of the reed on his coins.[41] Certainly the second comparison, 'one dressed in fine robes', is unmistakably directed at the Herodian court circles despite minor variations in the Lukan and Matthean versions. The 'royal palaces' (Lk.) or 'the houses of kings' (Mt.) can only refer in the context to the lifestyle of the Herodian court, either in Tiberias or Sepphoris.

It is significant, surely, that Josephus can speak of rivalry between the two cities because of the location of 'the royal bank and the records' (*Life*, 38). Royal banks and royal palaces go together and they send clear messages to the peasants who are expected to supply the resources to maintain both, irrespective of the impact on their own precarious existence. The additional comment in the Gospel of Thomas version of this saying, though probably reflecting its own Gnostic-style ethos, is quite apposite here also in unmasking the real problem with unbridled wealth: 'They are dressed in rich clothing, but they cannot understand the truth' (Gos.Thom. 78). Even though the Q passage goes on to draw a contrast between Jesus and John, the former enjoying conviviality and the latter living austerely, it is quite clear where Jesus' true sympathies lay (Mt. 11.16–19; Lk. 7.31–35). His hero, John, may be in prison but he should be assured that despite the different course that Jesus' ministry has taken, the prophetic promises of justice, equality and care for all were being realized in his ministry also (Mt. 11.2–11; Lk. 7.18–28).

Jesus and Herodian Rule: In addition to the stinging criticism of the luxurious lifestyle of the Herodians, the Jesus tradition also attacks their style of rule, proposing an alternative one based on the ruler as servant rather than as lord. Mark's version would appear to be particularly pointed towards Antipas with its qualification, 'those who regard themselves as rulers', whereas Matthew and Luke simply talk of rulers and kings. Antipas aspired to kingship in succession to his father who had been designated king of the Jews by the Roman senate, but he and his brothers were only given the title of tetrarch (literally, 'ruler of a quarter'). Despite the diminished status, Antipas could behave tyranically towards his subjects as the murder of the Baptist demonstrates, especially if his action might ingratiate him to his Roman overlords. Mark (followed by Matthew) seems to emphasize this aspect of Herodian rule by using two compound verbs to underline the repressive and insensitive nature of their rule, the standard for which had been set by Antipas' father, Herod – they are said 'to press *down*' and 'lord *over*' their subjects (Mk. 10.42). This statement about 'the kings of the gentiles' recalls the attack of 'the kings of the earth' on the Lord's anointed of the messianic psalm 2. It could, therefore, reflect a veiled allusion by Jesus to a different type of kingly rule associated with the messianic age, especially since the issue of styles of rule arose in the immediate context of the request from James and John for special places in the kingdom, which they assumed Jesus would soon establish in Jerusalem (Mk. 10.22–42).

As was noted above, there was a tradition of kingship based on harmony and peace-making associated with the messianic age, but this was less developed in later Jewish thinking than the notion of a war-like messiah who would conquer the nations. Indeed this is the case in Ps. 2, where the promise is made to the future Davidic ruler that he will break the kings of the earth 'with a rod of iron'. Recently, Gerd Theissen has proposed a different model for understanding Jesus' political stance in relation to popular expectations of kingship in his environment.[42] He suggests that Jesus engaged in the politics of 'symbols without coercion', thereby relying on the persuasiveness of his own charismatic gifts to legitimate his authority rather than the use of force or appeal to tradition. For Theissen, Jesus is the master of symbolic politics, proposing counter-symbols to those of Roman dominance, which, as we have seen, dotted the landscape of his ministry. His own actions are equally symbolic, not least the selection of the Twelve as leaders in his community, to whom he is now proposing a model that inverts the master/slave relationship as the correct pattern for ruling others. This model, according to Theissen, fits well with a long-standing tradition of humane kingship which operated in the ancient world and which Jesus is now proposing as an ideal for discipleship.

Such a context for understanding Jesus' critique of Herodian (and Roman) use of coercive power is indeed helpful in providing a broader perspective for interpreting Jesus' stance. There is evidence that it had entered Jewish thinking also in depicting the future humble king (Zech. 9.1–17), an image used for Jesus' entry into Jerusalem (Mk. 11.1–10). Luke too may have been familiar with a version of the humane ruler idea in his use of the term 'benefactor' (*euergetes*) for his rendering of the Markan passage under discussion, and his later application of this to Jesus' whole ministry in Galilee (Lk. 22.25; Acts 10.38). However, on its own it does not capture the radical challenge that Jesus' vision of the human community posed, which was prompted by the apocalyptic imagination of 'the kingdom of the holy ones' replacing earthly kingdoms and the participation of the wise in that triumph, with its echoes of the servant figure of Isaiah 53. In proposing the servant model of alternative rulership to that of the Herodians, Jesus' most immediate point of reference is not, it would seem, Greco-Roman traditions of humane rulers or benefactors, *pace* Luke, but that of Isaiah's suffering servant and Daniel's *maskilim*. This at least is Mark's point of view, with the concluding reflection placed on Jesus' lips being the clearest statement of his appropriation of the servant's role for himself (Mk. 10.46).

Sources of Power. That Jesus viewed the Herodian dynasty as doomed to apocalyptic annihilation becomes clearer from a consideration of the Beelzebul controversy in its political and cultural context. This episode is reported by both Mark and Q (Mk. 3.22–31; Mt. 12.22–30; Lk. 11.14–23), and there are further links between it and various allusions elsewhere in Jesus' sayings to houses and householders, thieves and robbers (Mt. 12.43–45; Lk. 11.24–26), which suggest political realities of the Herodian period.[43] The context of the Beelzebul controversy in both the Markan and Q versions is Jesus' practice of exorcism, which Mark in particular emphasizes, highlighting the apocalyptic tenor of his presentation of Jesus' career as a whole.

While the Q version suggests amazement by the crowd when Jesus effects an exorcism, it also shares the Markan perspective of some people attempting to discredit his activity by claiming that he was in league with Beelzebul, 'the prince of demons'. This type of negative labelling, amounting to vilification, is typical of situations where a particular individual or group is threatened by behaviour that is deemed to be deviant by the normal standards of the society. Mark gives a formal tone to the situation by suggesting a delegation sent from Jerusalem with the specific intention of discrediting Jesus with the 'unsuspecting' Galilean populace. This implicates the religious authorities and their retainers in the process of vilification, and by association suggests that his actions are dangerous in Roman eyes also, since his access to power did not come through the normal institutional channels, religious or secular.

Even independently of its Markan setting, the internal apocalyptic associations in the Beelzebul story are clear indicators of the political implications of Jesus' behaviour. Those who seek to discredit him do not call into question the fact of the exorcisms, but only the source of the power, by attributing it to the prince of demons. This charge immediately recalls the heavenly hosts and their angelic leaders, which were encountered in Daniel, and are frequently attested in Qumran also, especially in the War Scroll.[44] It was, as we saw, a feature of apocalyptic imagery to operate within a two-tiered universe, where earthly struggles mirror those in the heavens, sometimes actually merging into the one struggle between the forces of good and evil. How can exorcisms be regarded as politically threatening within such a scenario? To answer this question properly, the use of social theory in regard to labelling of deviancy in many societies has proved to be an important insight into the real, as distinct from the alleged, causes of opposition to Jesus.[45] Alleging demonic possession was (and often still is) a social instrument for excluding people who were deemed to be socially dangerous for one reason or another. Jesus' exorcisms were, therefore, not simply stories of healing, though in many cases they were seen as that also, since in the ancient world sickness or bodily abnormalities were attributed to invasive evil spirits. By ridding them of the demon, Jesus was restoring them again to the social world from which they had been excluded, and in doing so he was calling into question the norms by which they were deemed to be deviant in the first instance. In short, Jesus' exorcisms were a serious challenge to the prevailing norms and values concerning power and control in Herodian Galilee, and those of the Roman overlords who supported those norms. The only counter-strategy open to his opponents was to label him deviant and possessed also.

Jesus was acutely aware of the implications of his actions. He provided a proper context for understanding them by introducing the images of kingdom and house, both closely related politically. Oriental rulers such as Herod, but also the Romans, thought of their domains as households or houses over which they held absolute sway. Taxes and tributes were merely signs of their ownership of the realm and their rule was like that of a paterfamilias within a domestic household, absolute, universal and unquestioned. Divided kingdoms and divided houses could not hope to impose this system of rigid control, and for Jesus' audience the most obvious example of that maxim was surely that of the Herodian house itself. Herod the Great's final years were marked by bloodthirsty paranoia about his succession, and Rome had divided his kingdom between the three surviving sons, much to Antipas' chagrin. The source of Jesus' power was from God, not Satan, and his certainty about the fall of the oppressive rule was born of the belief that his actions were signs of the arrival of the kingdom of God now. That kingdom was not merely a judgement on all earthly kingdoms and their oppressive regimes, it called for the emergence of a new and different household which Jesus and his community of alternative values were in the process of re-assembling. It was to be a community where servanthood was the ideal for rulers and wisdom involved trusting in the creator God and his promises.

God or Caesar?

'Give back to Caesar what is Caesar's, and to God what is God's' – a call to accept Caesar's rule, or a declaration that only what belonged to God was of any consequence? There seems little doubt about Jesus' answer to his own question. Unlike some of his co-religionists who belonged to the retainer class, he was not prepared to accept the inevitability of Rome's rule as expressed in its propaganda (*JW* 2.348–361). Like other kingdoms, it too was doomed to pass. Despite Rome's claims, their peace could not be imposed. 'They make a desolation and call it peace' are words put on the lips of a British general Calgacus, by a Roman historian, Tacitus (*Agicola* 30.3–31). Jesus was not prepared to share the violent response to such conditions, espoused by many Jews throughout the first century, which eventually plunged the nation into a disastrous revolt. He believed in the power of symbols and symbolic action because he believed in a God of whom, unlike Caesar, no image could be made, and yet who summoned people to trust in his presence and his power. This was the risk of faith that Jesus was prepared to take. His was a faith that was grounded in a trust in the goodness of the creation as he had experienced it and reflected on its mysterious but hidden processes. It was also a faith that had been nourished by the apocalyptic imagination that this creator God was still in charge of his world and had the power to make all things new again. No human empire could be compared with this power, no matter how dominant it and its agents appeared to be. Caesar could have his image engraved on the coin of the tribute, but he could not control the power of the imagination that was fed by the tradition of God's mysterious but powerful presence in the world, to which no image could do justice.

6

DEATH IN JERUSALEM

Jerusalem, Jerusalem, you who kill the prophets and stone those who are sent to you ... (Mt. 23.37; Lk. 13.34)

The use of key aspects of Israel's story – the enjoyment of the fruits of the earth, the conquest of the land, the Zion traditions and resistance to imperial powers – for understanding the particular contours of Jesus' ministry in a Galilean setting has proved to be a productive exercise. Different views of all these topics were reflected in the Hebrew Scriptures, giving rise to intense debate and different responses within the changing social, political and religious environment of the later Second Temple period. Most of the literature that is now collected as the *Apocrypha and Pseudepigrapha of the Old Testament* (1983 and 1985) as well as the Dead Sea Scrolls can be seen as different interpretations and actualizations of aspects of the foundational literature of the *Torah* and the Prophets, representing various groups and circles, some of whom are known to us from other sources and some we can only dimly discern behind the various writings. The numerous versions of Jesus' life and teaching that circulated from a relatively early stage after his death can best be understood within that same milieu of 'exegetical communities' which the reception of the Hebrew Scriptures had generated. It has been the contention of this study that modern discussion of criteria for identifying the sayings of Jesus has had the effect of divorcing him from his own tradition, thereby also prohibiting him from participating in an active hermeneutical exercise in which he, like other Jews, was quite capable of engaging.

Undoubtedly, the Jesus-movement did continue this process after his death, stimulated in large part by the impact on them of that shocking event. This should not obscure the fact that Jesus also engaged in the quintessentially Jewish experience of 'searching the Scriptures' in order to discern more fully God's call for him in his own lifetime. Such a claim might well today meet the objection that Jesus was a Galilean, and that ascribing to him the kind of familiarity with his own tradition that the argument entails, is unrealistic, since it would locate him within the elitist scribal circles that had no interest in the 'little tradition' of the peasants or their social plight in Roman Palestine. Ironically, this type of modern objection echoes that of the Jerusalem establishment as represented in the Fourth Gospel, as well as by the local intellegenstia of his home-town, Nazareth (Jn. 7.15; Mk. 6.2). It attributes too little to peasant wisdom and too much to urban ideologues. The Jesus–movement is one of several bridging groups that functioned to bridge the yawning gap that had opened up between the Jerusalem priestly aristocracy and the country people from the Persian period onwards. The temple aristocracy, operating both as the spiritual leaders of the people and the agents of various ruling powers, were hopelessly compromised in redefining and leading a renewal of Israel. Both Jesus and the Pharisees shared a common cause in that regard, except that he operated from a prophetic point of view while they opted for the priestly one, leading inevitably to a clash of perspectives. Yet they both shared a common critique of those who controlled the actual temple system with its claim to unquestioning loyalty from the people at large in relation to the agricultural and other offerings. Such a system, so rich in its symbolic potential to express a shared heritage, became not just an irritant, but increasingly, an intolerable burden once the common vision no longer functioned. In the eyes of both Galilean and Judean peasants the temple aristocracy and their clientele had allied themselves with the imperial overlords and their value system.

The trend in recent scholarship to present the Jesus–movement in both its pre- and post-Easter phases as being radically opposed to Jerusalem, fails to recognize adequately the drawing power of the symbolic centre, even in a climate of hostility brought about by an unjust and exploitative system of control. To collapse that tension into either blind religious acceptance or hostile rejection of everything that Jerusalem stood for is to ignore the power of religious symbols when confronted with otherwise alienating circumstances. Jesus saw his own 'attack' on Jerusalem in the light of a history of prophetic challenges to the centre. After his death one group of his followers settled in the holy city, appropriating some of the Zion symbolism.[1] Even the Judean peasants who eventually stormed the temple in the early 60s did not attack the temple building, as they had done with Antipas' palace in Tiberias. They burned the debt records, attacked the royal palaces and murdered the high priest, electing by lot a peasant to the position (*JW* 2.42, 4.151–157). The Zion tradition, as explored earlier, had pointed the way towards deciphering Jesus' critical stance with regard to the temple in that he had opted, it was argued, for the servant-Zion role rather than that of triumphant Zion. If the *maskilim* of Daniel with their patient trust in God's graciousness when faced with imperial might had provided a model of resistance to the Jesus-movement in Galilee, the servant-Zion tradition in Isaiah offered possibilities for challenging the hegemony of the temple aristocracy in Jerusalem. It was there that Jesus was to encounter the collusion between the agents of both the state and the temple.

Jesus and the Temple

Jesus' journeys to Jerusalem were undertaken, it would appear, with a sense of foreboding. Quite independently of the threefold prediction of the passion, discussed in the previous chapter, there is the statement in Q which indicates that hostility is to be expected by any country prophet in Jerusalem, and that Jesus had made several unsuccessful efforts to win the hearts of the city (Mt. 23.37-39; Lk. 13.34-35). It would be convenient if one could confidently fill out this picture with some details from the Fourth Gospel, where the action in Jerusalem is repeatedly centred on the temple and the symbolic significance of the festivals – Passover, Tabernacles and Dedication.[2] However, the fact that these accounts are heavily weighted with Johannine theological concerns, suggests caution. Before dismissing the evidence entirely – the dominant attitude in historical Jesus studies since Strauss' *The Life of Jesus Critically Examined* (1835) – it should at least be noted that there is a correspondence between the pattern of repeated visits hinted at by Q, and the three years of public ministry conducted in both Judea and Jerusalem as well as in Galilee, in accordance with the Fourth Gospel's framework. A feature of the Johannine rhetoric of irony and misunderstanding, eventually leading to clarification on another level, is that it always begins in the 'real' world of Jewish life and experience, only to move to a higher plane as the discourse develops. In this regard it is noteworthy that John associates Jesus' visits with the festivals, something that historically is quite plausible, *pace* counter-claims that Galileans rarely if ever visited the temple, and that Jesus may have done so only once. This larger context of several and repeated encounters between Jesus and the temple authorities, particularly with regard to the meaning of the symbolism of the feasts, would provide a better vista for adjudicating on the one episode from the Synoptic gospels, that of the incident in the temple (Mk. 11.15–19), on which so much has been made to depend, including the arrest and handing over to the Romans as a treasonous and dangerous rebel.

Renewal, not Reform

The precise point of conflict between Jesus and the temple authorities has proved to be more illusive. The range of suggestions by modern scholars runs the whole gamut: a temple tantrum of minor consequence; critique of the commercial activity allowed in the environs of the temple; concern about the temple's purity and the correct application of the rules regarding offerings and sacrifices; a Zealot-style invasion and a desire to see a new temple as promised in various strands of restoration literature. Several of these suggestions are not mutually exclusive and some are more plausible than others. Since there is good evidence that Jesus actually predicted the imminent destruction of the present temple (Gos.Thom. 71; Mk. 13.1–2, 14.58, 15.29; Jn. 2.19), it must be assumed with Sanders that he had not reform, but radical renewal in mind.[3] The direct association of that event with his own ministry – '*I* will destroy this house' – appears in all three versions of the saying. His promise of a future building of a new temple is less certain since it is missing entirely from the Thomas version of the saying and in both the Markan and Johannine renderings the formulation is clearly influenced by later Resurrection faith.

The link between destruction and rebuilding should not be assumed, since, as Sanders notes, Jesus, like his namesake, the son of Ananias, could have been a prophet of doom with regard to the temple, the people and the city. However, from the discussion in previous chapters it is clear that Jesus of Nazareth did have a definite view on the restoration of Israel and of his own role with regard to that. Hopes for a new temple arose in various strands of the literature and for various reasons, it would seem. Sometimes it was a matter of human rebuilding (Tob. 14.5); sometimes it was done by God's agent (SibOr. 5.425; TBenj. 9.2), but more frequently by God himself (1 Enoch 90.28f.; Jub. 1.17; 11Q Temple 29.8–29). This last idea is represented in the Apocalyptic–Eschatological strand of the tradition, to which Jesus had been indebted, but the idea that he himself would have played a significant role in such an event should not be ruled out automatically. Because there is no double attestation for such a link, Crossan demurs at the suggestion.[4] Yet in the light of the discussion in the opening chapter of the need for a criterion of historical plausibility, it seems that the claim should be evaluated within the broader context of Jewish restoration hopes.

The Galilean context of any such claim is the chief focus of this study. A trawl through the sayings tradition does not yield any indication of a deep-seated animosity towards the temple and its institutions during the Galilean phase of Jesus' ministry. There is acknowledgement that the temple is to be identified with God's presence in the discussion about the 'offerings dedicated to the temple' (Mk. 7.11) and in the instruction about oaths (Mt. 5.34–37), but in the former case the institution of *korban* is criticized because of its casuistry in legitimating avoidance of more basic responsibilities, and in the latter, the device of swearing by the temple out of respect for God's name is unmasked, since the temple cannot be divorced from what it stands for, namely, God's presence. Both statements, therefore, suggest the use of the temple's sanctity for somewhat specious reasons. Criticism of the Pharisaic practices of insisting on the minutiae of the tithing laws while ignoring the weightier matters of the law – justice, mercy and faithfulness (Mt. 23.23; Lk. 11.42) follows the same lines and there is no hint of a desire to abolish the institution of tithing itself.[5] None of these implied criticisms would amount to a radical call for the present temple's destruction now. They point to the abuse of the temple's real significance for selfish ends or legislative practices, suggesting reform but not abolition. Is this then a matter of Jesus not taking the temple all that seriously while in Galilee, or did it impinge on his consciousness at a deeper level even there?

One preliminary clue to an adequate answer to this question is noted by Crossan, namely the use of the term 'house' for the temple in all three renderings of Jesus' statement. However, Crossan does not explore the possible significance of the choice of 'house' (*beth/oikos*) instead of 'temple'/'holy place' (*miqdash/hagion*) when discussing Jesus' action in the temple (Mk. 11, 15-19). Yet the citation from Isaiah that Mark attributes to Jesus in that context – 'my *house* shall be called a *house* of prayer for all nations' (Isa. 56, 7) – refers to the prophet's radical admission of gentiles to the altar with all the implications of such an action for the conventional temple worship. Thus, Jesus' use of spatial imagery calls for further investigation since it has several possible levels of reference – political, social and religious. As discussed previously, the imperial and/or the Herodian houses are destined for eschatological destruction in Jesus' view, and the reference to 'your house' in the lament for Jerusalem suggests that the temple was under judgement also. At the same time Jesus' use of familial imagery to describe the group of permanent followers with the Twelve at its centre (Mk. 3, 34), indicates a different understanding of Israel as a household, among whom kinship values of caring and community would be the norm. Such a broader understanding, indicated by the use of the term 'house', goes some distance towards explaining the vehemence of Jesus' action and saying. It would mean that his conception of the temple was radically different to the prevailing one, and that already in his Galilean ministry it was under attack insofar as a new image of Israel was being proposed, with definite implications for the nature of the temple community. Nevertheless, the saying about destroying the temple seems to have the physical building in its sights, and it is important to pursue the question further in the light of this consideration also.

Relations with the gentiles was a particular problem in the Galilean context, and it has been encountered more than once in this study. In dealing with the question of the admission of gentiles to the restored Israel it was suggested that Jesus was unlikely to have encouraged those who might have been inclined to take Isaiah literally, thereby seeking to claim their rights to offer sacrifices (not just gift offerings) in the Jerusalem temple, as envisaged by the prophet (Isa. 56.7). Such a frontal attack on the existing system could only have lead to violence and bloodshed.[6] What the eschatological temple was supposed to represent, at least as viewed within the Isaian trajectory, was the establishment of peace and harmony between all the children of the earth. While definite echoes of this hope can be heard in such writings as 1 Enoch (10.21, 90.28–90.38, 91.14, 100.6, 104.12–105.2) and the Sibylline Oracles (3.715), it is in the Jesus-movement alone that one finds any attempt to realize that dream. 'Galilee of the Gentiles' with its ambivalent connotations for many first-century Jews – symbol of hostility (1 Macc. 5.15) or beacon of hope for Jew and non-Jew alike (Isa. 8.23) – was the appropriate place for such a movement to appear. However, for its realization to actually take root it needed to be expressed and recognized at the centre also. Jesus had consistently refused to participate in any violent reclaiming of Israel's institutions in the name of his own eschatological vision, opting instead for the servant-role as depicted by Isaiah, and therefore leaving the future of the kingdom in God's hands. In dealing with the presence of Roman imperialism, his strategy was to rely on the power of symbolic speech and action. The same was likely to have been true in his 'attack' on the misappropriation of the religious symbols of his own tradition also, when existing practices were viewed from the perspective of his apocalyptic/eschatological awareness.

Isaiah was not the only prophet to have looked forward to an eschatological temple as part of Israel's restoration hopes. Ezekiel provides the most detailed account of such a building within the restored tribal territory (Ezck. 40–48). In direct contrast to Isaiah, however, he excludes all foreigners from any participation in the Jerusalem cult (Ezck. 44.6–9) and the resident aliens (*gerim*) are co-opted to become subject to Israelite law (Ezck. 47.23). His position was to prove highly influential among later Second Temple groups. The Book of Jubilees, a mid-second-century BCE reworking of Genesis, has close affinities with what later can be described as Essene ideas. In his world map of all the nations of the earth (Jub. 8.10–9.15), the author expands Ezekiel's notion of Jerusalem as the navel of the earth (Ezck. 38.12; cf. 5.5) by placing it at the centre of the territory of Shem, the most favoured of the sons of Noah, among whom the earth is divided. Shem is especially favoured because 'the Lord would dwell where Shem resided' (Jub. 7.12). Mt. Zion is described as 'the centre of the navel of the earth' and is situated between the Garden of Eden, described as the 'holy of holies' and Mt. Sinai, which is in the desert, 'three holy places one facing the other' (Jub. 8.12–21, especially v. 19). This linking of Zion, not only with Sinai, but with the Garden of Eden, is reflected in the manner in which the figure of Abraham of the Genesis account is changed to a Zion-centred exclusivist perspective. Abraham is here opposed to idolatry and the special covenant that was made with Israel is dated to him. His circumcision was expressive of true faithfulness, 'an eternal ordinance written in the heavenly tablets' (Jub. 15.23–32).[7]

Jubilees reflects the immediate aftermath of the reform of Antiochus and the desecration of the Jerusalem temple, so that its conservative attitude on the issue of the gentiles is, perhaps, understandable. A century later, the Psalms of Solomon, especially Ps. 17, is a response to Pompey's takeover of Jerusalem and his entry into the holy place in 67 BCE. It envisages the holy city being purged from all gentiles and the nations subjected to Israel's rule (Pss. of Sol. 17.20, 28, 30). It is among the Qumran sect that these xenophobic attitudes find their most extreme expression. Thus, 4Q Florilegium (4Q 174) declares that into the house which Yahweh will establish (Exod. 15.17f.) 'never will enter the Ammonite, the Moabite or the Bastard, or the foreigner or the proselyte, never, because there he will reveal his holy ones'. So absolute is the position adopted here that it could easily be read as a direct counter to the openness of Isa. 56.7 and the claims of those who were inspired by it. 11Q Temple Scroll is no more yielding on the subject of gentiles offering sacrifice in the temple. In the detailed plan of the temple put forward by this work the outer court is solely for women, unlike the Herodian temple, where the outer court was divided by a low wall that carried warning inscriptions, threatening the penalty of death for any gentile who might pass beyond that point (*JW* 5.193; *JA* 15.17).[8] This has given rise to the notion that there was 'a courtyard of the gentiles' in that temple, even though no ancient source mentions one. The wall and the inscription at least indicate that gentiles had been given some limited access to the temple area, but there is no question of their being able to approach the altar of sacrifice as Isaiah had foreseen.

The Temple in an Eschatological Setting

It has previously been suggested that Jesus was deeply influenced by Isaiah, both in regard to his understanding of God and his espousal of aspects of the image of the servant figure for his own role and that of his community. Might this same influence explain his attitude towards the Jerusalem temple, especially in the light of the more pressing issue in a Galilean setting of the place of the gentiles in the eschatological community that he believed was being inaugurated by his own ministry? Would their partial admission or exclusion – depending on what side of the dividing wall one stood – have in itself been sufficient to explain his extreme reaction of symbolically destroying the temple? The ingenuity of modern exegetes has been tested to the limits in deciphering the precise intention associated with the various actions attributed to Jesus in the different accounts – overturning of the tables of the money-changers and the seats of those who sold doves, driving out those who bought and sold in the temple courtyard, and forbidding anything to be carried through the temple and driving out the sheep and the cattle (Mk. 11.15f.;

Jn. 2.15f.). Do all these measures cohere? Are they all attributable to Jesus? What do they imply about temple practices? Rather than surveying the various opinions that have been put forward and adding to the suggestions, it is better to examine their overall thrust. Clearly, any one of these measures would seriously impair the functioning of the temple. However, as Sanders insists, on the hypothesis that the action and the declaration about destroying the temple go together, Jesus' attack was not about reforming the present practices. In that event one would expect the attack to be directed towards the priests and other temple officials. Instead, the attack is against the sacrificial system itself, insofar as the trade that was required for it to function was being abolished.

At first sight then, such an attitude would not seem to have been prompted by Isaiah's vision for the eschatological temple, since that envisaged gentiles actually performing priestly actions on the altar (Isa. 56.7, 66.21). Nevertheless, it seems important to explore the underlying implications of such a radical position. Rethinking the role of the temple and its functioning within an eschatological framework that included the full admission of gentiles, had given rise to a different understanding of God in the case of Isaiah. Does a similar shift of theological perspective play a role in Jesus' case also? Previously, it seemed permissible to postulate for him a more open attitude to gentiles than that of some of his Galilean co-religionists, yet there was no indication that they were the primary focus of his attention during the Galilean ministry. Perhaps, therefore, Crossan was correct in seeing Jesus' reaction in the temple as a sudden outburst because of its attitude towards the marginalized, in direct opposition to his own views of how things should be in the restored Israel. Not merely were gentiles kept at a safe distance, but women also were only allowed into the outer court. Yet in Jesus' circles women were admitted to his core group, it would seem, even if we do not hear their voices very often. While on the face of it Crossan's explanation does justice to the sudden and uncharacteristic nature of Jesus' action, it seems less than fully satisfying against the background of the discussion regarding the eschatological temple in contemporary sources.

One piece of evidence that may have particular relevance in this connection is the description of Enoch's revelatory experience in the so-called Book of the Watchers (1 Enoch 12–14).[9] There Enoch's heavenly journey and throne vision within the heavenly temple serve to confirm the judgement which he had already communicated to the Watchers of Heaven. This had entailed a severe sentence against them because of their sins in having intercourse with the daughters of men and revealing the secrets of heaven. This mythological story is based on the enigmatic episode of the fallen angels in Gen. 6.1–5, and is used here to explain the origins of evil in the world. Unable as they are 'to raise their eyes to heaven because of their sins', the Watchers ask Enoch, described as a 'scribe of righteousness', to intercede for them. He went and 'sat down by the waters of Dan – in Dan, which is southwest of Hermon' (1 Enoch 13.7), and engaged in reading the 'memorial prayers' until he fell asleep and experienced his dream vision. Whereas earlier in the narrative the Watchers are purely mythological characters, their identity as priests of the sanctuary becomes clearer in their discussion with Enoch, and their condemnation echoes other similar ones in the literature (Ezck. 9; Pss. of Sol. 8.11–15; CD 5.6–7): 'They have abandoned the high, holy and eternal heaven and slept with women and defiled themselves with the daughters of the people' when in fact they should have been 'interceding on behalf of men' (1 Enoch 15.2–4). Enoch's vision of the heavenly temple is so awe-inspiring that he cannot describe it in detail. It is a great house built on white marble which led to a second house, 'greater than the former', within which there was 'a lofty throne' and the Great Glory was sitting on it, wearing a gown 'brighter than the Sun' (1 Enoch 14.8–25). Within the dynamics of an apocalyptic myth, the vision is intended to reassure the circles that revered the figure of Enoch and his wisdom that the wicked priests would indeed be punished, but it also serves to confirm Enoch's wisdom and the righteousness that he teaches.

The possible significance of this vision for understanding Jesus' attack on the temple arises from its location in upper Galilee, a region which he also visited. The unusually specific description of the location and the procedure that Enoch went through in his preparation for the dream vision might well suggest that a mystic cult group existed in the region, as George Nickelsburg has tentatively suggested.[10] A bilingual inscription which reads in the Greek version, 'to the God who is in Dan', shows that worship continued there in Hellenistic times, long after the destruction of the Israelite shrine. That the author is critical of the temple establishment is certainly clear and the vision of the heavenly temple serves to suggest an alternative to the existing one. In this connection the choice of Dan is particularly ironic, since from an official point of view it was an illegitimate sanctuary associated with Jeroboam, the initiator of the schism between north and south in the ninth century (Judg. 17–19; 1 Kgs. 12.30). The setting for the vision might well have been chosen for polemical reasons, therefore, directed against the Jerusalem cult and its claims to be the sole centre of Yahweh worship. Even though it is difficult to offer a precise date for the Book of the Watchers, that suggested by Nickelsburg, prior to the death of Judas Maccabaeus, would point to the difficulties surrounding the restored priesthood after Antiochus' reform. As mentioned in the previous chapter, apocalyptic scenarios had a long 'shelf life' and there is evidence that Enoch's vision has influenced the Testament of Levi, itself also an attack on abuses among the Jerusalem priesthood, while profiling the eschatological high-priest to come. Of particular interest is the fact that Levi's call to the priesthood is also a dream vision on a high mountain (TLevi 2, 5f.). Could it be that a first-century Jewish prophet was also acquainted with this visionary tradition connected with upper Galilee and that this also played a role in developing his views on the Jerusalem temple and its personnel?

The answer to such a question must necessarily be extremely tentative, but the hypothesis raises again the purpose of Jesus' journeys to the villages of Cæsarea Philippi, since Dan is approximately 3 kilometres west of the site of that city. In the earlier discussions of that journey a possible visit to Hermon was not ruled out, given the character of the sacred mountain in the Jewish tradition also, as well as its ecological importance for Galilean life. Dew from Hermon had both spiritual and material significance for Galilean Jews, and their belief in the creator God as the giver of such blessings meant that the two aspects were inextricably bound together. Mark's mention of the villages of Cæsarea Philippi is tantalisingly vague and there is no explicit link with either Hermon itself or Dan. However, the visionary connection of the region seems to have been picked up by Matthew with the special commendation of Peter, whose confession of Jesus' messianic status is attributed to a special revelation (Mt. 16.16–18). Mark also seems to be aware of the links between the two locations, since he juxtaposes the confession about Jesus' identity on the way to the region with the scene of the Transfiguration on a high mountain (Mk. 8.27, 9.2). While no direct connection can be posited between Mark and Enoch, the apocalyptic tenor of the transfiguration story, especially its links with Dan 10, has long been noted by commentators. The brightness of Jesus' garb as well as the instruction by the voice from heaven 'to listen to him' correspond to Enoch's vision of the Great Glory and the acknowledgement that he is 'a scribe of righteousness'. If this Markan story is to be regarded as a transposed post-Resurrection story, as is frequently claimed, then at least Mark's association of the mount of revelation with an upper Galilean location is surely of some significance, pointing to his awareness of the symbolic importance of the region in terms of Jesus' Galilean ministry and its criticism of the Jerusalem temple's control of access to God's presence.

This discussion of the Galilean setting of Enoch's vision and its implications for Jesus' career add another element to a 'thick' description of his 'attack' on the temple. He, like Enoch, engaged in prayer in lonely places and he also enjoyed apocalyptic visionary experiences. His dissatisfaction with the existing temple did not have to await a journey to Jerusalem, therefore. The apocalyptic framework within which he operated provided him with an alternative symbolic universe within which the temple would have a very different function to that which currently operated. Unlike Jubilees, 1 Enoch has a universalist outlook in all sections of this composite work, but of particular significance for the discussion is the so-called Animal Apocalypse, because of the author's use of animal imagery for humans (1 Enoch 83–90). This account of Enoch's vision presupposes the earlier one from the Book of the Watchers, except that now he sees the transformation of the ancient house whose parts were all dismantled and taken away, only to be replaced by a new house which 'the Lord of the sheep' (the God of Israel) brought, 'new and greater than the first' (1 Enoch 90.28f.). The old house is to be removed because it was polluted from the very beginning and the sheep became dim-witted and their shepherds devoured them, so that they were scattered among the wild beasts (the gentiles) (1 Enoch 89.73–77). To this new house, however, Enoch sees those sheep who had survived as well as all the other animals and birds (the foreign nations) flocking, and making peace with each other (1 Enoch 90.30–35). Here the new temple has become a symbol for the reconciliation of all peoples before the God of Israel who has come down to them, and the concern about who might be allowed to offer sacrifices has disappeared from view.[11]

While the Jesus tradition too was familiar with the image of the sheep from the house of Israel who were lost (Mt. 10.5, 15.24), and the same image provides the raw material for one of his parables

(Lk. 15.4–6; Mt. 18.12f.; cf. also Jn. 10.1–18), it is the symbolic significance of the temple as the gathering place for Israel and the nations that is most suggestive. Could it be that Jesus' symbolic actions were performed because in his view, there would be no sacrifice in the eschatological temple, thus sharing the opinion of the author of the Animal Apocalypse, if not his views on the militant role attributed to the righteous? Sanders is uneasy about the notion of the temple being transformed from a place of sacrifice to one of prayer, as suggested by the Markan citation of Isa. 56.7, because it smacks of later Christian denigrating of Jewish religious practices. However, the Isaian reference to prayer along with sacrifices in Isa. 56.7 represents for Blenkinsopp a 'notable shift of emphasis' from the time of the kingdoms.[12] Prayer was an important element in the piety of visionary circles as evidenced by Daniel and Enoch, and apparently, Jesus also belonged to a similar tradition. This is not to ignore the fact that prayers accompanied the offering of various sacrifices in the temple, but it does point to the development of an alternative tradition among pious Jews, indicating that direct access to the divine was possible independently of the temple and its religious practices.

As a disciple of, and fellow-practitioner with John, of a baptism which apparently offered God's forgiveness independently of the temple rituals, Jesus had already distanced himself from the more essential redemptive media of his own religious tradition, such as sin-offerings and Yom-Kippur rituals. His creation-centred theology as reflected in the parables and other sayings suggested that the divine presence could be discovered in the everyday of people's lives and work. Isaiah had introduced a critical note to the 'Zionization' of God by assuring those who trembled at his word and who had been expelled from the cult, that the heavens were his throne and the earth his footstool, so that no house or place of rest was required for him (Isa. 66.1–4). This assurance was given in the context of the creation of a new heaven and a new earth, thereby eliminating the sense of God's withdrawal from an evil world that had infected so much of Second Temple Jewish thought (Isa. 65.17, 66.22). The 'globalization' of Israel's God had taken on a further dimension in the apocalyptic literature of resistance by highlighting Yahweh's kingship in opposition to various imperial powers, and Jesus participated in that image also.

These various strands provide a broader and richer set of associations for Jesus' word and deed against the temple, without in any sense removing him from his own tradition as this had been articulated by prophetic voices, Isaiah in particular, and had found further expression in later Jewish writings. It was a potent mix of wisdom and apocalyptic, creation and restoration, and Jesus' particular synthesis of the various strands, allied to his passionate concern for the poor, who had been marginalized by the temple system, help to make the incident both predictable and intelligible, but also a highly dangerous undertaking. Against this background one does not have to search too far for good evidence linking the incident with the arrest and death. Symbols speak to those with ears to hear, and in Jesus' case nobody, least of all the temple authorities and their retainers, could have been in any doubt as to what he was up to and why.

A Martyr's Death?

Mark, or his source, has combined a citation from the prophet Jeremiah with that from Isaiah, which he places on the lips of Jesus as commentary on his action in the temple. Instead of 'the house of prayer' for all nations that Isaiah had predicted, the temple had become 'a den of thieves', as Jeremiah had described the Jerusalem temple of his day (Mk. 11.17; Jer. 7.11). The cross-reference to Jeremiah is highly significant for a better understanding of Jesus also. His action in the temple is best understood as a symbolic act matching the word against the temple and his own role in its destruction. Of all the prophets, Jeremiah stands out as the master of the symbolic action to match the prophetic word. He is the one writing prophet whose personal biography becomes deeply inter-twined with his message, as Von Rad has noted.[13] While he did not suffer the ultimate fate, the combination of his actions and his words so incensed his contemporaries that they plotted to kill him:

> ' "Come on," they said, "let us concoct a plot against Jeremiah; the priest will not run short of instruction without him, nor the sage of advice, nor the prophet of the word. Come on let us hit at him with his own tongue; let us listen carefully to every word he says" '. (Jer. 18.18)

A Prophetic Forerunner?

Previously, Jeremiah had warned his contemporaries against a misplaced trust in Yahweh's presence in the temple, without any care for the ethical dimension of Israel's covenant obligations. The prophet relays Yahweh's invitation to them to go and visit the shrine of Shiloh 'where first I made my name to dwell' lying in ruins (Jer. 7.12). This incident receives a fuller treatment later in the book where again the ruined shrine from early Israel (Josh. 19.51; Judg. 21.12–21) is alluded to, leading to a formal decision: 'The priests and the prophets then addressed the officials and all the people: "This man deserves to die since he has prophesied against the city, as you have heard with your own ears" ' (Jer. 26.11f.). The sequel presents the reaction of the crowd, accepting Jeremiah's word as the word of Yahweh, and rejecting the call for his death, and thus he escapes with his life. In their response the people point to a pattern of such prophetic interventions, uttering the same call – Micah from Moresheth (cf. Mic. 3.12) and Uriah of Kiriath-jearim. This pattern was still continued in the first century CE, as previously noted, most notably in the figure of Jesus, son of Ananias, shortly before the first revolt. Jesus of Nazareth's repeated call to Jerusalem, as reflected in the Q saying and climaxing in the temple incident, was not without a well-remembered precedent, therefore.

Much had changed, however, in the period between Jeremiah's railings against syncretistic worship in the sixth century BCE and Jesus' dramatic action in the first century CE. The most notable difference between the two episodes is that whereas Jeremiah was operating within the context of an independent, though fragile Judah, soon to be taken over by the Babylonians, Jesus lived in Roman Palestine, dominated by imperial values as these were mediated by the Herodian dynasty. Successive foreign regimes had changed irrevocably the character and ethos of Judean life, and nowhere was this change more frequently registered and more keenly felt than with regard to the temple and its personnel at the religio-political centre of the nation. In Jesus' day, the architectural extension and enhancement of the courtyards and the splendid refurbishment of the sanctuary building gave outward expression to the radical transformation of the temple-system that had taken place and the values that now operated.[14]

Herod's lavish project with regard to the temple is often seen as his way of placating Jewish religious sensibilities. This judgement is not an adequate explanation, however, since he had introduced into Jerusalem other aspects of the gentile way of life, such as the amphitheatre, without any compunction (*JA* 15.268). His intentions are better understood as self-glorification in the best Hellenistic style by endowing Jerusalem with a temple that could match those of other great temple-cities of the east such as Palmyra, Jerash and Petra. He thus hoped to win good-will and admiration from the far-flung Jewish Diaspora, as well as recognition from his Roman patrons, who were not at all ill-disposed to religious shrines, provided they did not become centres of anti-Roman dissidence (*JA* 16.62–65).

This change in the symbolic status of the Jerusalem temple under Herodian patronage within the larger Roman world throws the magnitude of Jesus' symbolic action/word into bolder relief. Jeremiah's words were a reminder to his co-religionists that religious worship, devoid of ethical sincerity were valueless in the sight of Yahweh. Jesus' action, while affirming that aspect of prophetic insight, also represented a throwing down of the gauntlet to the imperial power that basked in the reflected glory of this extraordinary architectural statement. The enormity of the challenge was not lost on the author of the Fourth Gospel who places on the lips of Jesus' opponents the rhetorical question: 'It has taken forty-six years to build this sanctuary; will you rebuild it in three days?' (Jn. 2.20). The same commentator was later to acknowledge the political implications of Jesus' signs, most of them to do with the temple and its symbolism, by having the chief priests and the Pharisees complain: 'If we let him go on in this way, everybody will believe in him and the Romans will come and destroy our place [temple] and our nation' (Jn. 11.48). When one peels away the polemical irony of these statements, reflecting late first-century CE conflicts between the Johannine community and the synagogue, it is still possible to hear echoes of a keen awareness of the political as well as the religious implications of Jesus' attitude towards the temple. Johannine irony is always based in the real world and history often turns out to be deeply ironic.

Understanding Jesus' Death

Jesus cannot have been unaware of the consequences of his symbolic action for his own future. If, as Josephus claims (*JA* 18.118), his mentor John had met his death because of the potential threat to law and order of his preaching in remote Perea, he could scarcely have hoped for a lesser fate within the tinder-box that was the Jerusalem temple. While one must avoid psychologizing his intentions, it is a legitimate, if somewhat unfashionable, historical question to enquire as to what Jesus' possible attitudes to his impending death might have been, in the light of the overall contours of his ministry as these have been argued throughout this study. Or to put the question that has been posed more than once previously, how might a Galilean eschatological prophet have been inspired by his own tradition to face death in Jerusalem? In the two previous chapters the servant figure of Isaiah and the *maskilim* or wise ones of Daniel emerged as productive analogues for understanding aspects of Jesus and his group's stance. Indeed it would seem that Daniel's portrait of the *maskilim* had the figure of Isaiah's servant as its inspiration. Both include images of heroic acceptance of death, based on a confident hope in Yahweh's vindication. How helpful might this prove for understanding Jesus' approach to his death also?

As is well known, the historical questions surrounding Jesus' death are fraught with difficulties, because of the theological, apologetic and legal questions that the Passion narratives raise.[15] At least the fact that Jesus died by crucifixion is widely accepted, even if the full implications of this Roman form of execution are not always fully explicated.[16] Such a firm conclusion, need not, nor in my opinion, should not, exclude the involvement of the Jewish priestly aristocracy also, especially in view of the role they, like other native aristocracies in the East, were expected to play in maintaining the Roman peace.[17] However, in holding this opinion one should also fully acknowledge that the gospels' portrayal of Jewish involvement is seriously biased towards exonerating the Romans and blaming the Jews in general, rather than a particular element of the people. The fact is that Jesus was not the first Jew to have come to a violent end within his own community for espousing dissident religious views.[18] In this regard Jews were no different from other ethnic groups in antiquity for whom religious orthodoxy was seen as an expression of group loyalty that had to be safeguarded at all costs by those charged with maintaining a separate identity.

The theological implications of the Passion narratives are twofold. Firstly, the generalizing tendencies with regard to the Jewish involvement, especially in the First and Fourth Gospels, has promoted the charge of deicide being levelled at the whole Jewish people in later anti-Jewish, Christian polemic. This is a gross distortion of the historical facts, in view of the collaboration of interest, if not of sympathy, between the Roman provincial administration and the Jewish priestly aristocracy. The probability must be that they also collaborated in having Jesus removed. The same Jerusalem elite, it should be noted, had little compunction in advising Galilean pilgrims who were outraged at the murder by Samaritans of one of their members on his way to a festival in Jerusalem, not to cause a riot, 'but to take pity on the country and the sanctuary, their wives and children also, all of whom were in danger for the sake of avenging a single Galilean' (*JW* 2.237). For Jewish elites and Roman provincials alike, Galileans who were deemed to be troublesome in Jerusalem were utterly expendable (Lk. 13.1f.).

The second theological problem arising from the Passion stories is the tendency to read what are highly charged theological statements as though they were historical facts. Of course this is true with other parts of the gospels also, but the problem is accentuated in the case of the Passion stories since the Pauline theology of the cross was such a powerful influence in Christian theology and devotion in explaining the death of Jesus as an atoning sacrifice for the sins of the world (Rm. 3.21–31, 4.25, 5.1–11). Owing to this influence of later theology, the tendency has been, most shockingly of late in the movie *The Passion of the Christ*, to attribute to the historical Jesus a similar understanding of his death. This has had the effect not only that the charge of deicide could be levelled at Jews who are deemed to have murdered God's son, but that the purpose of Jesus' life is viewed as having solely to do with his death. It is clear that the death of Jesus did raise serious questions for his followers who continued to expect God's glorious reign to emerge in all its splendour, despite Jesus' teaching to the contrary, and they certainly were not disposed to accept the idea of a criminal's death in Jerusalem.

Thus, from a very early stage, the process of 'searching the Scriptures' in order to find meaning in this event became paramount. Paul tells us that he inherited the creedal formula, 'Christ died for our sins in accordance with the Scriptures', presumably when he joined the new movement (1 Cor. 15.3). He associates a similar understanding of Jesus' death with the celebration of the Lord's Supper, which he also inherited (1 Cor. 11.23–26). However, other circles seem to have adopted different models for seeing positive value in Jesus' death, most notably, those who continued the tradition of Jesus' sayings, which eventually crystallized in the Q document originating among a group of early believers, possibly in Galilee. Recent scholarship has sought to stress the fact that this document also should be labelled 'Gospel' in that it too presented a version of the career of Jesus which was 'good news' without having any Passion story as its conclusion.[19] For these early followers of Jesus, his words were understood as the words of Wisdom incarnate (Mt. 11.25–27; Lk. 10.21–22) and his death could be understood in the more general context of the trial, persecution and death of a wise man.[20] According to Nickelsburg, it is possible to identify such a literary genre within the Wisdom tradition, which includes the trial, death and vindication of the wise one. Elements of this genre are to be found in such writings as Daniel chs. 3 and 6; WisSol. 2–5; 2 Macc. 7 and Gen. 37–39.[21] The significance of such a conclusion for our present discussion of the historical Jesus' expectation of his own death, would be to suggest that if his first followers can be shown not to have had a definitive blueprint in advance for understanding his death, and so could develop different models from a very early stage of the post-Easter community, then it is unlikely that Jesus himself had made any clear or definitive statement on the matter.

Such a conclusion need not, however, undermine the working hypothesis of this study, namely, that the historical Jesus saw his career in the light of his own inherited religious tradition and that he was inspired by particular aspects of that tradition in the choices which he made during his public ministry. In suggesting that the suffering servant of Isaiah and the *maskilim* of Daniel were likely background figures for Jesus' public ministry, the argument was not based on a one-to-one correspondence between the prophetic texts and aspects of Jesus' ministry, including his death. Jesus was no literalist even in dealing with the most sensitive and pertinent aspects of his own tradition. Even those earlier scholars who maintained direct influence on Jesus' understanding of his death of Isa. 53, especially v. 10f., with its reference to the servant's death as a 'sin offering', have had to acknowledge that instances of direct verbal links are rare and uncertain.[22] What is being proposed in this study is that such images provided significant analogues for Jesus' public ministry, and that there are sufficient indicators in its broad contours for the claim that they played a decisive role in shaping key aspects of that ministry, including, I believe, acceptance of the inevitability of his death.

The development of the 'biography' of the servant figure within the prophetic book – from prophet servant with a mission to Israel and the nations (Isa. 49) to suffering servant, whose life and example generated a following of servants (Isa. 53) who continued the lifestyle and values of the original figure, thereby winning the commendation of Yahweh, but exclusion by their fellows who gloried in the triumphant Zion ideology (Isa. 61, 65 and 66) – this development corresponds with that of the basis-biography, with its genuine historical intention in regard to Jesus' life, which was posited in the opening chapter of this study. The correspondence extends beyond the outline to the shared values of both the servant and Jesus – openness to outsiders, critique of wealth and rejection of triumphalist attitudes arising from God's vindication of Israel's case. In the final analysis the correspondences are based on a shared belief in the creator God whose care extends to all his creation and who will vindicate those who seek to witness to that care in their lives. The *maskilim* of Daniel were an important link in the chain of reception of this ideal for a restored Israel within the Second Temple's chequered history of competing ideologies of restoration and different strategies of resistance to imperial powers. They sought to instruct the many in righteousness in a time of severe crisis, and faced with the threat of violent destruction, they persisted in their particular way of faithfulness to the covenant values, eschewing the allurement of either violent revolution or instant martyrdom. Like the servant who will be raised very high, their hope too was to enjoy astral immortality, shining like the stars for ever (Dan. 11.31–33; 12.2–3).

It is this strand of Jewish non-violent resistance with its critique of both religious and political imperialism that would appear best to characterize the particular aspects of the Jesus-movement that we can discern behind the different versions of the gospels' narratives in both their Galilean and Jerusalem situations. The term martyr is not used of Jesus himself within the New Testament, with the sole, but important, exception of the Book of Revelation of John, where he is described as the *pistos martys*, 'the faithful witness' (Rev. 1.5), the circumstances of whose death had inspired others to resist imperial Rome in the province of Asia Minor towards the end of the first century CE. In the subsequent heavenly vision of the seer they are described as 'those who have come out of the great ordeal; they have washed their robes in the blood of the lamb' – a great throng, representative of both the twelve tribes of Israel and every nation, tribe and tongue (Rev. 7.5–17). In Luke's gospel, written about the same time, we can see the beginnings of the transition in the semantics of the word *martys*, with its forensic connotation of witness in a law-court to a more general meaning of publicly attesting to one's convictions even when confronted with hostile reaction, and in this sense it could well be applied to Jesus also.[23]

This transition within early Christianity from the more typical terminology for missionary endeavours – *kerysein* and *eyangelizesthai*, 'to herald' and 'to announce good news' – to the more ominous idea of witnessing, suggests a background of growing Roman awareness of the threat which the new movement posed. The Fourth Gospel also speaks repeatedly of Jesus 'bearing witness (*martyrein*) to the truth', and while this is usually in the context of polemics against the Jews, Jesus' coming can also be described as the *krisis*/crisis-judgement of the world (Jn. 9.39). Soon the term martyr would return to its original setting of the law-courts where Christians would be tried before local magistrates for refusing to worship the emperor and condemn Christ. Thereafter it has been preserved in Church circles solely for those who in fact have sealed their commitment to Christ with their blood in contexts of oppression and violence. In these circumstances, Christ has become the object of the witnessing rather than the witness, yet the term encapsulates well his apocalyptically inspired challenge to both Roman imperialism and the collaboration with it of the Jewish religious aristocracy of his own day. Jesus did not opt for the more glamorous modes of resistance of some of his contemporaries, such as those who took their lives at Masada, rather than submit to Rome.[24] He chose the way of the *maskilim*, teaching the many righteousness and trusting in God to make things right. He would render to God what was God's, and leave it to the creator God to make all things new.

EPILOGUE: RETURN TO GALILEE

Contextual plausibility as formulated by Gerd Theissen provided the key for reading the Jesus-story. This allows Jesus and his movement to take their place within the variegated setting of different communities of interpretation which had been generated by the reception of the Hebrew Scriptures of the Second Temple period. Contextual plausibility does not mean that Jesus should be made to conform to any one of the known groups of first-century Palestine, but implies only that 'positive connections can be established between the Jesus tradition and the Jewish context'. The criterion does not, therefore, exclude Jesus' own selection and reworking of various aspects of that shared tradition. Rather, it implies a distinctive and personal approach that was occasioned by the circumstances of both the Galilean and Judean social and religious worlds as he encountered them in his role as a prophet of restoration during the reign of Antipas.

The closing injunction of Mark's gospel that the disciples should 'go back to Galilee' (Mk. 16.7) indicates that the region continued to play an important role in the post-Easter memory of Jesus' followers. While various scholars have argued for a Galilean setting for both Mark and Q, thereby providing a possible link between Jesus' first followers and later 'Galilean Christianity', there is, unfortunately, no clear evidence from the earliest phase of the new movement for such a development independently of the two works in question.[1] In his account of the development of the mission in Acts of the Apostles, a mission which was to extend from 'Jerusalem, in all Judea and Samaria, and to the end of the earth' (Acts 1.8), Luke merely mentions Galilee in passing (Acts 9.31). However, this virtual silence need not be interpreted to suggest either lack of interest or information about the Jesus-movement there. Following Roman administrative nomenclature, Luke may have included Galilee in his reference to 'all Judea' since in his day the region was part of the extended province of Judea in the wake of the first Jewish revolt, whereas during Jesus' lifetime it was recognized as the independently ruled tetrarchy of Antipas. Without dismissing the value of 'reading Q in Galilee' as suggested recently by John Kloppenborg, the methodological difficulty of extrapolating from intra-textual references to Galilean locations such as Corazin, Bethsaida and Caphernaum, to extra-textual communities of Jesus-followers in these places has been highlighted by literary critics who stress the 'fictional' character of all narratives, even history-writing.[2] The same objection would hold for attributing Mark's gospel to Galilean communities of Jesus' followers, simply because of its geographical references to the region and a general correspondence between the narrated social world and that which can be stipulated for first-century Galilee from archaeology and other sources such as Josephus.

Theissen's criterion includes the plausibility of effects as well as of context, and this may prove the safer route for exploring the continued importance of the Galilean Jesus for early Christianity in all its manifestations. E. P. Sanders has given his own version of this criterion when he suggests that any account of the historical Jesus which explains the origins of a movement in his name later, is inherently more plausible than one which does not see such an outcome as relevant.[3] Such a criterion insists on a greater role for memory in the development of early Christianity than that which has dominated the discussion since Bultmann's description of the sources for the historical Jesus' life and personality as fragmentary and legendary. The gulf that was thereby opened up between the *kerygma* about Jesus of the early preaching and the historical Jesus was only partially bridged by Bultmann's own students when Käsemann and others argued for the historical nature of the *kerygma*. For these 'new questers' the *kerygma* was related solely to the Pauline version of the cross and resurrection and did not take sufficient account of the earthly career of Jesus as a whole as an essential element of the early preaching.

That the career of Jesus in Galilee as well as its outcome in Jerusalem was important for the first Christians is borne out by the fact of its inclusion in the outline 'basis-biographie' of Acts 10.37–41, cited in the opening chapter of this book. This brief reference to Galilee is a pointer to the importance of Jesus' Galilean ministry, as more expanded written accounts were developed, either of the Markan or the Q variety. The tenacity of interest in the past of Jesus continued to assert itself as other tendencies of developing faith in him as the risen Lord and Saviour pulled in the opposite direction. The bitter disputes in the Johannine community reflected in the First Epistle are a clear indication of the resistance to such trends, even in a community which itself had developed the most elevated understanding of Jesus within early Christianity. It was not just a matter of confessing that Jesus was the Christ and that he had come in the flesh (1 Jn. 2.22, 4.2–3), but of walking in the light as he had walked (1 Jn. 3.3.7). Living a life as Jesus had lived his became an essential component of the early Christian *kerygma*; orthopraxis, or proper behaviour, became as important as, indeed was an expression of, orthodoxy or right belief.

This was a message that was as important for Christians in Rome, Asia Minor and elsewhere in the Mediterranean world as it was for those communities of Jesus' followers who may have regrouped in Galilee after his death. The demand for written accounts of Jesus' life and their early and wide dissemination suggests that while these writings may have originated in particular local settings, the process of textualization of the oral tradition meant that these early 'lives' of Jesus travelled as the movement itself travelled. Remembering Jesus was not just a matter of recalling the past but of probing its meaning more deeply to meet the demands of new situations. Here again the emphasis on the role of memory in the Johannine community as expressed in Jn. 2.22 and Jn. 12.16 – the beginning and end of the description of Jesus' public ministry, according to the schema of the Fourth Gospel – is highly significant. There it suggests a process of reflection leading to a deepening appreciation of the events that they had experienced, and possibly points to a particular ethos of the group who stand behind this work, especially in the light of their understanding of the role of the Spirit to lead them into the fullness of truth. But they were not alone among the Jesus-groups in engaging in such a process of remembering Jesus, as the description of the eucharist as an *anamnesis* of Jesus clearly indicates. Such remembering included not only the account of his death but also his association with socially despised outsiders (Mk. 14.9). Perhaps the best indication of the central importance of the historical Jesus and his life's work for early Christian identity is the fact that pagan and Jewish detractors alike focused not just on the theological claims about Jesus but on aspects of his human life and conduct also. Origen's *Contra Celsum*, demonstrates that the process of vilification of aspects of Jesus' life and ministry as a form of counter-gospel was clearly well established by the second century CE, if not earlier still.

The suggestion of this book that Jesus had seen his own role in the light both of the servant of Yahweh and the *maskilim* of Daniel may provide some of the historical links between him and the movement that originated in his name which have been missing in many recent treatments which isolate him from both his Jewish heritage *and* his Christian reception. The remembering of Jesus that I have been postulating took place within a group or groups of followers who saw themselves as following him in precisely the same manner as the servants of the Lord of Isaiah and the *maskilim* of Daniel had understood themselves to be following in the footsteps of a particular figure whose life and death had inspired radical styles of resistance. For Jesus' first followers, therefore, 'Going back to Galilee' was neither an exercise of nostalgia nor a return to the everyday of their past lives, but a recalling of the mission and ministry that had challenged them initially in Galilee, and that was now about to make new and dangerous demands if they were to be true to the call of the rejected servant whom they believed had been exalted by God.

NOTES

Chapter 1

1 Albert Schweitzer, *The Quest of the Historical Jesus*, reprint of English translation W. Montgomery, New York: Macmillan, 1968; James M. Robinson, *A New Quest of the Historical Jesus*, London: SCM, 1959.

2 John Dominic Crossan, *The Historical Jesus, The Life of a Mediterranean Jewish Peasant*, Edinburgh: T&T Clark, 1991, xxviii.

3 John P. Meier, *A Marginal Jew. Rethinking the Historical Jesus*, 3 vols., The Anchor Bible Reference Library, New York and London: Doubleday, 1991, 1993, 2001. Here vol. 1, 4–6 and 21–31.

4 Sandra M. Schneiders, *The Revelatory Text. Interpreting the New Testament as Sacred Scripture*, New York: HarperCollins, 1991, 97–110.

5 Crossan, *The Historical Jesus*, xxx.

6 Rudolph Bultmann, *Jesus and the Word*, London: Collins, 1926, 14.

7 Ernst Käsemann, 'The Problem of the Historical Jesus' (1953) reprinted in *id.*, *Essays on New Testament Themes*, London: SCM Press, 1964, 15–47 (46).

8 Sean Freyne, 'Early Christian Imagination and the Gospels', in Charles Horton ed., *The Earliest Gospels. The Origin and Transmission of the Earliest Christian Gospel – the Contribution of the Chester Beatty Gospel Codex, P45, JSNTSS* 258, London: T&T Clark, 2004, 2–12.

9 Dirk Frikenschmidt, *Evangelium als Biographie. Die Vier Evangelien im Rahmen antiker Erzälkunst*, Tübingen: Franke Verlag, 1997, especially 192–209.

10 Steve Mason, *Life of Josephus. Translation and Commentary*, Leiden: Brill, 2001.

11 Sean Freyne, *Galilee from Alexander the Great to Hadrian. A Study of Second Temple Judaism*, Wilmington, DL: Michael Glazier, 1980 (reprint Edinburgh: T&T Clark, 2000).

12 S. F. G. Brandon, *Jesus and the Zealots*, Manchester: Manchester University Press, 1967; Geza Vermes, *Jesus the Jew*, London: Collins, 1973; F. G. Downing, *Cynics and Christian Origins*, Edinburgh: T&T Clark, 1992.

13 Walter Grundmann, *Jesus der Galiläer und das Judentum*, Leipzig: Georg Wigand, 1941, 175.

14 Sean Freyne, *Galilee, Jesus and the Gospels. Literary Approaches and Historical Investigations*, Dublin and Minneapolis: Gill-Macmillan and Augsburg, 1988.

15 Sean Freyne, 'The Geography of Restoration. Galilee-Jerusalem Relations in early Judaism and early Christianity', *NTS* 47(2001) 289–311.

16 Halvor Moxnes, *Putting Jesus in His Place. A Radical Vision of Household and Kingdom*, Louisville and London: Westminster John Knox Press, 2003, especially 1–21.

17 See the collection of essays in R. S. Sugirtharajah ed., *Voices from the Margin, Interpreting the Bible in the Third World*, London: SPCK, 1991.

18 Moxnes, *Putting Jesus in His Place*, 12.

19 Jonathan Z. Smith, *To Take Place*, Chicago: University of Chicago Press, 1992, 30.

20 Ernest Renan, *Vie de Jésus*, Paris: Michel Levy, 1863 (ET *The Life of Jesus*, Buffalo: Prometheus Books, 1991), 56f.

21 David Friedrich Strauss, *The Life of Jesus Critically Examined*, reprinted English translation, London: SCM, 1972, 264.

22 Susannah Heschel, *Abraham Geiger and the Jewish Jesus*, Chicago: Chicago University Press, 1998.

23 Gösta Lindeskog, *Die Jesusfrage im Neuzeitlichen Judentum*, reprint Darmstadt: Wissenschaftliche Buchgesellschaft, 1973; Werner Volger, *Jüdische Jesusinterpretation in christlicher Sicht*, Weimar: Herman Böhlaus, 1988.

24 Heschel, *Abraham Geiger*, 76–105.

25 Samuel Klein, *Galiläa von der Makkabäerseit bis 67*, Berlin, 1923. Adolf Büchler, *Die Priester und der Cultus im letzten Jahrzenten des Jerusalemishen Tempels*, Vienna, 1895; id., *The Political and Social Leaders of the Jewish Community of Sepphoris in the Second and Third Centuries*, Jewish College Publications 6, London, 1914.

26 Heschel, *Abraham Geiger*, 233–235.

27 E. P. Sanders, *Jesus and Judaism*, London: SCM Press, 1985; *Paul and Palestinian Judaism*, Philadelphia: Fortress Press, 1978.

28 Bruce D. Chilton, *A Galilean Rabbi and his Bible. Jesus' Use of the Interpreted Scripture of his Time*, Wilmington, DL: Michael Glazier, 1984.

29 Norman Perrin, *Rediscovering the Teaching of Jesus*, London: SCM Press, 1967, 39.

30 Gerd Theissen and Annette Merz, *The Historical Jesus. A Comprehensive Guide*, English translation, John Bowden, London: SCM Press, 115–118 (117).

31 John Dominic Crossan and Jonathan L. Reed, *Excavating Jesus. Beneath the Stones, Behind the Texts*, New York: HarperCollins, 2001, is an interesting combination of an archaeologist (Reed) and a literary historian (Crossan) collaborating on a book about the historical Jesus.

32   For a brief account of the history of Galilean scholarship, including archaeology of the region see Sean Freyne, *Galilee and Gospel, Selected Essays, WUNT* 125, Tübingen: J. C. B. Mohr, 2000, 1–26.

33   John J. Collins and Gregory E. Sterling eds., *Hellenism in the Land of Israel*, Notre Dame, IN: University of Notre Dame, 2001 and Lee I. Levine, *Judaism and Hellenism in Antiquity, Conflict or Confluence?* Peabody, MA: Hendrikson Publishers, 1998, are two up-to-date discussions of the issues.

34   Sean Freyne, 'Archaeology and the Historical Jesus', in Freyne, *Galilee and Gospel*, 160–182, especially 176–182; Jonathan Reed, *Archaeology and the Galilean Jesus. A Re-Examination of the Evidence*, Harrisburg, PA: Trinity Press, 2000, especially 23–61.

35   Richard A. Horsley, *Galilee. History, Politics, People*, Valley Forge, PA: Trinity Press, 1995; *id., Archaeology, History and Society in Galilee. The Social Context of Jesus and the Rabbis*, Valley Forge, PA: Trinity Press, 1996.

36   Rebecca Martin Nagy and Eric M. Meyers eds., *Sepphoris in Galilee. Crosscurrents of Culture*, Raleigh: North Carolina Museum of Modern Art, 1996; Eric M. Meyers ed., *Galilee through the Centuries. Confluence of Cultures*, Winona Lake, IN: Eisenbrauns, 1999.

37   Marianne Sawicki, *Crossing Galilee, Architectures of Contact in the Occupied Land of Jesus*, Harrisburg, PA: Trinity Press, 1998, 61–80 (68).

38   George W. E. Nickelsburg, *Ancient Judaism and Christian Origins. Diversity, Continuity and Change*, Minneapolis: Fortress Press, 2003, 10f.

39   Catherine Hezser, *Jewish Literacy in Roman Palestine, TSAJ* 81, Tübingen: J. C. B. Mohr, 2001.

40   For a discussion of oral memory with regard to the New Testament see Birger Gerhardsson, *Memory and Manuscript. Oral Tradition and Written Transmission in Rabbinic Judaism and Early Christianity*, Lund: G. W. K. Gleerup, 1961; Richard A. Horsley with Jonathan Draper, *Whoever Hears You Hears Me. Prophets, Performance and Tradition in Q*, Harrisburg, PA: Trinity Press, 1998, especially 125–150.

41   Bruce Chilton and Craig Evans, 'Jesus and Israel's Scriptures', in *id.* eds., *Studying the Historical Jesus. Evaluations of the State of Current Research*, Brill: Leiden, 1994, 281–336, is particularly pertinent to this study because of the discussion of Jesus' prophetic use of Scripture, especially 309–333.

Chapter 2

1   Gerhard Von Rad, *Old Testament Theology*, 2 vols., English translation, D. M. G. Stalker, Edinburgh: Oliver and Boyd, 1962, especially vol. I, and Oscar Cullmann, *Salvation in History*, English translation, Sidney G. Sowers, London: SCM Press, 1967, are influential examples of the concern with salvation history in both Old and New Testament studies.

2   As a representative of the influential Albright School, which combined biblical interpretation and archaeological investigation to highlight Israel's uniqueness, see George Ernest Wright, *The Old Testament Against its Environment*, London: SCM Press, 1950.

3   Arlene Miller Rosen, 'Paleoenvironmental Reconstruction', in Eric M. Meyers ed., *The Oxford Encyclopaedia of Archaeology in the Near East*, 5 vols., New York and Oxford: Oxford University Press, 1997, vol. 4, 200–205, is a good introduction to these developments in archaeology today with further bibliography.

4   Elizabeth Schüssler Fiorenza, *Jesus, Miriam's Child, Sophia's Prophet: Critical Issues in Feminist Christology*, New York: Crossroad, 1994; Ingrid Rosa Kitzberger ed., *Transformative Encounters. Jesus and Women Re-viewed*, Leiden: Brill, 2000; Kathleen E. Corley, *Women and the Historical Jesus. Feminist Myths of Christian Origins*, Santa Rosa, CA: Polebridge Press, 2002.

5   For a discussion of the connection between the instrumentalizing of nature and the domination of women in western thought, see eco-feminist philosopher Val Plumwood, *Feminism and the* Mastery *of Nature*, London and New York: Routledge, 1993, 41–68 (46f.).

6   Renan, *Vie de Jésus*, 39.

7   George Adam Smith, *The Historical Geography of the Holy Land*, London, 1924, 273.

8   Ps. 74.13–14,19; 89.9–10, 104.26; Isa. 27.1; Job 3.8, 7.12, 40.25f. In the Babylonian mythology of the Enuma Elish, Tiamat (the Deep) co-operated in the birth of the Gods only to be ousted in a revolt of the younger gods, led by Marduk. She responds by the creation of monsters but they were not able to defeat Marduk. The extent of the influence of this myth on the Israelite creation traditions is debated among scholars, even though there appears to be a shared world-view.

9   Claus Westerman, *Genesis 1–11. A Commentary*, Minneapolis: Augsburg Press, 1984; Bernhard Anderson ed., *Creation in the Old Testament*, London: SPCK, 1984.

10 Norman C. Habel, *The Land is Mine. Six Biblical Ideologies*, Overtures to Biblical Theology, Minneapolis: Fortress Press, 1995, 17–36.

11 Oded Borowski, *Agriculture in Iron Age Israel*, Boston, MA: American School of Oriental Research, 2002, 127.

12   Habel, *The Land is Mine*, 97–114.

13   *The Land is Mine*, 103f.

14   Von Rad, *Old Testament Theology*, I, 418–441 (419).

15   Lynn White Jr, 'The Historical Roots of our Ecological Crisis', *Science* 155(1967) 1203–1207, reprinted in S. Gottlieb ed., *The Sacred Earth. Religion, Nature and the Environment*, London: Routledge, 1996, 183–193.

16   Jacob Neusner, *Judaism. The Evidence of the Mishnah*, Chicago: Chicago University Press, 1981, 230–239.

17   Alan Avery-Peck, *Mishnah's Division of Agriculture. A History and Theology of Seder Zeraim*, Brown Judaic Series 79, Chico, Cal: Scholars Press, 1985, 15–20.

18   Menahen Stern, *Greek and Latin Authors on Jews and Judaism*, 3 vols., Jerusalem: The Israel Academy of Sciences and Humanities, 1976–84, vol. I, 288 and 469.

19   R. Frankel, N. Getzov, M. Aviam, A. Degani, *Settlement Dynamics and Regional Diversity in Ancient Upper Galilee*, IAA Reports, 14, Jerusalem: Israel Antiquities Authority, 2001, 1–8, especially 2f. on aerial photography of the region.

20   F. Lang, ' "Über Sidon mitten ins Gebiet der Dekapolis''. Geographie und Theologie in Markus 7, 31', *ZDPV* 94(1978) 145–160; T. Schmeller, 'Jesus im Umland Galiläas: zu den Markinischen Berichten vom Aufenthalt Jesu in den Gebieten von Tyros, Cæsarea Philippi und der Dekapolis', *BZ* 38(1994) 44–66.

21   Dean W. Chapman, 'Locating the Gospel of Mark: A Model of Agrarian Geography', *BTB* 25(1995) 24–37.

22   For a detailed discussion of all aspects of Jesus' relations to John see John P. Meier, *A Marginal Jew*, vol. II, 19–236, especially 42–56.

23   Sean Freyne, 'Jesus, Prayer and Politics', in L. Hogan and B. Fitzgerald eds., *Between Poetry and Politics*, Dublin: Columba Press, 2003, 67–85.

24   Borowski, *Agriculture in Iron Age Israel*, 128f.

25   D. H. K. Amiram, 'Sites and Settlements in the Mountains of Lower Galilee', *IEJ* 6(1956) 69–77.

26   J. Murphy-O'Connor, 'John the Baptist and Jesus', *NTS* 36(1990) 359–374.

27   As reported privately by Mr. Ros Voss, the archaeologist, conducting the excavation, 1999.

28   Reed, *Archaeology and the Galilean Jesus*, especially 23–61. M. Aviam, 'The Hasmonean Dynasty's Activities in Galilee', in *id Jews, Pagans and Christians in the Galilee*, Rochester, NY: University of Rochester Press, 2004, 41–50.

29 Sean Freyne, 'Jesus and the Urban Culture of Galilee', in *Galilee and Gospel, Selected Essays*, WUNT 215, Tübingen: J. C. B. Mohr, 2000, 183–207.

30 David Fiensy, *The Social History of Palestine in the Herodian Period*, Lewiston, NY: Edwin Mellon Press, 1991.

31 Z. Tzuk, 'The Water Installations at Sepphoris', in Nagy and Meyers eds., *Sepphoris in Galilee. Cross-Currents of Culture*, 45–50.

32 Adrian M. Leske, 'Mt 6, 25–34: Human Anxiety and the Natural World', in Norman C. Habel and Vicki Balabanski eds., *The Earth Story in the New Testament*, The Earth Bible, vol. 5, London and New York: Sheffield Academic Press, 2002, 15–27.

33 Denis Baly, *The Geography of the Bible*, New York: Harper and Row, 1957, 191–210.

34 Mendel Nun, *Ancient Anchorages and Harbours around the Sea of Galilee*, Kibbuz Ein Gev: Kinnereth Sailing Company, 1988.

35 On the impact of the Ptolemaic administration on Galilee in the third century BCE, see Victor Tcherikover, *Palestine under the Ptolemies. A Contribution to the Study of the Zenon Papyri*, Mizraim, vols. IV and V, New York: G. E. Stechert, 1937.

36 Graham Horsley, 'A Fishing Cartel in First-Century Ephesos', in *id.*, *New Documents Illustrating Early Christianity*, 5(1989) Macquarrie University, Sydney: The Ancient History Research Centre, 1989, 95–114.

37 Peregrine Horden and Nicholas Purcell, *The Corrupting Sea. A Study of Mediterranean History*, Oxford: Blackwell, 2000, 190–197.

38 For discussion of the fish industry on the Sea of Galilee, see K. C. Hanson and Douglas Oakman, *Palestine in the Time of Jesus. Social Structures and Social Conflicts*, Minneapolis: Fortress Press, 1998, 106–110.

39 Marianne Sawicki, *Crossing Galilee*, 143–153.

40 Gerd Theissen, ' "Meer" und "See" in den Evangelien: Ein Beitrag zur Lokalcoloritforschung', *Studien zum Neuen Testament und seiner Umwelt*, 10(1985) 5–25.

41 Baly, *The Geography of the Bible*, 152–163; Freyne, *Galilee from Alexander the Great to Hadrian*, 9–16.

42 Mark Smith, 'Ugaritic Studies and Israelite Religion: A Retrospective View', *Near Eastern Archaeology* (formerly *Biblical Archaeology*) 65(2002) 17–29.

43 Horden and Purcell, *The Corrupting Sea*, 403–460.

44 Mary Beagon, *Roman Nature. The Thought of Pliny the Elder*, Oxford: Clarendon Press, 1992, 26–34.

45 Sean Freyne, 'Jesus the Wine-Drinker: A Friend of Women', in *Galilee and Gospel*, 271–286.

46   Hippocrates, *Airs, Waters, Places*, Loeb Classical Library, Cambridge, MA: Harvard University Press, 1923.
47   This inscription was discovered by the explorer Sir Charles Warren in 1870 and published by the French explorer, Ch. Clérmont-Ganneau, 'Le Mont Hermon et son dieu d'après une inscription inédite', *Receuil d'Archeologie Orientale* 5(1903) 346–366. The Christian writer, Eusebius (fourth century CE), mentions continued pagan practice there in his day. The identity of the God in question is uncertain, but Zeus, the head of the Greek pantheon or Helios the Sun god, are two possibilities.

Chapter 3

1   Albrecht Alt, 'Galiläische Probleme, 1937–40', in *Kleine Schriften zur Geschichte des Volkes Israel*, 3 vols., Munich: Ch. Beck, 1953–64, vol. II, 363–435.
2   Richard A. Horsley, *Galilee. History, Politics, People*, Valley Forge, PA: Trinity Press, 1995, 25–29.
3   Freyne, *Galilee from Alexander the Great to Hadrian*, 23–26; *Galilee, Jesus and the Gospels*, 170f., based on the findings of Zvi Gal, *Lower Galilee During the Iron Age*, ASOR Dissertation Series 8, Winona Lake: Eisenbrauns, 1992.
4   K. Lawson Younger Jr, 'The Deportation of the Israelites', *JBL* 117(1998) 201–227.
5   William Dever, ' "Will the Real Israel Please stand up?" Archaeology and Historiography: Part I', *BASOR* 297(1995) 61–80; 'Histories and Non-Histories of Ancient Israel', *BASOR* 316(1999) 89–105; Israel Finkelstein and Neil Asher Silberman, *The Bible Unearthed. Archaeology's New Vision of Ancient Israel and its Sacred Texts*, New York, London: Simon and Schuster, 2001; Keith W. Whitelam, 'Recreating the History of Israel', *JSOT* 35(1986) 45–70.
6   A. D. H. Mayes, 'The Period of the Judges and the Rise of the Monarchy', in John H. Hayes and J. Maxwell Miller eds., *Israelite and Judean History*, Philadelphia: The Westminster Press, 1977, 285–331 (299–307).
7   Hans Zobel, *Stammesspruch und Geschichte*, BZAT 95, Berlin: Topelmann, 1965, 53–59.
8   Norman C. Habel, *The Land is Mine, Six Biblical Ideologies*, Overtures to Biblical Theology, Minneapolis: Fortress Press, 1995, 36–53.
9   Habel, *The Land is Mine*, 115–133 (129f.).
10   Joseph Fitzmyer, *The Genesis Apocryphon of Qumran Cave I, A Commentary*, Biblica et Orientalia 18, Rome: Pontifical Biblical Institute, 1966, 12–17 and 127–149.

11   N. Na'aman, *Borders and Districts in Biblical Historiography*, Jerusalem: Simor, 1986, 40–66.

12   Na'aman, *Borders and Districts*, 75–79. David's census, on which the topography of these accounts is deemed to have been based, describes the border as having included the territory from Dan around to Sidon, coming to the fortress (or fountain) of Tyre (2 Sam. 24, 6f.).

13   Na'aman, *Borders and Districts*, 60–62; Z. Kallai, *Historical Geography of the Bible. The Tribal Territories of Israel*, Jerusalem, The Magnes Press, 1986, 204–224; Y. Aharoni, *The Land of the Bible. A Historical Geography*, London: Burns and Oates, 1967, 237f.

14   Na'aman, *Borders and Districts*, 95–98.

15   Doron Mendels, *The Rise and Fall of Jewish Nationalism*, New York: Doubleday, 1992, 81–106.

16   F. Lang, ' "Über Sidon mittens ins Gebiet der Dekapolis" ', *ZDPV* 94(1978) 145–159; T. Schmeller, 'Jeus im Umland Galiläas', *BZ* 38(1994) 44–66; Heinz-Wolfgang Kuhn, 'Jesu Hinwendung zu den Heiden im Markusevangelium im Verhältnis zu Jesu historischem Wirken in Betsaida', in Klaus Krämmer and Ansgar Paus eds., *Die Weite des Mysteriums. Christliche Identität im Dialog*, Freiburg and Basel: Herder, 2000, 204–240.

17   A. N. Sherwin-White, *Roman Society and Roman Law in the New Testament*, Oxford: Clarendon Press, 1963, 127–133. J. Rich and A. Wallace-Hadrill eds., *City and Country in the Ancient World*, London and New York: Routledge, 1991.

18   G. Stemberger, 'Die Bedeutung des "Landes Israel" in der rabbinischen Tradition', *Kairos* 25(1983) 176–199 (193); M. Hengel, '*Ioudaia* in der geographischen Liste Apg 2, 9–11 und Syrien als "Grossjudäa" ', *RHPR* 80(2000), 51–68 (62–65).

19   R. Frankel, N. Getzov, M. Aviam, A. Degani, *Settlement Dynamics and Regional Diversity*, IAA Reports, 14, Jerusalem Israel Antiquities Authority, 2001, 110–114.

20   Sean Freyne, 'The Geography of Restoration: Galilee-Jerusalem Relations in Early Judaism and early Christianity', *NTS* 47(2001) 289–311, especially 293–295.

21   Emil Schürer, *The History of the Jewish People in the Age of Jesus Christ*, revised edition and translation, G. Vermes, F. Millar and M. Black, 4 vols., Edinburgh: T&T Clark, 1973–85, vol. 2, 10f.

22   Freyne, *Galilee from Alexander the Great to Hadrian*, 43–45; *Galilee and Gospel*, 129.

23   Doron Mendels, *The Land of Israel as a Political Concept in Hasmonean Literature*, TSAJ 15, Tübingen: J. C. B. Mohr, 1987, 145–154.

24   R. Frankel, 'Har Mispe Yamim – 1988/89', *ESI* 9(1989/90) 100–102; R. Frankel and R. Ventura, 'The Mispe Yamim Bronzes', *BASOR* 311(1998) 39–55.

25   D. Goodblatt, 'From Judeans to Israel. Names of Jewish States in
     Antiquity', *JSJ* 31 (1998) 1–37.

26   Frankel, Getzov, Aviam, Degani, *Settlement Dynamics and Regional
     Diversity*, 109–110.

27   Jonathan Reed, 'The Identity of the Galileans: Ethnic and Religious
     Considerations', in *Archaeology and the Historical Jesus*, 2000, 23–61,
     especially 49–51.

28   D. Adan-Bayewitz and M. Aviam, 'Iotapata, Josephus and the Siege
     of 67: Preliminary Report on the 1992–94 Season', *JRA* 10(1997)
     131–165; A. M. Berlin, 'Romanization and anti-Romanization in
     pre-Revolt Galilee', in Andrea M. Berlin and J. Andrew Overman
     eds., *The First Jewish Revolt. Archaeology, History and Ideology*, London
     and New York: Routledge, 2002, 57–73.

29   Sanders, *Jesus and Judaism*, 264–267; cf. Freyne, *Galilee, Jesus and the
     Gospels*, 247–268.

30   Sean Freyne, 'Galileans, Phoenicians and Itureans: A Study of
     Regional Contrasts in the Hellenistic Age', in Collins and Sterling
     eds., *Hellenism in the Land of Israel*, 184–217, especially 184–188 and
     199–205.

31   S. Herbert and A. Berlin, 'A New Administrative Centre for Persian
     and Hellenistic Galilee: Preliminary Report of the University of
     Minnesota Excavations at Kadesh', *BASOR* 329 (2002) 13–59.

32   D. Barag, 'Tyrian Currency in Galilee', *Israel Numismatic Journal*, 6/
     7(1982/83) 7–13; U. Rappaport, 'Phoenicia and Galilee. Economy,
     Territory and Political Relations', *Studia Phoenicia* IX(1992) 262–268.

33   D. Adan-Bayewitz and M. Aviam, 'Iotapata, Josephus and the Siege
     of 67', 161 and 164f.; D. Syon, 'The Coins from Gamla. An Interim
     Report', *Israel Numismatic Journal* 12(1992/93) 34–55.

34   D. Adan-Bayewitz, *Common Pottery in Roman Galilee. A Study of Local
     Trade*, Ramat Gan: Bar-Ilan University Press, 1993.

35   A. Berlin, 'From Monarchy to Markets', *BASOR* 306(1997) 75–86.

36   Frankel, Getzov, Aviam, Degani, *Settlement Dynamics and Regional
     Diversity*, 112.

37   Jonathan Reed, 'The Sign of Jonah: Q 11, 29–32', in *Archaeology and
     the Galilean Jesus*, 197–211, especially 204–211.

38   John P. Meier, *A Marginal Jew*, vol. II, 659f.

39   T. Rajak, 'Greeks and Barbarians in Josephus', in Collins and Sterling
     eds., *Hellenism in the Land of Israel*, 246–263.

40   U. Rappaport, 'Jewish-Pagan Relations and the Revolt against
     Rome, 66–70 C.E.', in L. Levine ed., *The Jerusalem Cathedra*,
     Jerusalem: Yad Izhak Ben-Zvi Institute, 1981, 81–95.

41   Gerd Theissen, *The Gospels in Context*, English translation, Linda M.
     Maloney, Edinburgh: T&T Clark, 1992, 60–80 (79).

Chapter 4

1   Bruce Chilton and Craig Evans, 'Jesus and Israel's Scriptures', in *Studying the Historical Jesus*, 1994, 309–314.

2   John J. Collins, *The Scepter and the Star. The Messiahs of the Dead Sea Scrolls and Other Ancient Literature*, New York and London: Doubleday, 1995, 117–122.

3   David Catchpole, *The Quest for Q*, Edinburgh: T&T Clark, 1993, 271–280; Sean Freyne, 'Geography of Restoration', *NTS* 47(2001) 307–310.

4   J. Kloppenborg, 'City and Wasteland: The Narrative World and the Beginnings of the Sayings' Gospel (Q)', *Semeia*, 52(1990) 145–160; *id., Excavating Q. The History and Setting of the Sayings' Gospel*, Edinburgh: T&T Clark, 2000, 255–259; Jonathan Reed, 'The Sayings Source Q in Galilee', in *Archaeology and the Galilean Jesus*, 212–221, especially 186–189.

5   John Dominic Crossan, *The Historical Jesus*, 360; *The Birth of Christianity. Discovering What Happened in the Years Immediately after the Execution of Jesus*, New York: HarperCollins, 1998, 6.

6   Kim Huat Tan, *The Zion Traditions and the Aims of Jesus, SNTSMS,* Cambridge: Cambridge University Press, 1997.

7   Norman C. Habel, *The Land is Mine*, 17–31.

8   M. Noth, 'Jerusalem und die Israelitische Tradition', in *Gesammelte Studien zum Alten Testament*, Munich: Kaiser Verlag, 1957, 172–178.

9   E. Zenger, 'Der Psalter als Buch. Beobachtungen zu seiner Entstehung, Komposition und Funktion', in *id.* ed., *Der Psalter in Judentum, und Christentum*, Freiburg: Herder, 1998, 1–57.

10 Joseph Blenkinsopp, *The Anchor Bible 19, Isaiah* I–39. *A New Translation and Commentary*, New York: Doubleday, 2000, 76f.

11 This is Blenkinsopp's description of the present situation with regard to the study of the book *Isaiah 1–39*, 73f. See U. Berges, 'Zur Zionstheologie des Buches Jesaja', *Estudios Biblicos* LVIII(2000) 167–198, especially here 171–175.

12 Joseph Blenkinsopp, *The Anchor Bible 19B, Isaiah 56–66. A New Translation and Commentary*, New York: Doubleday, 2003, 27–37; U. Berges, 'Zur Zionstheologie des Buches *Jesaja', Estudios Biblicos* LVIII(2000) 167–198, at 176–180.

13 A. Alt, 'Jesaja 8.23–9.6. Befreiungsnacht und Krönungstag', *Kleine Schriften*, vol. 2, 206–225; Blenkinsopp, *Isaiah 1–39*, 247f.

14 Blenkinsopp, *Isaiah 1–39*, 265.

15 Blenkinsopp, *Isaiah* 267, and *Isaiah 56–66*, 36f.

16 Blenkinsopp, *Isaiah 56–66*, 307 and 313.

17 Daniel Smith-Christopher, 'Between Ezra and Isaiah: Exclusion, Transformation, and Inclusion of the "Foreigner" in Post-Exilic

Biblical Theology', in Mark Brett ed., *Ethnicity and the Bible*, Leiden: Brill, 1996, 117–143, (140).

18   Berges, 'Zionstheologie', 190–195.

19   Blenkinsopp, *Isaiah 56–66*, 80–88, especially 83, also 314f.

20   H. J. Hermisson, 'Frau Zion', in J. van Ruiten and M. Vervenne eds., *Studies in the Book of Isaiah F.S. W. A. M. Beuken*, Leuven, 1997, 19–39.

21   As Blenkinsopp notes, *Isaiah 56–66*, 221, the investiture of this prophetic person here recalls the role of the servant of Yahweh in the second section of the book, especially the endowment of the Spirit (42.1) and the mission to preach good news (40.9, 41.27, 52.7).

22   J. Blenkinsopp, 'A Jewish Sect of the Persian Period', *CBQ* 52(1990) 5–20.

23   Blenkinsopp, *Isaiah 56–66*, 292–301.

24   Brooks Schramm, *The Opponents of Third Isaiah, Reconstructing the Cultic History of the Restoration, JSOTSS.* 193, 1995.

25   Shaye Cohen, *The Beginnings of Jewishness: Boundaries, Varieties, Uncertainties*, Berkley: University of California Press, 1999.

26   Sanders, *Jesus and Judaism*, 220f.

27   Richard Horsley, *Jesus and the Spiral of Violence*, San Francisco: Harper and Row, 1987, 172–177; Bruce Chilton, *Pure Kingdom. Jesus' Vision of God*, Grand Rapids, MI: William Eerdmans, and London: SPCK, 1996, 81f. See, however, Gerd Theissen, *The Gospels in Context*, 43–59 (46).

28   1 Macc. 4.38-60, 5.54, 6.48–64; 2 Macc. 10.1–9. In recounting the Roman general Pompey's invasion of Jerusalem 100 years after Antiochus, Josephus describes the city and the temple as a fortress (*JA* 14.57, 15.247f.; cf. *JW* 5.136–141).

29   D. Syon, 'The Coins from Gamla. An interim Report', *Israel Numismatic Journal* 12(1992/93), 34–55(40–41).

30   Blenkinsopp, *Isaiah 56–66*, 229–230 with references.

31   Blenkinsopp, *Isaiah 56–66*, 274.

32   Bryan, *Jesus and Israel's Traditions of Judgement and Restoration*, 81–86.

33   Jonathan Reed, 'The Sign of Jonah: Q 11.29–32, in *Archaeology and the Galilean Jesus*, 197–211.

34   Moxnes, *Putting Jesus in His Place*, 72–90.

Chapter 5

1   Chilton, *Pure Kingdom*, 31–34 and 146–163.

2   Blenkinsopp, *Isaiah 1–39*, 183, 186; Chilton, *Pure Kingdom*, 146.

3   Ephraim Stern, *Archaeology of the Land of the Bible*, vol. II, New York and London: Doubleday, 2001, 14–58 and Zvi Gal, *Lower Galilee*

During the Iron Age, ASOR Dissertation Series 8, Winona Lake, IN: Eisenbrauns, 1992, deal with the archaeological evidence for the Assyrian devastation of the north; Lawson Younger, 'The Deportations of the Israelites', *JBL* 117(1998) 201–227, deals with the evidence from the Assyrian royal archives.

4   Hans M. Barstad, *The Myth of the Empty Land*, Oslo: Scandinavian University Press, 1996 and Oded Lipschits and Joseph Blenkinsopp eds., *Judah and Judeans in the Neo-Babylonian Period*, Winona Lake, IN: Eisenbrauns, 2003, deal with both the archaeological and the literary evidence for Judah after the Babylonian exile.

5   Seth Schwartz, *Imperialism and Jewish Society, 200 B.C.E. to 640 C.E.*, Princeton and Oxford: Princeton University Press, 2001, 49–99 (98).

6   For recent discussions of the multi-faceted impact of Hellenism on Jewish life cf. Lee I. Levine, *Judaism and Hellenism in Antiquity. Conflict or Confluence?*, Peabody, MA: Hendrikson Publishers, 1998; John J. Collins and Gregory E. Sterling eds., *Hellenism in the Land of Israel*, Notre Dame, IN: University of Notre Dame, 2001; Erich S. Gruen, *Heritage and Hellenism. The Reinvention of Jewish Tradition*, Berkley: University of California Press, 1998.

7   John J. Collins, *Daniel, A Commentary on the Book of Daniel* Hermeneia. A Critical and Historical Commentary on the Bible Minneapolis: Augsburg-Fortress, 1993, 24–38.

8   John J. Collins, 'Temporality and Politics in Jewish Apocalyptic Literature', in Christopher Rowland and John Barton eds., *Apocalyptic in History and Tradition*, *JSP* Supplement Series 43, Sheffield: Sheffield Academic Press, 2002, 26–43 (29).

9   Adela Yarbro Collins, 'The Influence of Daniel on the New Testament', in Collins, *Daniel*, 90–112, especially 92–96.

10 For details and background see Collins, *Daniel*, 274–324.

11 Collins, *Daniel*, 385 and 393.

12 Collins, *Daniel*, 62–69.

13 H. Ginsberg, 'The Oldest Interpretation of the Suffering Servant', *VT* 3(1953) 400–404; Sean Freyne, 'The Disciples in Mark and the *Maskilim* in Daniel. A Comparison', *JSNT* 16(1982) 7–23; George W. E. Nickelsburg, *Ancient Judaism and Christian Origins. Diversity, Continuity and Change*, Minneapolis: Fortress Press, 2003, 17–20.

14 John J. Collins, *The Apocalyptic Vision of the Book of Daniel*, Missoula, MO: Scholars Press, 1997, 191–218.

15 John J. Collins, 'The Mythology of the Holy War in Daniel and the Qumran War Scroll: A Point of Transition in Jewish Apocalyptic', *VT* 25(1975) 596–612.

16 Collins, *The Scepter and the Star*; Sean Freyne, 'Messiah and Galilee', in *Galilee and Gospel*, 230–270.

17 Gerbern G. Oegma, *The Anointed and his People. Messianic Expectation from the Maccabees to Bar Cochba*, Sheffield: Sheffield Academic Press, 1998, 103–108.

18 For an interesting discussion of the Pharisees' role as retainers, cf. Anthony J. Saldarini, *Pharisees, Scribes and Sadducees in Palestinian Society*, Edinburgh: T&T Clark, 1988.

19 Sean Freyne, 'The Geography, Politics and Economics of Galilee and the Quest for the Historical Jesus', in Bruce Chilton and Craig Evans eds., *Studying the Historical Jesus*, 75–122.

20 Sean Freyne, 'Jesus and the Urban Culture of Galilee', in *Galilee and Gospel*, 183–207.

21 K. C. Hanson, 'Jesus and the Social Bandits', in Wolfgang Stegemann, Bruce J. Malina and Gerd Theissen eds., *The Social Setting of Jesus and the Gospels*, Minneapolis: Fortress Press, 2002, 283–300.

22 Ernst Bammel and C. F. D. Moule eds., *Jesus and the Politics of his Day*, Cambridge and New York: Cambridge University Press, 1984, contains a collection of articles discussing various aspects of this hypothesis. Cf. in particular, E. Bammel, 'The Revolution Theory from Reimarus to Brandon', 11–68.

23 Richard A. Horsley, *Galilee. History, Politics, People*, Valley Forge, PA: Trinity Press, 1995, 258f; David M. Rhoads, *Israel in Revolution. 6–74 C.E. A Political History Based on the Writings of Josephus*, Philadelphia: Fortress Press, 1976, 97–111.

24 Freyne, *Galilee from Alexander the Great to Hadrian*, 208–255.

25 For a review of the evidence see Meier, *A Marginal Jew*, II, 237–270.

26 Crossan, *The Historical Jesus*, 76.

27 Crossan, *The Historical Jesus*, 292.

28 Horsley, *Jesus and the Spiral of Violence; Sociology and the Jesus Movement*, New York: Crossroad, 1989; *Jesus and Empire. The Kingdom of God and the New World Disorder*, Minneapolis: Fortress Press, 2003.

29 C. Hempel, A. Lange, H. Lichtenberger eds., *The Wisdom Texts from Qumran and the Development of Sapiential Thought*, Leuven: Leuven University Press, 2002. Crossan acknowledges the links between the two genres, yet curiously he decides to ignore this, *The Historical Jesus, 291f.*

30 Sean Freyne, 'Galilean Questions to Crossan's Mediterranean Jesus', in *Galilee and Gospel*, 208–229.

31 Bruce Chilton, 'The Kingdom of God in Recent Discussion', in Chilton and Evans eds., *Studying the Historical Jesus*, 255–280.

32 William A. Beardslee, *Literary Criticism of the New Testament*, Philadelphia: Fortress Press, 1970, 53–63.

33 Bruce J. Malina, 'Christ and Time: Swiss or Mediterranean?, in *id.*, *The Social World of Jesus and the Gospels*, London: Routledge, 1996, 179–216.

34 Collins, *Daniel*, 318. In one of the recently published Wisdom fragments from Qumran we read with reference to the heavenly rewards of the wise ones that 'among all the godly ones God has cast your lot and has magnified your glory greatly, and has appointed you as first-born, saying "I will bless you".'

35 Daniel J. Harrington, *Wisdom Texts from Qumran*, London and New York: Routledge, 1996, 40–59 for text and exposition. See also his remarks on the relevance of these texts for the historical Jesus debate (90f.).

36 Freyne, 'Jesus, Prayer and Politics', in Hogan and Fitzgerald eds., *Between Poetry and Politics*, 67–85.

37 Meier, *A Marginal Jew*, I, 56–69, discusses the later Christian interpolations in this text.

38 Paul Corby Finney, 'The Rabbi and the Coin Potrait (Mk. 12.15b, 16): Rigorism Manqué', *JBL* 112(1993) 629–644 suggests that the coin was probably a silver *denarius* of Tiberias with a crowned head of the emperor bearing the inscription 'Tiberias Caesar Augustus, son of the Divine Augustus' on the obverse, and on the reverse a seated female figure robed and with a diadem, holding a sceptre in the right hand and an olive in the left. In all probability this is Peace personified in the guise of a priestess, possibly Augustus' daughter Livia, since the inscription on this side reads 'high priest' (632f.).

39 Contrast Horsley, *Jesus and the Spiral of Violence*, 306–317 and *Jesus and Empire*, 98f. with F. F. Bruce, 'Render to Caesar', in Bammel and Moule eds., *Jesus and the Politics of his Day*, 265–286.

40 Sean Freyne, 'Jesus and the Urban Culture of Galilee', in *Galilee and Gospel*, 199–206.

41 Theissen, *The Gospels in Context*, 26–39.

42 Gerd Theissen, 'The Political Dimension of Jesus' Activities', in Stegemann, Malina, Theissen eds., *The Social Setting of Jesus and the Gospels*, 225–250.

43 Douglas Oakman, 'Rulers' Houses, Thieves and Usurpers. The Beelzebul Pericope', *Forum* 4,3 (1988) 109–123.

44 Collins, *Daniel*, 313–317.

45 Santiago Guijarro, 'The Politics of Exorcism', in Stegemann, Malina, Theissen eds., *Jesus and the Gospels*, 159–174.

Chapter 6

1 See Ben Meyer, *The Early Christians. Their World Mission and Self-Discovery*, Wilmington, DE: Michael Glazier, 1986, 53–66.

2 See now, however, the collection of articles in Robert T. Fortna and Tom Thatcher eds., *Jesus in the Johannine Tradition*, Louisville and London: Westminster John Knox, 2001.

3 E. P. Sanders, *Jesus and Judaism*, London: SCM Press, 1985, 61–76, especially 66. For a discussion of most of the recent proposals see Adela Yarbro Collins, 'Jesus' Action in Herod's Temple', in Adela Yarbro Collins and Margaret Mitchell eds., *Antiquity and Humanity. Essays in Ancient Religion and Philosophy Presented to Hans Dieter Betz*, Tübingen: J. C. B. Mohr, 2001, 45–61; Stephen M. Bryan, *Jesus and Israel's Traditions of Judgement and Restoration*, SNTSMS 117, Cambridge: Cambridge University Press, 2002, 206–225; Kim Haut Tan, *The Zion Traditions and the Aims of Jesus*, 158–196.

4 Crossan, *The Historical Jesus*, 359f.

5 E. P. Sanders, *Jewish Law from Jesus to the Mishnah*, London: SCM Press, 1990, 48f.

6 See Daniel R. Schwartz, 'On Sacrifice by Gentiles in the Temple of Jerusalem', in *Studies in the Jewish Background of Christinity*, Tübingen: J. C. B. Mohr, 1992, 102–116.

7 James C. Vander Kam, *The Book of Jubilees*, Sheffield: Sheffield Academic Press, 2001, 40–45; Nickelsburg, *Ancient Judaism and Christian Origins*, 75–79.

8 Bryan, *Jesus and Israel's Traditions of Judgement and Restoration*, 199–202.

9 George Nickelsburg, *Jewish Literature from the Bible to the Mishnah*, London: SCM Press, 1981, 48–55.

10 George Nickelsburg, 'Enoch, Levi and Peter: Recipients of Revelation in Upper Galilee', *JBL* 100(1981) 575–600.

11 John J. Collins, *The Apocalyptic Imagination*, Missoula, MO: Scholars Press, 1977, 53–56.

12 Sanders, *Jesus and Judaism*, 63; Blenkinsopp, *Isaiah 56–66*, 141.

13 Von Rad, *Old Testament Theology*, vol. II, 193–201.

14 Peter Richardson, *City and Sanctuary. Religion and Architecture in the Roman Near East*, London: SCM Press, 2002, 130–160.

15 For an excellent discussion see Theissen and Merz, *The Historical Jesus. A Comprehensive Guide*, 449–469.

16 Martin Hengel, *Crucifixion*, Philadelphia: Fortress Press, 1977, has a detailed account of attitudes to this form of execution in the Roman world.

17 Martin Goodman, *The Ruling Class of Judea. The Origins of the Jewish Revolt against Rome* A.D. *66–70*, 29–50.

18 800 opponents crucified by Alexander Jannaeus (*JA* 13.380–383); 4QpNahum, 3–4, col.1; Onias, 'the just, who was dear to God', stoned to death because he refused to pray for God's vengeance against opponents in the context of a civil strife in Jerusalem (JA 14.22–25); the teacher of righteousness from Qumran who was persecuted by the wicked priest, 1QpHab, 9.9–10, 11.4–7.

19 John S. Kloppenborg, *Excavating Q*, Edinburgh: T&T Clark, 2000, 398–408.

20 QLk 6.22f., 7.31–35, 11.47–51, 13.34–35, 14.27.

21 George Nickelsburg, 'The Genre and Function of the Markan Passion Narrative', *HTR* (1980) 153–184, especially 155–163; Kloppenborg, *Excavating Q*, 369–374.

22 Vincent Taylor, *The Gospel According to Mark*, London: Macmillan and Company, 1963, 445f.; Joachim Jeremias, 'The Servant of God in the New Testament', in Walter Zimmerli and Joachim Jeremias eds., *The Servant of God*, London: SCM Press, 1957, 80–106, especially 88–94.

23 Sean Freyne, 'Jesus the Martyr', in Teresa Okure, Jon Sobrino, Felix Wilfrid eds., *Concilium. Rethinking Martyrdom*, London: SCM Press, 2003/1, 39–48.

24 Arthur J. Droge and James D. Tabor, *A Noble Death. Suicide and Martyrdom among Christians and Jews in Antiquity*, New York: HarperCollins, 1992.

Epilogue

1 S. Freyne, 'Christianity in Sepphoris and Galilee', in *Galilee and Gospel*, 299–308.

2 Kloppenborg, *Excavating Q*, 214–261; cf. Elizabeth Struthers Malbon, 'Galilee and Jerusalem: History and Literature in Markan Interpretation', *CBQ* 44(1982) 242–255.

3 Sanders, *Jesus and Judaism*, 318–335 (334).

SELECT BIBLIOGRAPHY

Adan-Bayewitz, David, *Common Pottery in Roman Galilee. A Study of Local Trade*, Ramat Gan: Bar-Ilan University Press, 1993.
—— and Aviam, M., 'Iotapata, Josephus and the Siege of 67: Preliminary Report on the 1992–94 Season', *JRA* 10(1997) 131–165.
Aharoni, Y., *The Land of the Bible. A Historical Geography*, London: Burns and Oates, 1967.
Alt, Albrecht, 'Galiläische Probleme, 1937–40', in *Kleine Schriften zur Geschichte des Volkes Israel*, 3 vols., Munich: Ch.Beck, 1953–64, vol. II, 363–435.
Amiram, D. H. K., 'Sites and Settlements in the Mountains of Lower Galilee', *IEJ* 6(1956) 69–77.
Anderson, Bernhard ed., *Creation in the Old Testament*, London: SPCK, 1984.
Avery-Peck, Alan, *Mishnah's Division of Agriculture. A History and Theology of Seder Zeraim*, Brown Judaic Series 79, Chico, Cal: Scholars Press, 1985.
Aviam, Mordechai, *Jews, Pagans and Christians in the Galilee*, Land of Galilee Studies 1, Rochester, NY: University of Rochester Press, 2004.
Baly, Denis, *The Geography of the Bible*, New York: Harper and Row, 1957.
Bammel, E., 'The Revolution Theory from Reimarus to Brandon', in Bammel and Moule eds., *Jesus and the Politics of his Day*, 11–68.
Bammel Ernst and Moule C. F. D. eds., *Jesus and the Politics of his Day*, Cambridge and New York: Cambridge University Press, 1984.
Barag, D., 'Tyrian Currency in Galilee', *Israel Numismatic Journal*, 6/7(1982/83) 7–13.
Barstad, Hans M., *The Myth of the Empty Land*, Oslo: Scandinavian University Press, 1996.
Beagon, Mary, *Roman Nature. The Thought of Pliny the Elder*, Oxford: Clarendon Press, 1992.
Beardslee, William A., *Literary Criticism of the New Testament*, Philadelphia: Fortress Press, 1970.
Berges, U., 'Zur Zionstheologie des Buches Jesaja', *Estudios Biblicos* LVIII(2000) 167–198.
Berlin, A. M., 'Romanization and anti-Romanization in pre-Revolt Galilee', in Berlin and Overman eds., *The First Jewish Revolt*, 57–73.
Berlin, A., 'From Monarchy to Markets', *BASOR* 306(1997) 75–86.
Berlin, Andrea M. and Overman, Andrew eds., *The First Jewish Revolt. Archaeology, History, and Ideology*, London: Routledge, 2002.
Blenkinsopp, Joseph, The Anchor Bible 19, *Isaiah 1–39*, New York: Doubleday, 2000.
—— The Anchor Bible 19B, *Isaiah 56–66. A New Translation and Commentary*, New York: Doubleday, 2003.
—— 'A Jewish Sect of the Persian Period', *CBQ* 52(1990) 5–20.
Borowski, Oded, *Agriculture in Iron Age Israel*, Boston, MA: American School of Oriental Research, 2002.
Brandon, S. F. G., *Jesus and the Zealots*, Manchester: Manchester University Press, 1967.
Brett, Mark ed., *Ethnicity and the Bible*, Leiden: Brill, 1996.
Bryan, Stephen M., *Jesus and Israel's Traditions of Judgement and Restoration*, SNTSMS 117, Cambridge: Cambridge University Press, 2002.

Büchler, Adolf, *Die Priester und der Cultus im letzten Jahrzent des Jerusalemishen Tempels*, Vienna, 1895.

—— *The Political and Social Leaders of the Jewish Community of Sepphoris in the Second and Third Centuries*, Jewish College Publications 6, London, 1914.

Bultmann, Rudolph, *Jesus and the Word*, London: Collins, 1926.

Bruce, F. F., 'Render to Caesar', in Bammel and Moule eds., *Jesus and the Politics of his Day*, 265–286.

Catchpole, David, *The Quest for Q*, Edinburgh: T&T Clark, 1993.

Chapman, Dean W., 'Locating the Gospel of Mark: A Model of Agrarian Geography', *BTB* 25(1995) 24–37.

Charlesworth, James H. ed., *The Old Testament Pseudepigrapha*, 2 vols., London: Darton, Longman and Todd, 1983 and 1985.

Chilton, Bruce D., *A Galilean Rabbi and his Bible. Jesus' Use of the Interpreted Scripture of his Time*, Wilmington, DL: Michael Glazier, 1984.

Chilton, Bruce, *Pure Kingdom. Jesus' Vision of God*, Grand Rapids, MI: William Eerdmans, and London: SPCK, 1996.

—— and Evans, Craig, 'Jesus and Israel's Scriptures', in *id., Studying the Historical Jesus*, 281–336.

Chilton, Bruce, 'The Kingdom of God in Recent Discussion', in *id., Studying the Historical Jesus*, 255–280.

—— and Evans, Craig eds., *Studying the Historical Jesus. Evaluations of the State of Current Research*, Leiden: Brill, 1994.

Clérmont-Ganneau, Ch., 'Le Mont Hermon et son dieu d'après une inscription ined
itè', *Receuil d'Archeologie Orientale* 5(1903) 346–366.

Cohen, Shaye, *The Beginnings of Jewishness: Boundaries, Varieties, Uncertainties*, Berkley: University of California Press, 1999.

Collins, Adela Yarbro, 'The Influence of Daniel on the New Testament', in Collins, *Daniel*, 90–112.

— 'Jesus' Action in Herod's Temple', in Adela Yarbro Collins and Margaret Mitchell eds., *Antiquity and Humanity. Essays in Ancient Religion and Philosophy Presented to Hans Dieter Betz*, Tübingen: J. C. B. Mohr, 2001, 45–61.

Collins, John J., 'The Mythology of the Holy War in Daniel and the Qumran War Scroll: A Point of Transition in Jewish Apocalyptic', *VT* 25(1975) 596–612.

—— *The Apocalyptic Vision of the Book of Daniel*, Missoula, MO: Scholars Press, 1977.

—— *Daniel, A Commentary on the Book of Daniel*, Hermeneia. A Critical and Historical Commentary on the Bible, Minneapolis: Augsburg-Fortress, 1993.

—— *The Scepter and the Star. The Messiahs of the Dead Sea Scrolls and Other Ancient Literature*, New York and London: Doubleday, 1995.

—— 'Temporality and Politics in Jewish Apocalyptic Literature', in Christopher Rowland and John Barton eds., *Apocalyptic in History and Tradition*, JSP Supplement Series 43, Sheffield: Sheffield Academic Press, 2002, 26–43.

—— and Sterling, Gregory eds., *Hellenism in the Land of Israel*, Notre Dame, IN: Notre Dame University Press, 2001.

Corley, Kathleen E., *Women and the Historical Jesus. Feminist Myths of Christian Origins*, Santa Rosa, CA: Polebridge Press, 2002.

Crossan, John Dominic, *The Historical Jesus, The Life of a Mediterranean Jewish Peasant*, Edinburgh: T&T Clark, 1991.

—— *The Birth of Christianity. Discovering What Happened in the Years Immediately after the Execution of Jesus*, New York: HarperCollins, 1998.

—— and Reed, Jonathan L., *Excavating Jesus. Beneath the Stones, Behind the Texts*, New York: HarperCollins, 2001.

Cullmann, Oscar, *Salvation in History*, English translation, Sidney G. Sowers, London: SCM Press, 1967.

Dever, William, ' "Will the Real Israel Please stand up?" Archaeology and Historiography: Part I', *BASOR* 297(1995) 61–80.

—— 'Histories and Non-Histories of Ancient Israel', *BASOR* 316(1999) 89–105.

Downing, F. G., *Cynics and Christian Origins*, Edinburgh: T&T Clark, 1992.

Droge, Arthur J. and Tabor, James, D., *A Noble Death. Suicide and Martyrdom among Christians and Jews in Antiquity*, San Francisco: HarperSanFrancisco, 1992.

Fiensy, David, *The Social History of Palestine in the Herodian Period*, Lewiston, NY: the Edwin Mellon Press, 1991.

Finkelstein, Israel and Silberman, Neil Asher, *The Bible Unearthed. Archaeology's New Vision of Ancient Israel and its Sacred Texts*, New York, London: Simon and Schuster, 2001.

Finney, Paul Corby, 'The Rabbi and the Coin Portrait (Mk 12, 15b.16): Rigorism Manqué', *JBL* 112(1993) 629–644.

Fiorenza, Elizabeth Schüssler, *Jesus, Miriam's Child, Sophia's Prophet: Critical Issues in Feminist Christology*, New York: Crossroad, 1994.

Fitzmyer, Joseph, *The Genesis Apocryphon of Qumran Cave I, A Commentary*, Biblica et Orientalia 18, Rome: Pontifical Biblical Institute, 1966.

Fortna, Robert T. and Thatcher, Tom eds., *Jesus in the Johannine Tradition*, Louisville and London: Westminster John Knox, 2001.

Frankel, R., 'Har Mispe Yamim – 1988/89', *ESI* 9(1989/90) 100–102.

—— and Ventura, R., 'The Mispe Yamim Bronzes', *BASOR* 311(1998) 39–55.

——, Getzov, N., Aviam, M., Degani, A., *Settlement Dynamics and Regional Diversity in Ancient Upper Galilee*, IAA Reports, 14, Jerusalem: Israel Antiquities Authority, 2001.

Freyne, Sean, *Galilee from Alexander the Great to Hadrian. A Study of Second Temple Judaism*, Wilmington, DL: Michael Glazier, 1980 (reprint Edinburgh: T&T Clark, 2000).

—— 'The Disciples in Mark and the *Maskilim* in Daniel. A Comparison', *JSNT* 16(1982) 7–23.

—— *Galilee, Jesus and the Gospels. Literary Approaches and Historical Investigations*, Dublin and Minneapolis: Gill-Macmillan and Augsburg, 1988.

—— 'The Geography, Politics and Economics of Galilee and the Quest for the Historical Jesus', in Chilton and Evans eds., *Studying the Historical Jesus. Evaluations of the State of Current Research*, 75–122.

—— *Galilee and Gospel, Selected Essays*, WUNT 125, Tübingen: J. C. B. Mohr, 2000.

—— 'The Geography of Restoration. Galilee-Jerusalem Relations in early Judaism and early Christianity', *NTS* 47(2001) 289–311.

—— 'Galileans, Phoenicians and Itureans: A Study of Regional Contrasts in the Hellenistic Age', in Collins and Sterling eds., *Hellenism in the Land of Israel*, 184–217.

—— 'Jesus, Prayer and Politics', in L. Hogan and B. Fitzgerald eds., *Between Poetry and Politics*, Dublin: Columba Press, 2003, 67–85.

—— 'Jesus the Martyr', in *Concilium. An International Journal of Theology*, London: SCM 39(2003) 39–48.

—— 'Early Christian Imagination and the Gospels', in Charles Horton ed., *The Earliest Gospels. The Origin and Transmission of the Earliest Christian Gospel – the Contribution of the*

Chester Beatty Gospel Codex, P45, JSNTSS 258, London: T&T Clark International, 2004, 2–12.

Frikenschmidt, Dirk, *Evangelium als Biographie. Die Vier Evangelien im Rahmen antiker Erzälkunst*, Tübingen: Franke Verlag, 1997.

Gal, Zvi, *Lower Galilee During the Iron Age*, ASOR Dissertation Series 8, Winona Lake, IN: Eisenbrauns, 1992.

Gerhardsson, Birger, *Memory and Manuscript. Oral Tradition and Written Transmission in Rabbinic Judaism and Early Christianity*, Lund: G. W. K. Gleerup, 1961.

Goodblatt, D., 'From Judeans to Israel. Names of Jewish States in Antiquity', *JSJ* 31(1998) 1–37.

Goodman, Martin, *The Ruling Class of Judaea. The Origins of the Jewish Revolt against Rome. A.D. 66–70*, Cambridge: Cambridge University Press, 1987.

Ginsberg, H., 'The Oldest Interpretation of the Suffering Servant', *VT* 3(1953) 400–404.

Gruen, Erich S., *Heritage and Hellenism. The Reinvention of Jewish Tradition*, Berkley: University of California Press, 1998.

Grundmann, Walter, *Jesus der Galiläer und das Judentum*, Leipzig: Georg Wigand, 1941.

Guijarro, Santiago, 'The Politics of Exorcism', in Stegemann, Malina, Theissen eds., *The Social Setting of Jesus and the Gospels*, 159–174.

Habel, Norman C., *The Land is Mine. Six Biblical Ideologies*, Overtures to Biblical Theology, Minneapolis: Fortress Press, 1995.

Hanson, K. C., 'Jesus and the Social Bandits', in Stegemann, Malina, Theissen eds., *The Social Setting of Jesus and the Gospels*, 283–300.

—— and Oakman, Douglas, *Palestine in the Time of Jesus. Social Structures and Social Conflicts*, Minneapolis: Fortress Press, 1998.

Harrington, Daniel J., *Wisdom Texts from Qumran*, London and New York: Routledge, 1996.

Hempel, C., Lange, A., Lichtenberger, H., *The Wisdom Texts from Qumran and the Development of Sapiential Thought*, Leuven: Leuven University Press, 2002.

Hengel, Martin, *Crucifixion*, Philadelphia: Fortress Press, 1977.

—— 'Ioudaia in der geographischen Liste Apg 2, 9–11 und Syrien als "Grossjudäa" ', *RHPR* 80(2000), 51–68.

Hermisson, H. J., 'Frau Zion', in J. van Ruiten and M. Vervenne eds., *Studies in the Book of Isaiah F.S.W.A.M. Beuken*, Leuven: Leuven University Press, 1997, 19–39.

Herbert, S. and Berlin, A., 'A New Administrative Centre for Persian and Hellenistic Galilee: Preliminary Report of the University of Minnesota Excavations at Kadesh', *BASOR* 329 (2003) 13–59.

Heschel, Susannah, *Abraham Geiger and the Jewish Jesus*, Chicago: Chicago University Press, 1998.

Hezser, Catherine, *Jewish Literacy in Roman Palestine*, TSAJ 81, Tübingen: J. C. B. Mohr, 2001.

Hippocrates, *Airs, Waters, Places*, Loeb Classical Library, Cambridge, MA: Harvard University Press, 1923.

Horden, Peregrine, and Purcell, Nicholas, *The Corrupting Sea. A Study of Mediterranean History*, Oxford: Blackwell, 2000.

Horsley, Graham, 'A Fishing Cartel in First-Century Ephesos', in *id., New Documents Illustrating Early Christianity*, 5(1989) Macquarrie University, Sydney: The Ancient History Research Centre, 1989, 95–114.

Horsley, Richard A., *Jesus and the Spiral of Violence. Popular Jewish Resistance in Roman Palestine*, San Francisco: Harper and Row, 1987.
—— *Sociology and the Jesus Movement*, New York: Crossroad, 1989.
—— *Galilee. History, Politics, People*, Valley Forge, PA: Trinity Press, 1995.
—— *Archaeology, History and Society in Galilee. The Social Context of Jesus and the Rabbis*, Valley Forge, PA: Trinity Press, 1996.
—— *Jesus and Empire. The Kingdom of God and the New World Disorder*, Minneapolis: Fortress Press, 2003.
—— with Draper, Jonathan, *Whoever Hears You Hears Me. Prophets, Performance and Tradition in Q*, Harrisburg, PA: Trinity Press, 1998.
Jeremias, Joachim, 'The Servant of God in the New Testament', in Walter Zimmerli and Joachim Jeremias eds., *The Servant of God*, London: SCM Press, 1957, 80–106.
Kallai, Z., *Historical Geography of the Bible. The Tribal Territories of Israel*, Jerusalem: The Magnes Press, 1986.
Käsemann, Ernst, 'The Problem of the Historical Jesus', (1953), reprinted in *id.*, *Essays on New Testament Themes*, London: SCM, 1964, 15–47.
Kitzberger, Ingrid Rosa ed., *Transformative Encounters. Jesus and Women Re-viewed*, Leiden: Brill, 2000.
Klein, Samuel, *Galiläa von der Makkabäerseit bis 67*, Berlin, 1923.
Kloppenborg, J., 'City and Wasteland: The Narrative World and the Beginnings of the Sayings' Gospel (Q)', *Semeia*, 52(1990) 145–160.
—— *Excavating Q: The History and Setting of the Sayings' Gospel*, Edinburgh: T&T Clark, 2000.
Kuhn, Heinz-Wolfgang, 'Jesu Hinwendung zu den Heiden im Markusevangelium im Verhältnis zu Jesu historischem Wirken in Betsaida', in Klaus Krämmer and Ansgar Paus eds., *Die Weite des Mysteriums. Christliche Identität im Dialog*, Freiburg and Basel: Herder, 2000, 204–240.
Lang, F., ' "Über Sidon mitten ins Gebiet der Dekapolis". Geographie und Theologie in Markus 7, 31', *ZDPV* 94(1978) 145–159.
Leske, Adrian M., 'Mt 6, 25–34: Human Anxiety and the Natural World', in Norman C. Habel and Vicki Balabanski eds., *The Earth Story in the New Testament*, The Earth Bible, vol. 5, London and New York: Sheffield Academic Press, 2002.
Levine, L. ed., *The Jerusalem Cathedra*, Jerusalem: Yad Izhak Ben-Zvi Institute, 1981.
Levine, Lee I., *Judaism and Hellenism in Antiquity, Conflict or Confluence?*, Peabody, MA: Hendrikson Publishers, 1998.
Lindeskog, Gösta, *Die Jesusfrage im Neuzeitlichen Judentum*, reprint Darmstadt: Wissenschaftliche Buchgesellschaft, 1973.
Lipschits, Oded and Blenkinsopp, Joseph eds., *Judah and Judeans in the Neo-Babylonian Period*, Winona Lake, IN: Eisenbrauns, 2003.
Malina, Bruce J., 'Christ and Time: Swiss or Mediterranean?', in *id.*, *The Social World of Jesus and the Gospels*, London: Routledge, 1996, 179–216.
Mason, Steve, *Life of Josephus. Translation and Commentary*, Leiden: Brill, 2001.
Mayes, A. D. H. 'The Period of the Judges and the Rise of the Monarchy', in John H. Hayes and J. Maxwell Miller eds., *Israelite and Judean History*, Philadelphia: The Westminster Press, 1977, 285–331.
Meier, John P., *A Marginal Jew. Rethinking the Historical Jesus*, 3 vols., The Anchor Bible Reference Library, New York and London: Doubleday, 1991, 1993, 2001.

Mendels, Doron, *The Land of Israel as a Political Concept in Hasmonean Literature*, TSAJ 15, Tübingen: J. C. B. Mohr, 1987.

—— *The Rise and Fall of Jewish Nationalism*, New York: Doubleday, 1992.

Meyer, Ben, *The Early Christians. Their World Mission and Self-Discovery*, Wilmington, DL: Michael Glazier, 1986.

Meyers, Eric M. ed., *The Oxford Encyclopaedia of Archaeology in the Near East*, 5 vols., New York and Oxford: Oxford University Press, 1997.

—— (ed.), *Galilee through the Centuries. Confluence of Cultures*, Winona Lake, IN: Eisenbrauns, 1999.

Moxnes, Halvor, *Putting Jesus in His Place. A Radical Vision of Household and Kingdom*, Louisville and London: John Knox Press, 2003.

Murphy-O'Connor, Jerome, 'John the Baptist and Jesus', *NTS* 36(1990) 359–374.

Na'aman, Nadav, *Borders and Districts in Biblical Historiography*, Jerusalem: Simor Jerusalem, 1986.

Nagy, Rebecca Martin and Meyers, Eric M. eds., *Sepphoris in Galilee. Crosscurrents of Culture*, Raleigh: North Carolina Museum of Modern Art, 1996.

Neusner, Jacob, *Judaism. The Evidence of the Mishnah*, Chicago: Chicago University Press, 1981.

Nickelsburg, George, 'The Genre and Function of the Markan Passion Narrative', *HTR* (1980) 153–184.

—— *Jewish Literature from the Bible to the Mishnah*, London: SCM Press, 1981.

—— 'Enoch, Levi and Peter: Recipients of Revelation in Upper Galilee', *JBL* 100(1981) 575–600.

—— *Ancient Judaism and Christian Origins. Diversity, Continuity and Change*, Minneapolis: Fortress Press, 2003.

Noth, M., *Gesammelte Studien zum Alten Testament*, Munich: Kaiser Verlag, 1957.

Nun, Mendel, *Ancient Anchorages and Harbours around the Sea of Galilee*, Kibbuz Ein Gev: Kinnereth Sailing Company, 1988.

Oakman, Douglas, 'Rulers' Houses, Thieves and Usurpers. The Beelzebul Pericope', *Forum* 4.3 (1988) 109–23.

Oegma, Gerbern G., *The Anointed and his People. Messianic Expectation from the Maccabees to Bar Cochba*, Sheffield: Sheffield Academic Press, 1998.

Perrin, Norman, *Rediscovering the Teaching of Jesus*, London: SCM Press, 1967.

Plumwood, Val, *Feminism and the Mastery of Nature*, London and New York: Routledge, 1993.

Rajak, T., 'Greeks and Barbarians in Josephus', in Collins and Sterling eds., *Hellenism in the Land of Israel*, 246–263.

Rappaport, U., 'Jewish-Pagan Relations and the Revolt against Rome, 66–70 C.E.', in Levine ed., *The Jerusalem Cathedra*, 81–95.

—— 'Phoenicia and Galilee. Economy, Territory and Political Relations', *Studia Phoenicia* IX(1992) 262–268.

Reed, Jonathan, *Archaeology and the Galilean Jesus. A Re-Examination of the Evidence*, Harrisburg, PA: Trinity Press, 2000.

Renan, Ernest, *Vie de Jésus*, Paris: Michel Levy, 1863, English translation, New York: Prometheus Books, 1991.

Rhoads, David M., *Israel in Revolution. 6–74 C.E. A Political History Based on the Writings of Josephus*, Philadelphia: Fortress Press, 1976.

Rich, J. and Wallace-Hadrill, A. eds., *City and Country in the Ancient World*, London and New York: Routledge, 1991.

Richardson, Peter, *City and Sanctuary. Religion and Architecture in the Roman Near East*, London: SCM Press, 2002.

Robinson, James M., *A New Quest of the Historical Jesus*, London: SCM, 1959.

Rosen, Arlene Miller, 'Paleoenvironmental Reconstruction', in Meyers ed., *The Oxford Encyclopaedia of Archaeology in the Near East*, vol. 4, 200–205.

Saldarini, Anthony J., *Pharisees, Scribes and Sadducees in Palestinian Society*, Edinburgh: T&T Clark, 1988.

Sanders, E. P., *Jesus and Judaism*, London: SCM Press, 1985.

—— *Paul and Palestinian Judaism*, Philadelphia: Fortress Press, 1978.

—— *Jewish Law from Jesus to the Mishnah*, London: SCM Press, 1990.

Sawicki, Marianne, *Crossing Galilee, Architectures of Contact in the Occupied Land of Jesus*, Harrisburg, PA: Trinity Press, 1998.

Schmeller, T., 'Jesus im Umland Galiläas: zu den Markinischen Berichten vom Aufenthalt Jesu in den Gebieten von Tyros, Cæsaea Philippi und der Dekapolis', *BZ* (1994) 44–66.

Schneiders, Sandra M., *The Revelatory Text. Interpreting the New Testament as Sacred Scripture*, New York: HarperCollins, 1991.

Schürer, Emil, *The History of the Jewish People in the Age of Jesus Christ*, revised edition and translation, G. Vermes, F. Millar and M. Black, 4 vols., Edinburgh: T&T Clark, 1973–1985.

Schramm, Brooks, *The Opponents of Third Isaiah, Reconstructing the Cultic History of the Restoration*, *JSOTS* 193, 1995.

Schwartz, Daniel R., *Studies in the Jewish Background of Christianity*, Tübingen: J. C. B. Mohr, 1992.

Schwartz, Seth, *Imperialism and Jewish Society, 200 B.C.E. to 640 C.E.*, Princeton and Oxford: Princeton University Press, 2001.

Schweitzer, Albert, *The Quest of the Historical Jesus*, reprint of English translation, W. Montgomery, New York: the Macmillan Company, 1968.

Sherwin-White, A. N., *Roman Society and Roman Law in the New Testament*, Oxford: Clarendon Press, 1963.

Sloan, Robert B. Jr, *The Favorable Year of the Lord. A Study of Jubilary Theology in the Gospel of Luke*, Austin, TX: Scholars Press, 1977.

Smith, George Adam, *The Historical Geography of the Holy Land*, London: 1924.

Smith, Jonathan, Z., *To Take Place*, Chicago: University of Chicago Press, 1992.

Smith, Mark S., 'Ugaraitic Studies and Israelite Religion: A Retrospective View', *Near Eastern Archaeology* 65 (2002), 17–29.

Smith-Christopher, Daniel, 'Between Ezra and Isaiah: Exclusion, Transformation, and Inclusion of the "Foreigner" in Post-Exilic Biblical Theology', in Brett ed., *Ethnicity in the Bible*, 117–143.

Stegemann, Wolfgang, Malina, Bruce J., Theissen, Gerd, eds., *The Social Setting of Jesus and the Gospels*, Minneapolis: Fortress Press, 2002.

Stemberger, G., 'Die Bedeutung des "Landes Israel" in der rabbinischen Tradition', *Kairos* 25(1983) 176–199.

Stern, Ephraim, *Archaeology of the Land of the Bible*, vol. II, New York and London: Doubleday, 2001.

Stern, Menahen, *Greek and Latin Authors on Jews and Judaism*, 3 vols., Jerusalem: The Israel Academy of Sciences and Humanities.

Strauss, David Friedrich, *The Life of Jesus Critically Examined*, reprinted English translation, London: SCM, 1972.

Struthers-Malbon, Elizabeth, 'Galilee and Jerusalem: History and Literature in Markan Interpretation', *CBQ* 44(1982) 242–255.

Sugirtharajah, R. S. ed., *Voices from the Margin, Interpreting the Bible in the Third World*, London: SPCK, 1991.

Syon, D., 'The Coins from Gamla. An Interim Report', *Israel Numismatic Journal* 12(1992/93) 34–55.

Tan, Kim Huat, *The Zion Traditions and the Aims of Jesus, SNTSMS*, Cambridge: Cambridge University Press, 1997.

Taylor, Vincent, *The Gospel According to Mark*, London: Macmillan and Company, 1963.

Tcherikover, Victor, *Palestine under the Ptolemies. A Contribution to the Study of the Zenon Papyri*, Mizraim, vols. IV–V, New York: G. E. Stechert, 1937.

Theissen, Gerd, '"Meer" und "See" in den Evangelien: Ein Beitrag zur Lokalcoloritforschung', *Studien zum Neuen Testament und seiner Umwelt*, 10(1985) 5–25.

—— *The Gospels in Context*, English translation, Linda M. Maloney, Edinburgh: T&T Clark, 1992.

—— 'The Political Dimension of Jesus' Activities', in Stegemann, Malina, Theissen, eds., *Jesus and the Gospels*, 225–250.

—— and Merz, Annette, *The Historical Jesus. A Comprehensive Guide*, English translation, John Bowden, London: SCM Press, 1996.

Tzuk, Z., 'The Water Installations at Sepphoris', in Nagy, Meyers, eds., *Sepphoris in Galilee. Cross-Currents of Culture*, 45–50.

Vander Kam, James C., *The Book of Jubilees*, Sheffield: Sheffield Academic Press, 2001.

Vermes, Geza, *Jesus the Jew*, London: Collins, 1973.

Volger, Werner, *Jüdische Jesusinterpretation in christlicher Sicht*, Weimar: Herman Böhlaus, 1988.

Von Rad, Gerhard, *Old Testament Theology*, 2 vols., English translation, D. M. G. Stalker, Edinburgh: Oliver and Boyd, 1962.

Westerman, Claus, *Genesis 1–11. A Commentary*, English translation, Minneapolis: Augsburg Press, 1984.

White, Lynn Jr, 'The Historical Roots of our Ecological Crisis', *Science* 155(1967) 1203–1207, reprinted in S. Gottlieb ed., *The Sacred Earth. Religion, Nature and the Environment*, London: Routledge, 1996, 183–193.

Whitelam, Keith W., 'Recreating the History of Israel', *JSOT* 35(1986) 45–70.

Wright, George Ernest, *The Old Testament Against its Environment*, London: SCM Press, 1950.

Younger, K. Lawson Jr, 'The Deportation of the Israelites', *JBL* 117(1998) 201–227.

Zenger, E., *Der Psalter in Judentum, und Christentum*, Freiburg: Herder, 1998, 1–57.

Zobel, Hans, *Stammesspruch und Geschichte, BZAT* 95, Berlin: Topelmann, 1965.

INDEX OF REFERENCES